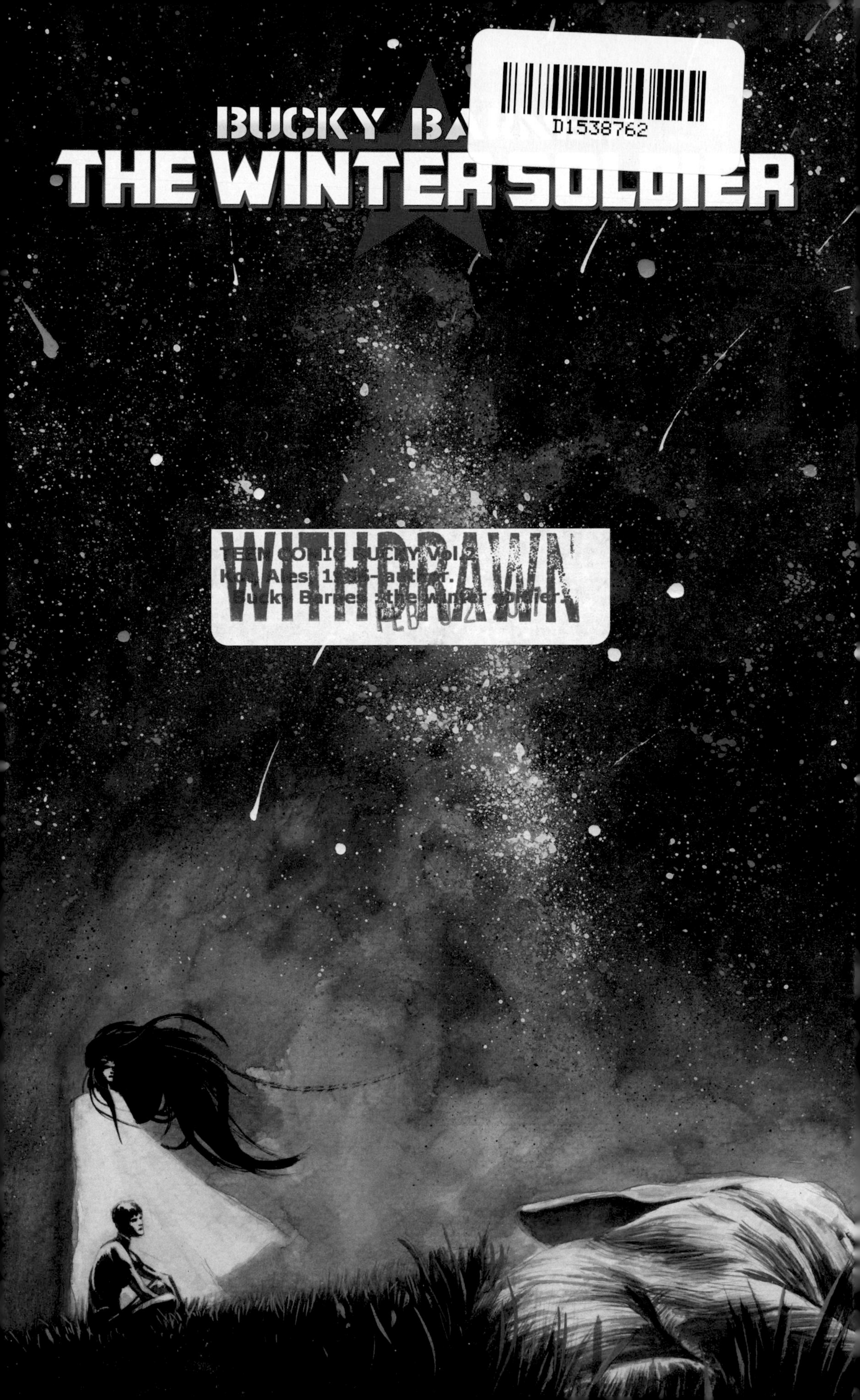
BUCKY BA
THE WINTER SOLDIER

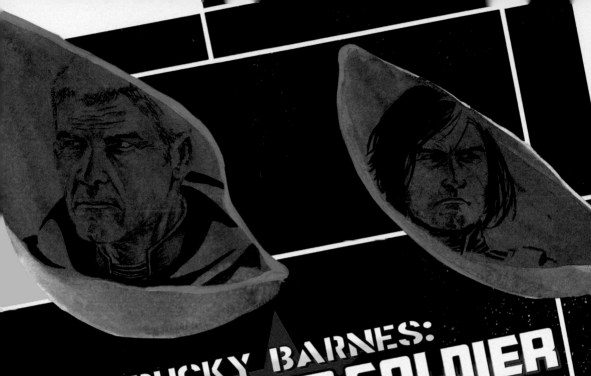

# BUCKY BARNES:
# THE WINTER SOLDIER

**WRITER: ALES KOT**
**ARTISTS:**
**MARCO RUDY**
(#6, PP. 1-9, 15-20; #8-10; #11, PP. 7-11, 17-20) &

**LANGDON FOSS**
(#6, PP. 10-14; #7; #11, PP. 1-6, 12-16)

**WITH MICHAEL WALSH** (#11, PP. 1-6, 12-16)

**BUCKY BARNES CREATED BY**
**JOE SIMON & JACK KIRBY**

**COLOR ARTISTS:**
**JORDAN BOYD** (#6, PP. 10-14 & #11, PP. 1-6, 12-16)
**WITH MICHAEL WALSH** (#11, PP. 1-6, 12-16) &
**RACHELLE ROSENBERG** (#7)

**LETTERER: VC'S CLAYTON COWLES**
**COVER ART: MICHAEL DEL MUNDO**
**ASSISTANT EDITOR: JON MOISAN**
**EDITOR: WIL MOSS**

COLLECTION EDITOR: **SARAH BRUNSTAD**
ASSOCIATE MANAGING EDITOR: **ALEX STARBUCK**
EDITORS, SPECIAL PROJECTS: **JENNIFER GRÜNWALD &**
**MARK D. BEAZLEY**
SENIOR EDITOR, SPECIAL PROJECTS: **JEFF YOUNGQUIST**
SVP PRINT, SALES & MARKETING: **DAVID GABRIEL**

EDITOR IN CHIEF: **AXEL ALONSO**
CHIEF CREATIVE OFFICER: **JOE QUESADA**
PUBLISHER: **DAN BUCKLEY**
EXECUTIVE PRODUCER: **ALAN FINE**

BUCKY BARNES: THE WINTER SOLDIER VOL. 2. Contains material originally published in magazine form as BUCKY BARNES: THE WINTER SOLDIER #6-11. First printing 2015. ISBN# 978-0-7851-8930-5. Published by MARVEL WORLDWIDE, INC., a subsidiary of MARVEL ENTERTAINMENT, LLC. OFFICE OF PUBLICATION: 135 West 50th Street, New York, NY 10020. Copyright © 2015 MARVEL No similarity between any of the names, characters, persons, and/or institutions in this magazine with those of any living or dead person or institution is intended, and any such similarity which may exist is purely coincidental. **Printed in Canada.** ALAN FINE, President, Marvel Entertainment; DAN BUCKLEY, President, TV, Publishing and Brand Management; JOE QUESADA, Chief Creative Officer; TOM BREVOORT, SVP of Publishing; DAVID BOGART, SVP of Operations & Procurement, Publishing; C.B. CEBULSKI, VP of International Development & Brand Management; DAVID GABRIEL, SVP Print, Sales & Marketing; JIM O'KEEFE, VP of Operations & Logistics; DAN CARR, Executive Director of Publishing Technology; SUSAN CRESPI, Editorial Operations Manager; ALEX MORALES, Publishing Operations Manager; STAN LEE, Chairman Emeritus. For information regarding advertising in Marvel Comics or on Marvel.com, please contact Jonathan Rheingold, VP of Custom Solutions & Ad Sales, at jrheingold@marvel.com. For Marvel subscription inquiries, please call 800-217-9158. **Manufactured between 8/28/2015 and 10/5/2015 by SOLISCO PRINTERS, SCOTT, QC, CANADA.**

10 9 8 7 6 5 4 3 2 1

# #6

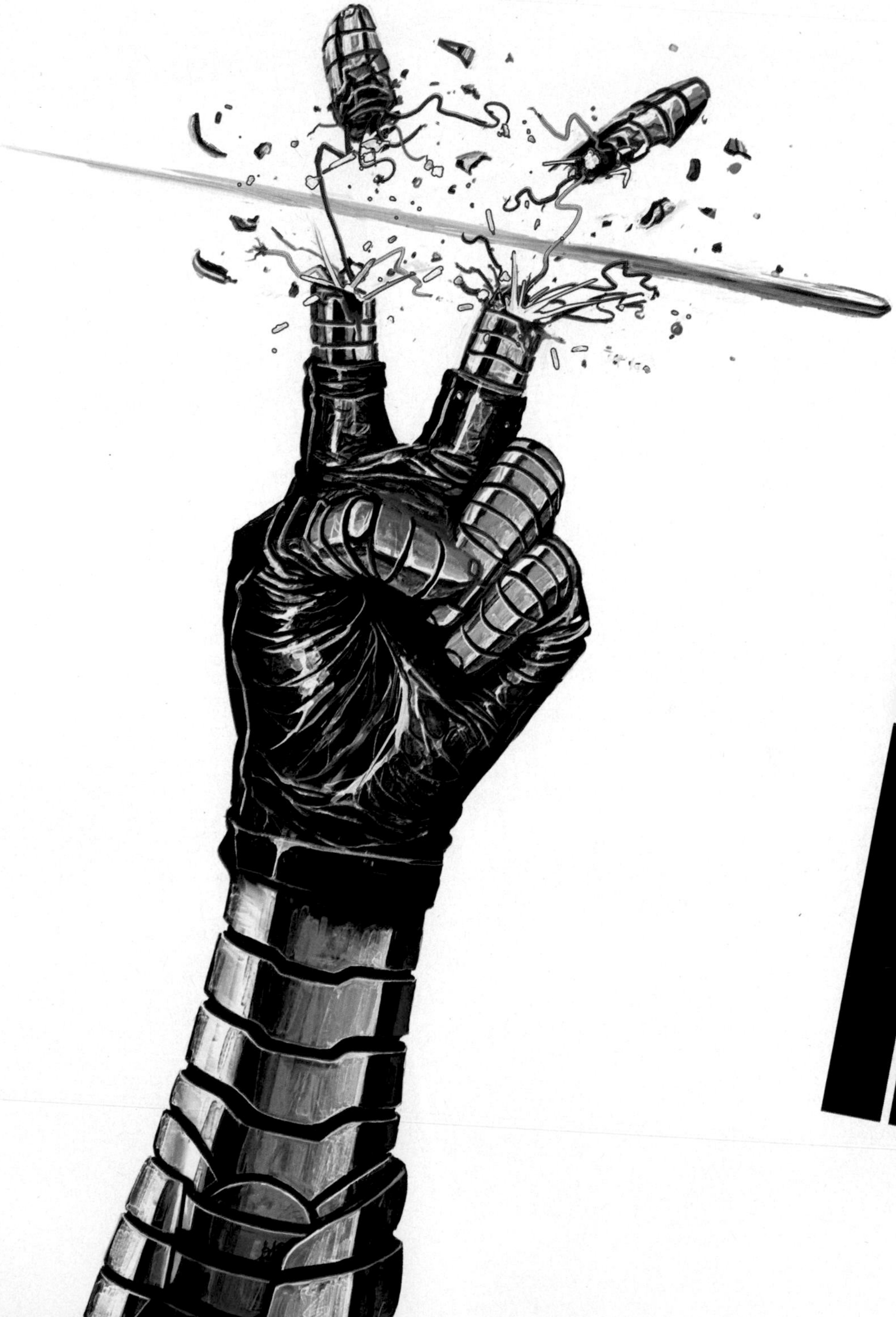

# PEACE TALKS

JAMES BUCHANAN BARNES FOUGHT FOR THE U.S. DURING
WORLD WAR II AS BUCKY, THE TEENAGE SIDEKICK OF CAPTAIN
AMERICA. THEN HE FOUGHT FOR SOVIET RUSSIA AS A
BRAINWASHED ASSASSIN CODE-NAMED THE WINTER SOLDIER.
THEN HE FOUGHT TO HONOR HIS MENTOR'S LEGACY WHEN HE
BRIEFLY SERVED AS CAPTAIN AMERICA.

NOW BUCKY BARNES FIGHTS FOR EVERYONE. HE IS "THE MAN
ON THE WALL," CLANDESTINELY PROTECTING EARTH FROM ALL
THREATS WITH HIS PARTNER, DAISY "QUAKE" JOHNSON.

TWO HUNDRED YEARS FROM NOW, BUCKY LIVES IN A UNIVERSE
OF UTTER PEACE. BUT AFTER A REVIEW OF THE LIVES OF HIS
VARIOUS SELVES ACROSS THE MULTIVERSE SHOWED HIM THE
BUCKY OF THIS UNIVERSE BEING UNEXPECTEDLY MURDERED
IN THE PRESENT, HE DECIDED TO TRAVEL BACK IN TIME TO
PREVENT IT.

BUT IT LOOKS LIKE HE IS TOO LATE. BUCKY OF THE PRESENT
AND DAISY WERE ON A MISSION TO TAKE OUT VENTOLIN,
THE LEADER OF THE PAO'REE PEOPLE AND QUEEN OF THE
PLANET MER-Z-BOW. BUT BUCKY FELL IN LOVE WITH HER
INSTEAD. AND NOW A SEEMINGLY DIFFERENT VERSION OF
THE MERCENARY KNOWN AS CROSSBONES HAS ARRIVED TO
DO WHAT BUCKY COULD NOT: DETONATING THE TOWER THAT
BUCKY, DAISY AND VENTOLIN WERE IN, AS BUCKY OF THE
FUTURE HELPLESSLY WATCHED...

BUCKY BARNES:
THE WINTER SOLDIER

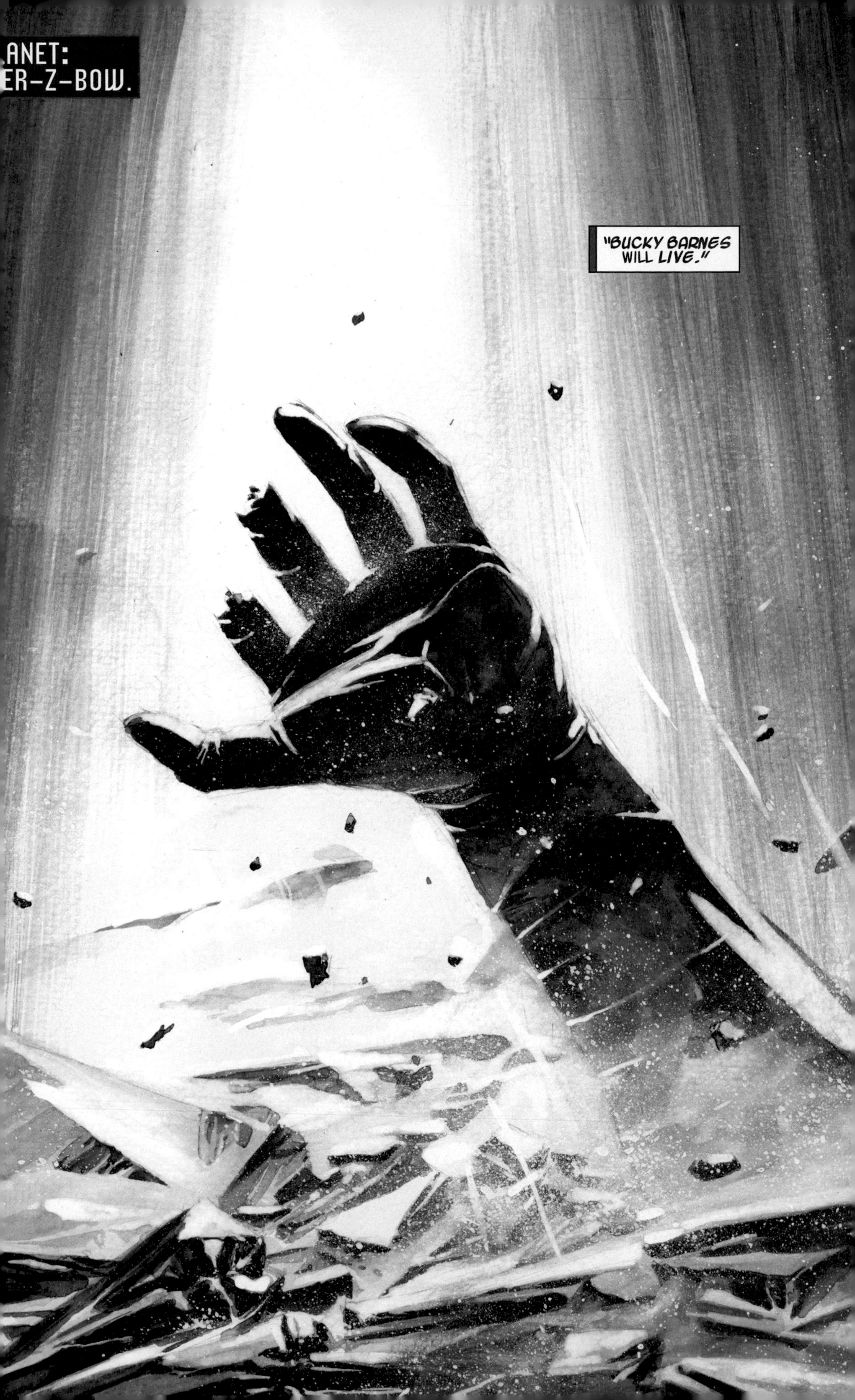
ANET:
ER-Z-BOW.
"BUCKY BARNES WILL LIVE."

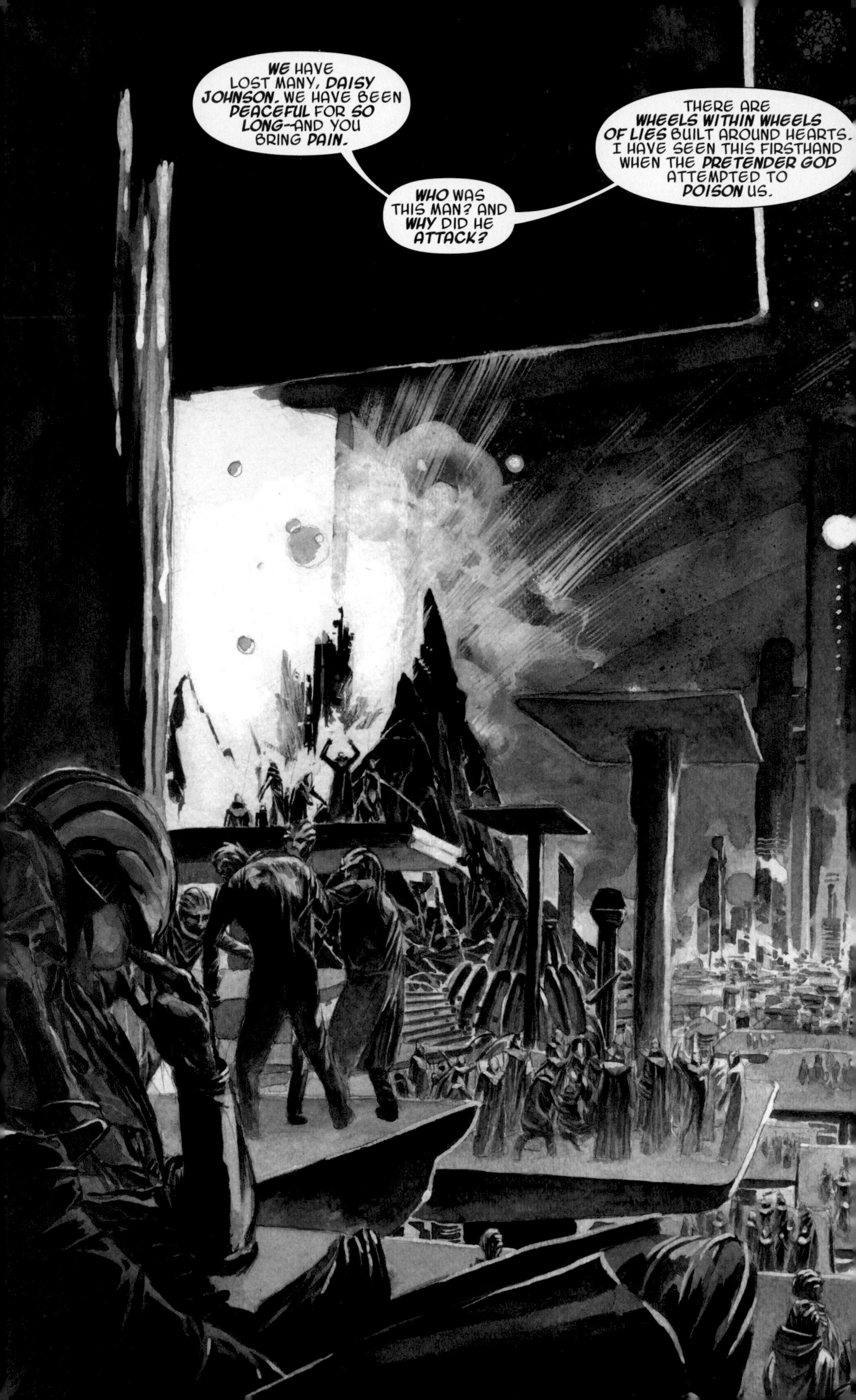
WE HAVE LOST MANY, DAISY JOHNSON. WE HAVE BEEN PEACEFUL FOR SO LONG--AND YOU BRING PAIN.
WHO WAS THIS MAN? AND WHY DID HE ATTACK?
THERE ARE WHEELS WITHIN WHEELS OF LIES BUILT AROUND HEARTS. I HAVE SEEN THIS FIRSTHAND WHEN THE PRETENDER GOD ATTEMPTED TO POISON US.

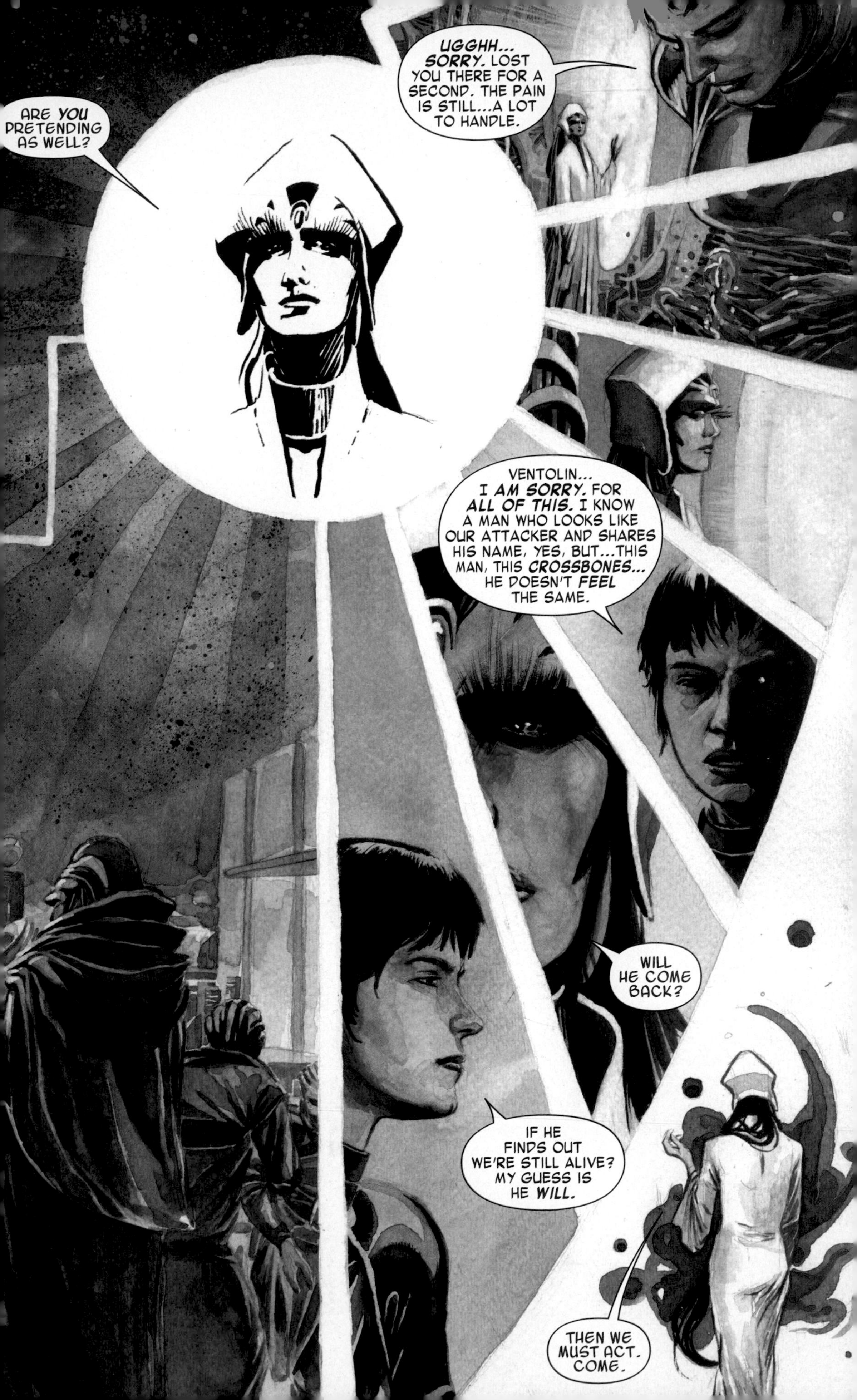
ARE YOU PRETENDING AS WELL?
UGGHH... SORRY. LOST YOU THERE FOR A SECOND. THE PAIN IS STILL...A LOT TO HANDLE.
VENTOLIN... I AM SORRY. FOR ALL OF THIS. I KNOW A MAN WHO LOOKS LIKE OUR ATTACKER AND SHARES HIS NAME, YES, BUT...THIS MAN, THIS CROSSBONES... HE DOESN'T FEEL THE SAME.
WILL HE COME BACK?
IF HE FINDS OUT WE'RE STILL ALIVE? MY GUESS IS HE WILL.
THEN WE MUST ACT. COME.

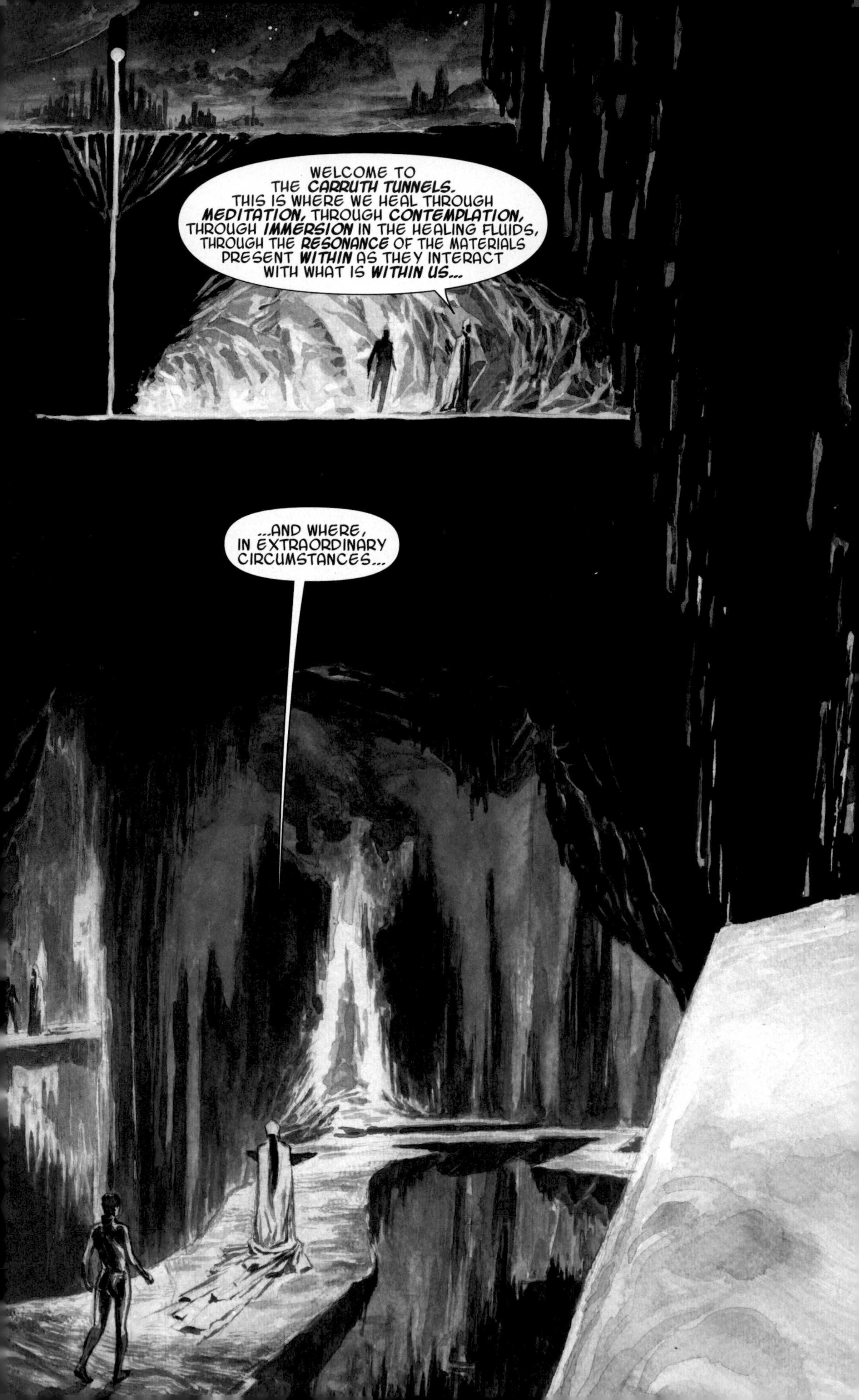
WELCOME TO THE CARRUTH TUNNELS. THIS IS WHERE WE HEAL THROUGH MEDITATION, THROUGH CONTEMPLATION, THROUGH IMMERSION IN THE HEALING FLUIDS, THROUGH THE RESONANCE OF THE MATERIALS PRESENT WITHIN AS THEY INTERACT WITH WHAT IS WITHIN US...
...AND WHERE, IN EXTRAORDINARY CIRCUMSTANCES...

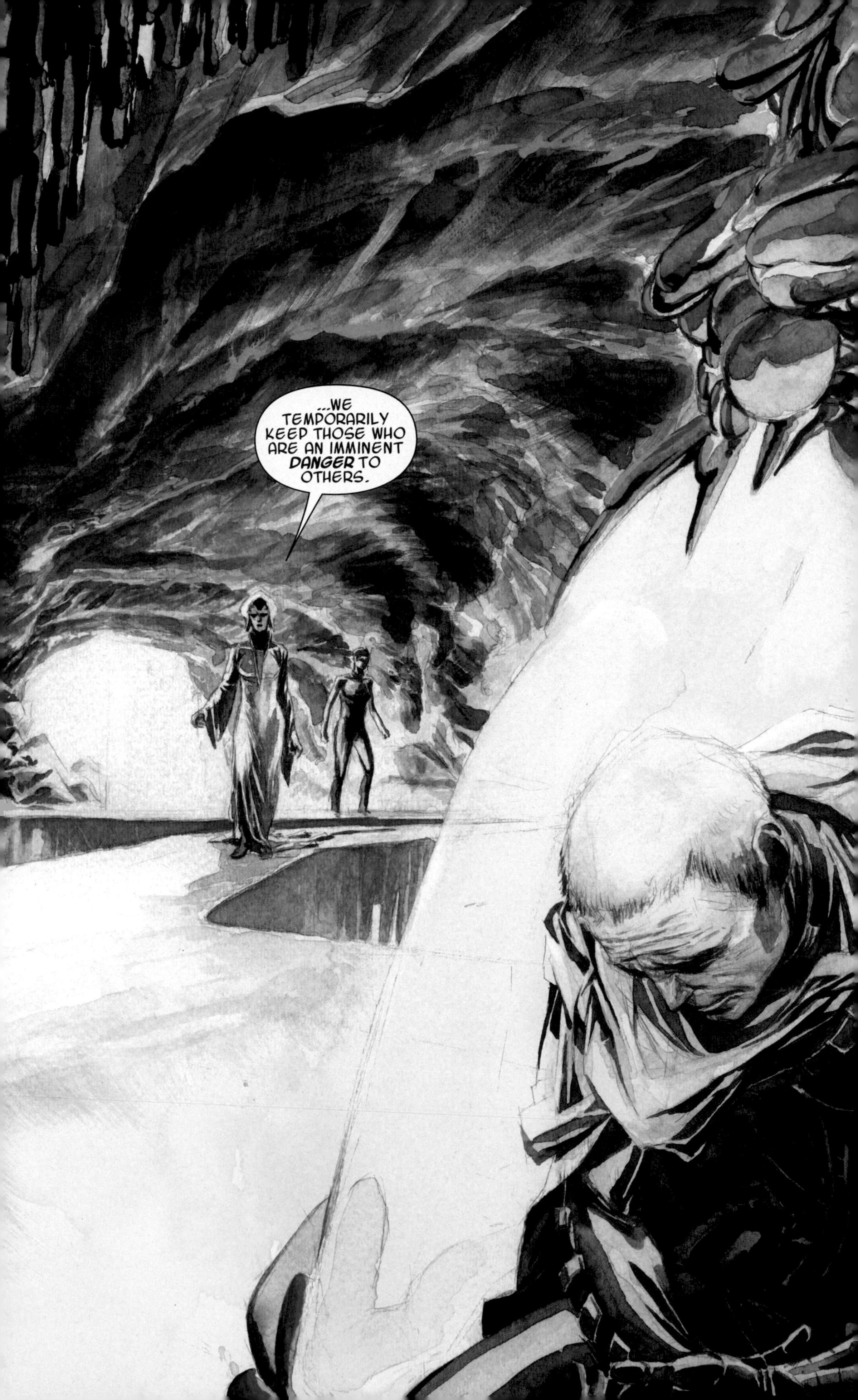
...WE TEMPORARILY KEEP THOSE WHO ARE AN IMMINENT DANGER TO OTHERS.

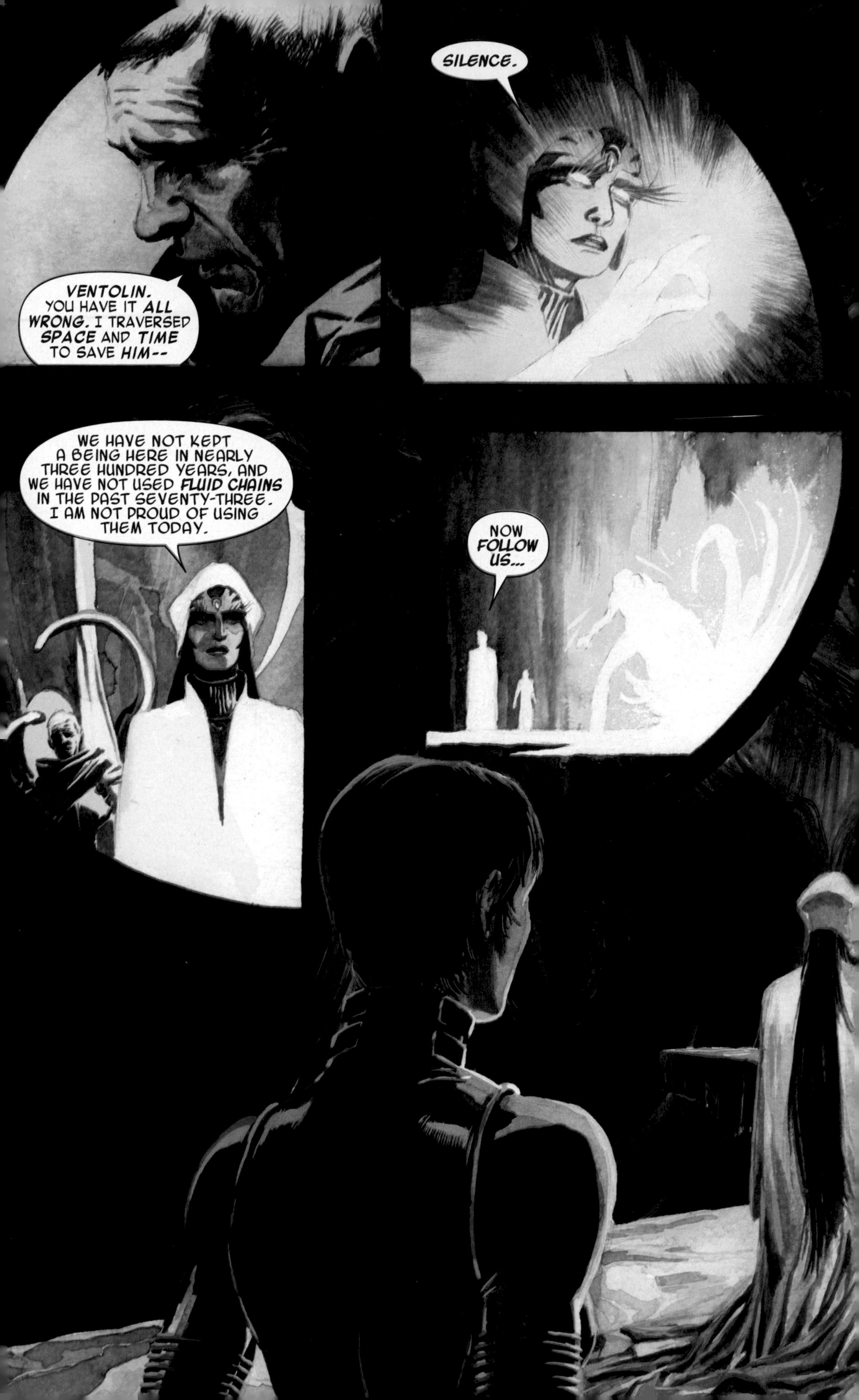
VENTOLIN. YOU HAVE IT ALL WRONG. I TRAVERSED SPACE AND TIME TO SAVE HIM--
SILENCE.
WE HAVE NOT KEPT A BEING HERE IN NEARLY THREE HUNDRED YEARS, AND WE HAVE NOT USED FLUID CHAINS IN THE PAST SEVENTY-THREE. I AM NOT PROUD OF USING THEM TODAY.
NOW FOLLOW US...

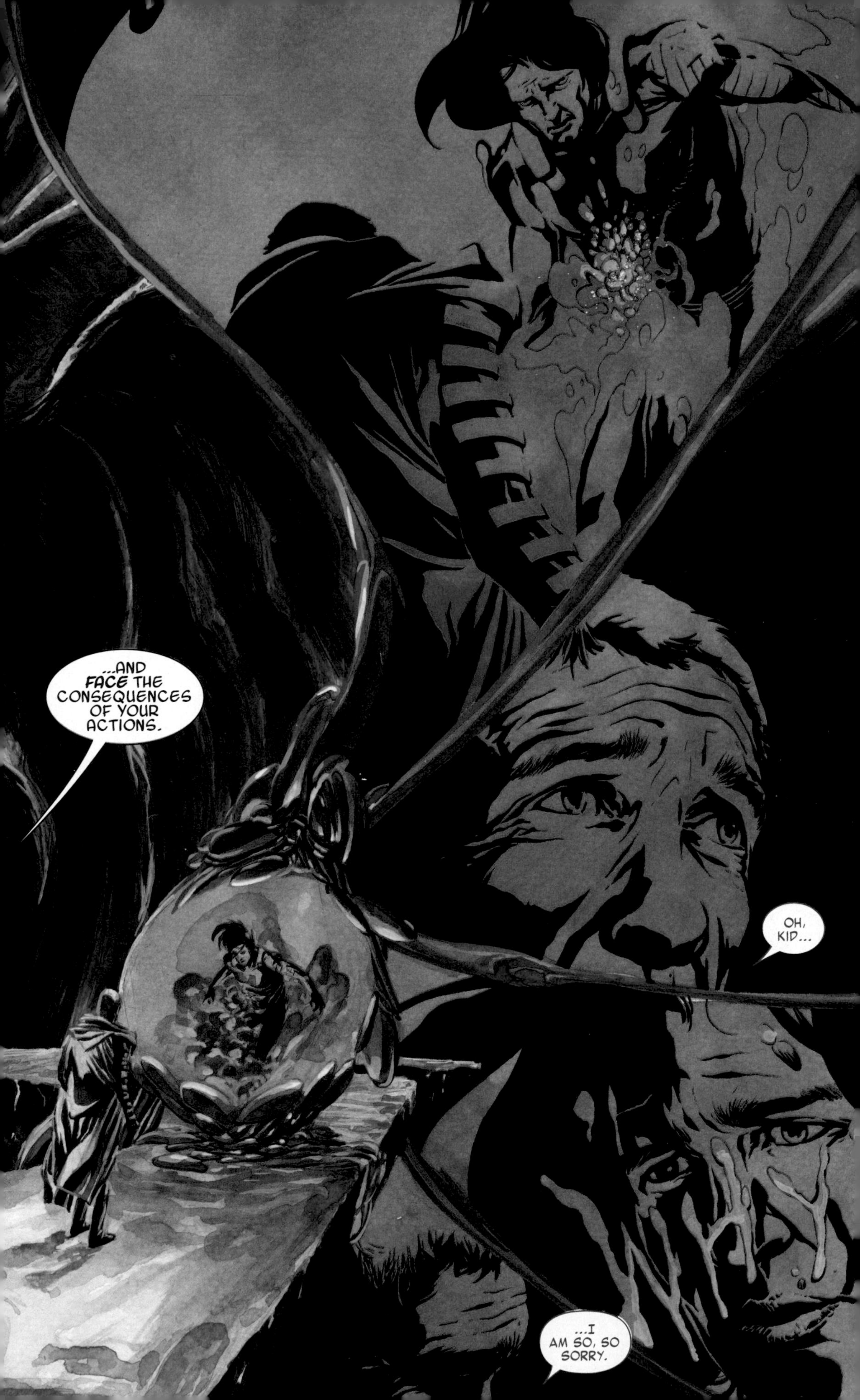
...AND FACE THE CONSEQUENCES OF YOUR ACTIONS.
OH, KID...
...I AM SO, SO SORRY.

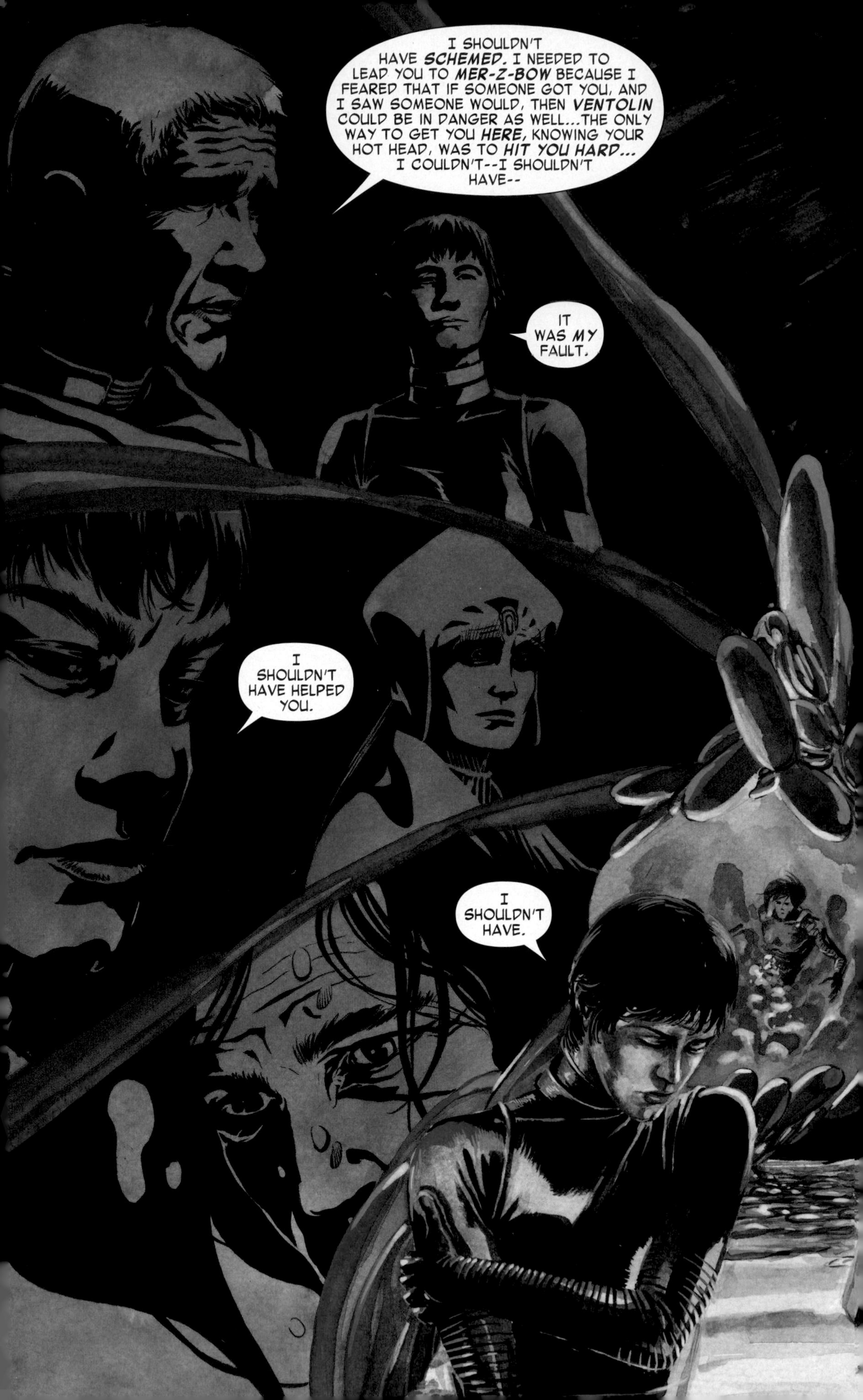
I SHOULDN'T HAVE SCHEMED. I NEEDED TO LEAD YOU TO MER-Z-BOW BECAUSE I FEARED THAT IF SOMEONE GOT YOU, AND I SAW SOMEONE WOULD, THEN VENTOLIN COULD BE IN DANGER AS WELL...THE ONLY WAY TO GET YOU HERE, KNOWING YOUR HOT HEAD, WAS TO HIT YOU HARD... I COULDN'T--I SHOULDN'T HAVE--
IT WAS MY FAULT.
I SHOULDN'T HAVE HELPED YOU.
I SHOULDN'T HAVE.

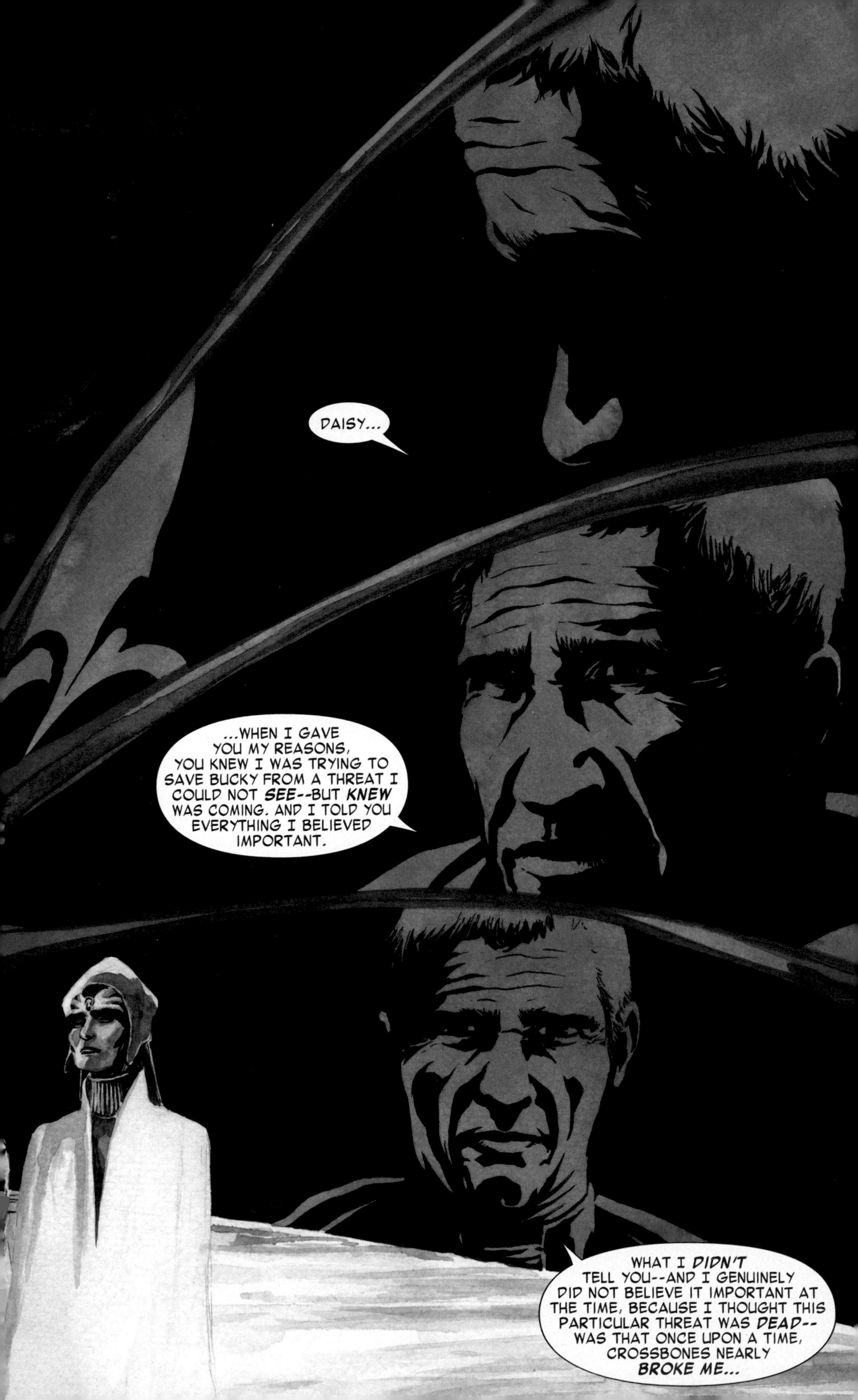
DAISY...
...WHEN I GAVE YOU MY REASONS, YOU KNEW I WAS TRYING TO SAVE BUCKY FROM A THREAT I COULD NOT SEE--BUT KNEW WAS COMING. AND I TOLD YOU EVERYTHING I BELIEVED IMPORTANT.
WHAT I DIDN'T TELL YOU--AND I GENUINELY DID NOT BELIEVE IT IMPORTANT AT THE TIME, BECAUSE I THOUGHT THIS PARTICULAR THREAT WAS DEAD--WAS THAT ONCE UPON A TIME, CROSSBONES NEARLY BROKE ME...

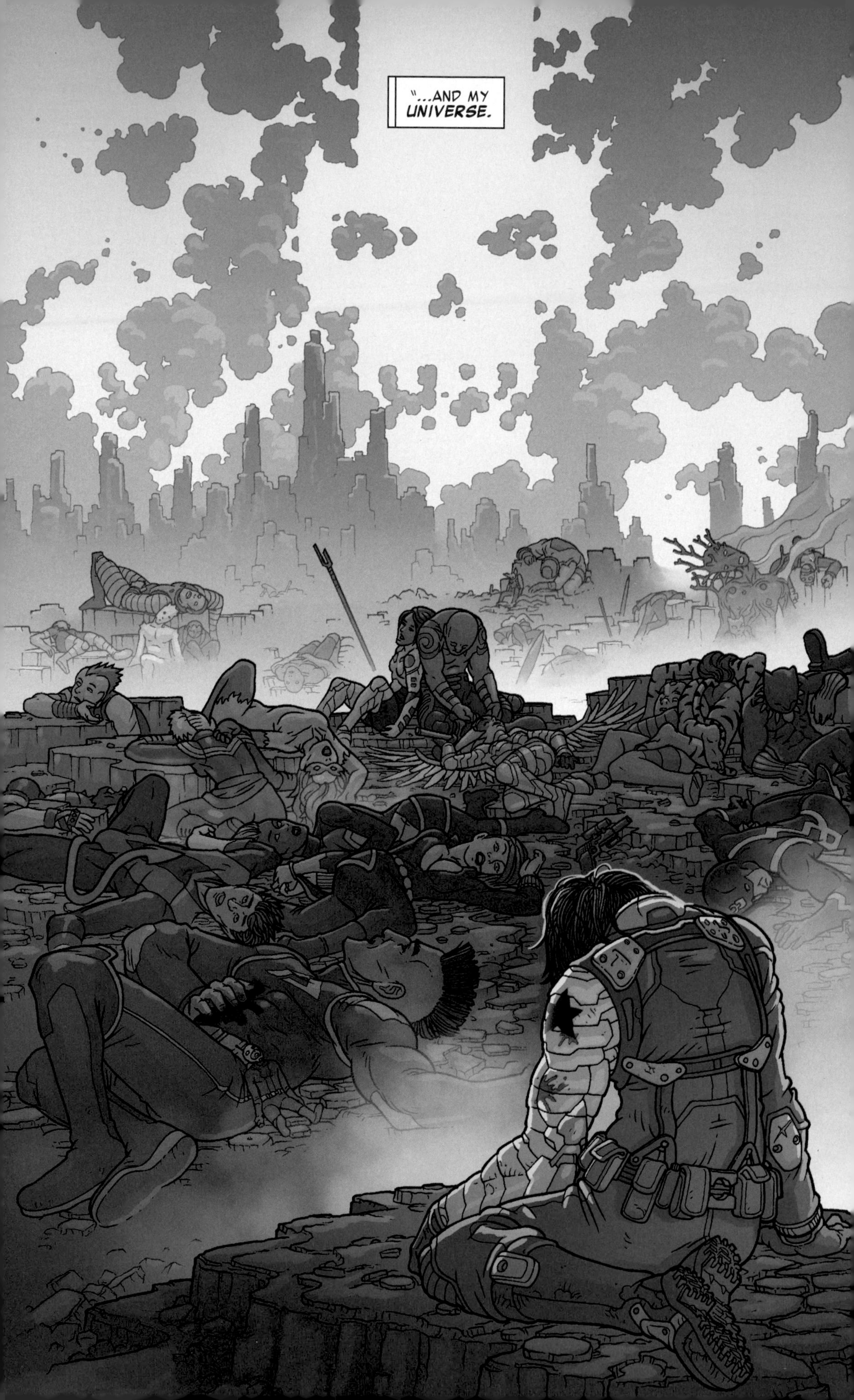
"...AND MY UNIVERSE.

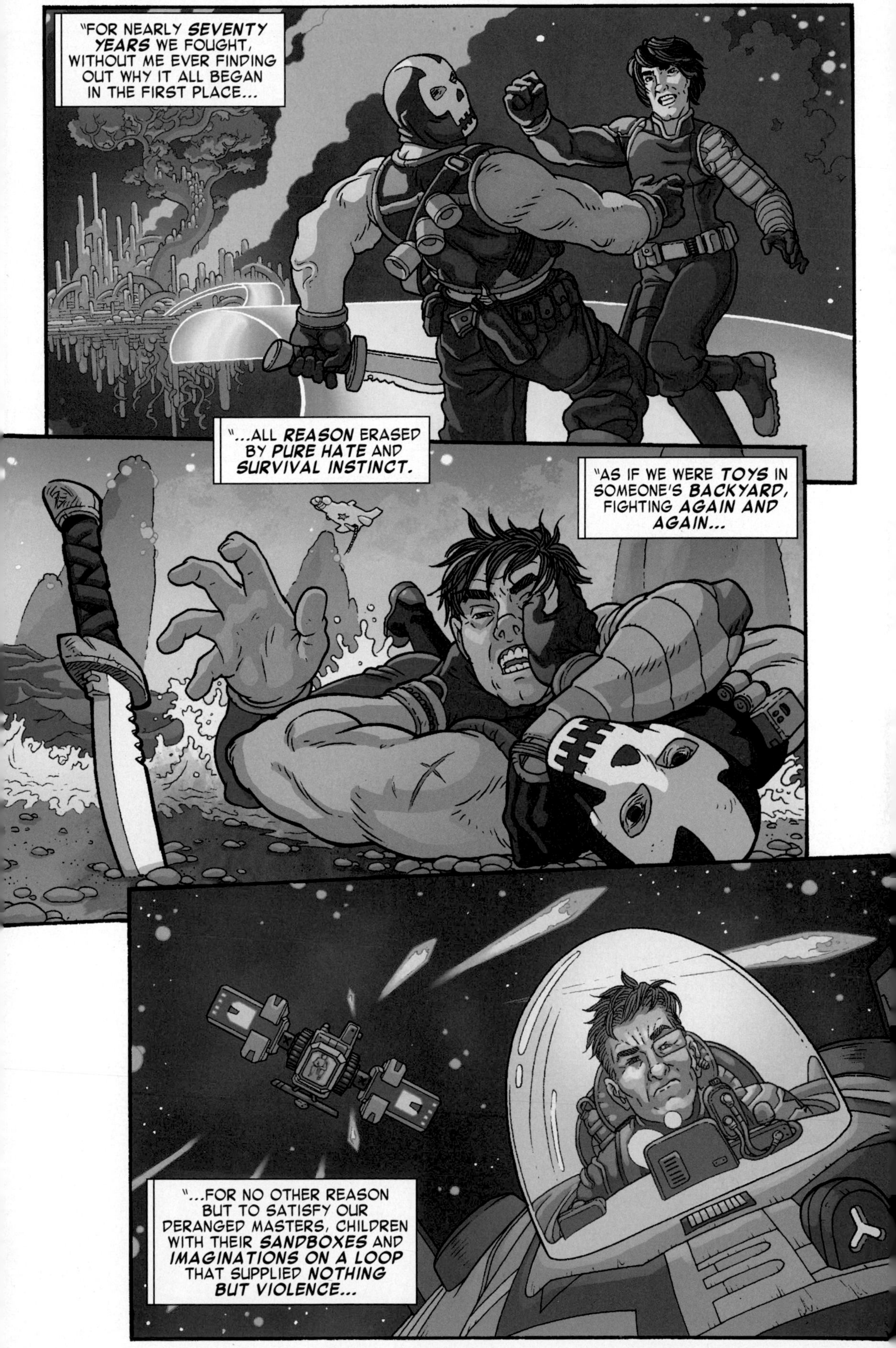
"FOR NEARLY SEVENTY YEARS WE FOUGHT, WITHOUT ME EVER FINDING OUT WHY IT ALL BEGAN IN THE FIRST PLACE...
"...ALL REASON ERASED BY PURE HATE AND SURVIVAL INSTINCT.
"AS IF WE WERE TOYS IN SOMEONE'S BACKYARD, FIGHTING AGAIN AND AGAIN...
"...FOR NO OTHER REASON BUT TO SATISFY OUR DERANGED MASTERS, CHILDREN WITH THEIR SANDBOXES AND IMAGINATIONS ON A LOOP THAT SUPPLIED NOTHING BUT VIOLENCE...

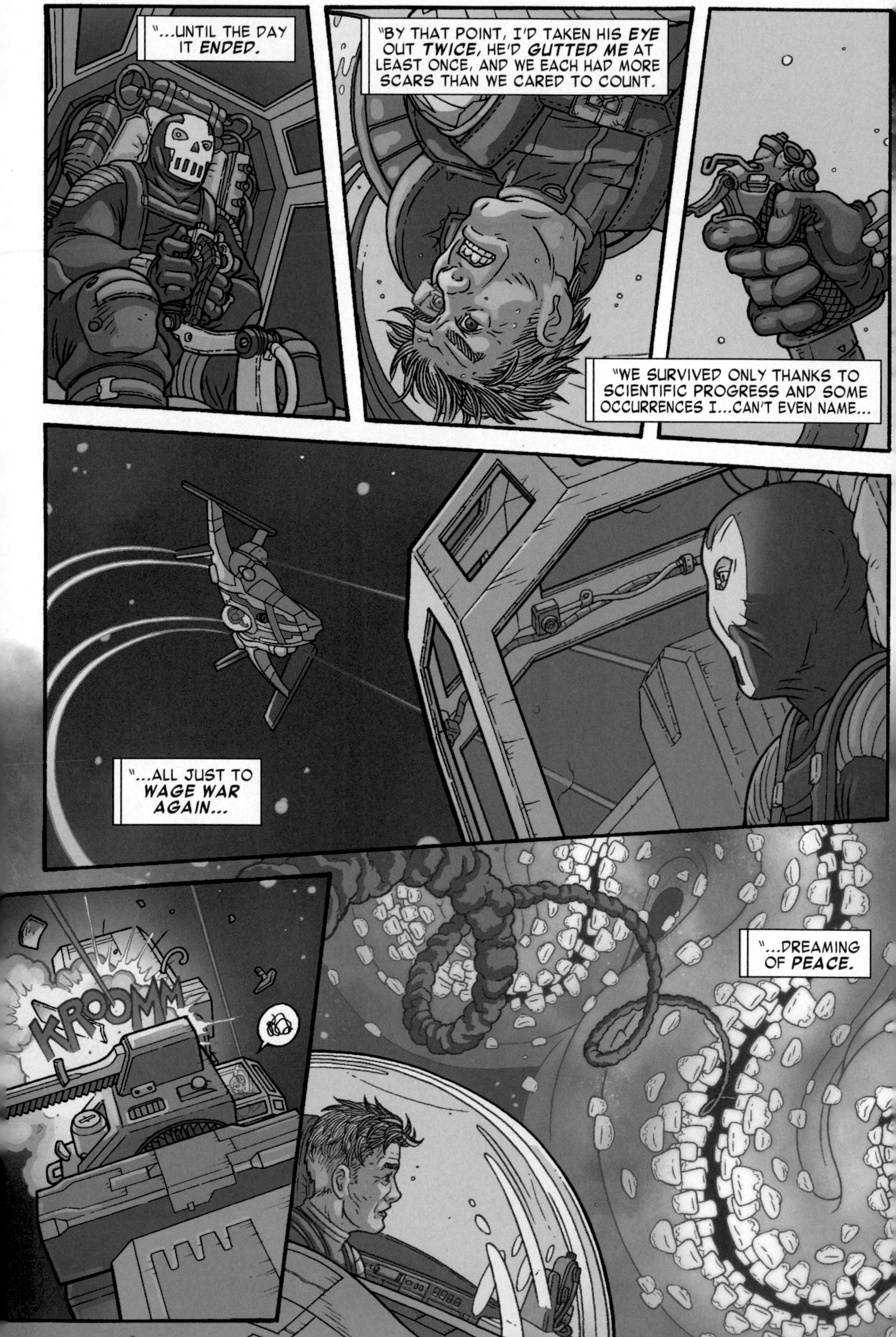
"...UNTIL THE DAY IT ENDED.
"BY THAT POINT, I'D TAKEN HIS EYE OUT TWICE, HE'D GUTTED ME AT LEAST ONCE, AND WE EACH HAD MORE SCARS THAN WE CARED TO COUNT.
"WE SURVIVED ONLY THANKS TO SCIENTIFIC PROGRESS AND SOME OCCURRENCES I...CAN'T EVEN NAME...
"...ALL JUST TO WAGE WAR AGAIN...
KROOMM
"...DREAMING OF PEACE.

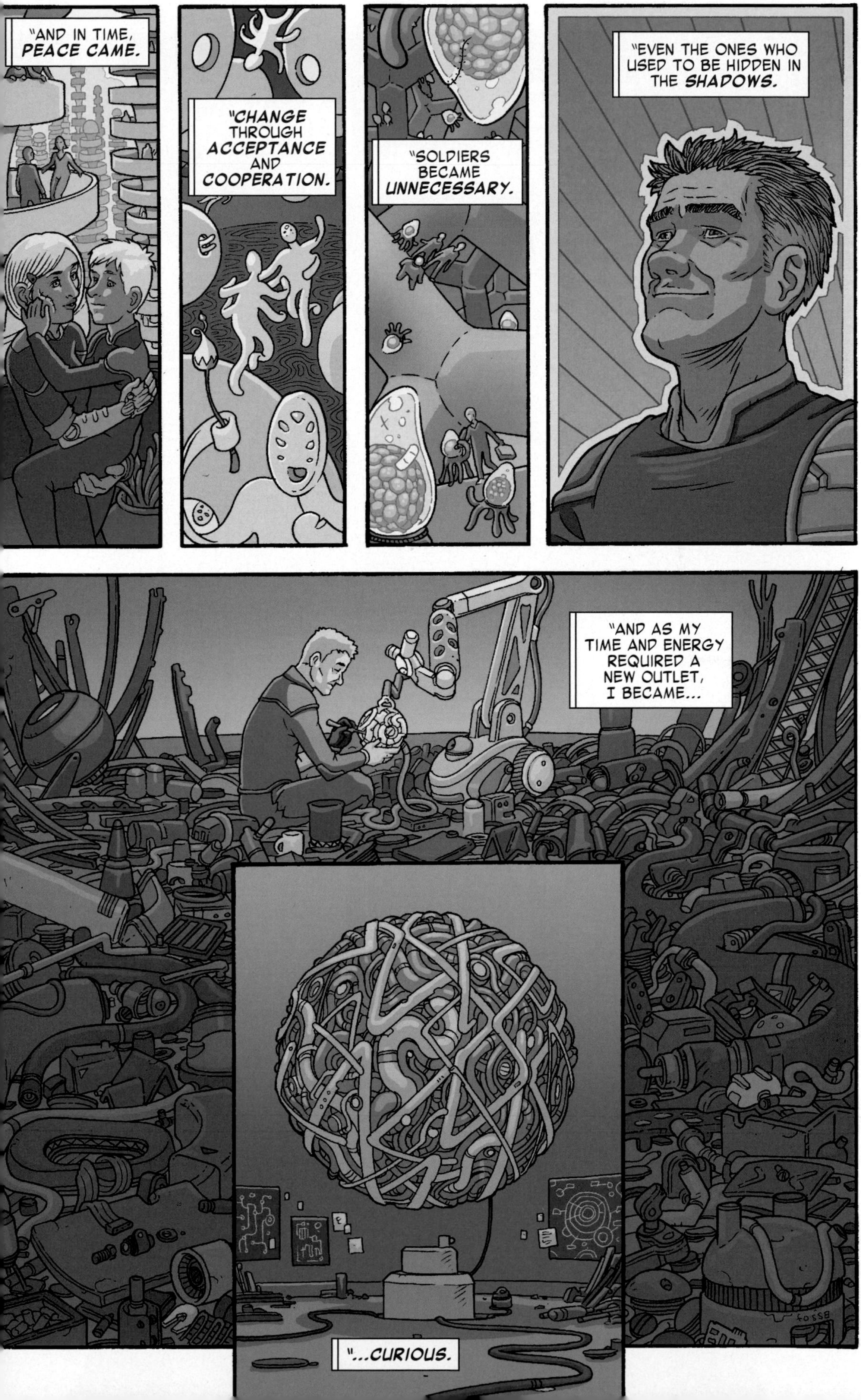
"AND IN TIME, PEACE CAME.
"CHANGE THROUGH ACCEPTANCE AND COOPERATION.
"SOLDIERS BECAME UNNECESSARY.
"EVEN THE ONES WHO USED TO BE HIDDEN IN THE SHADOWS.
"AND AS MY TIME AND ENERGY REQUIRED A NEW OUTLET, I BECAME...
"...CURIOUS.

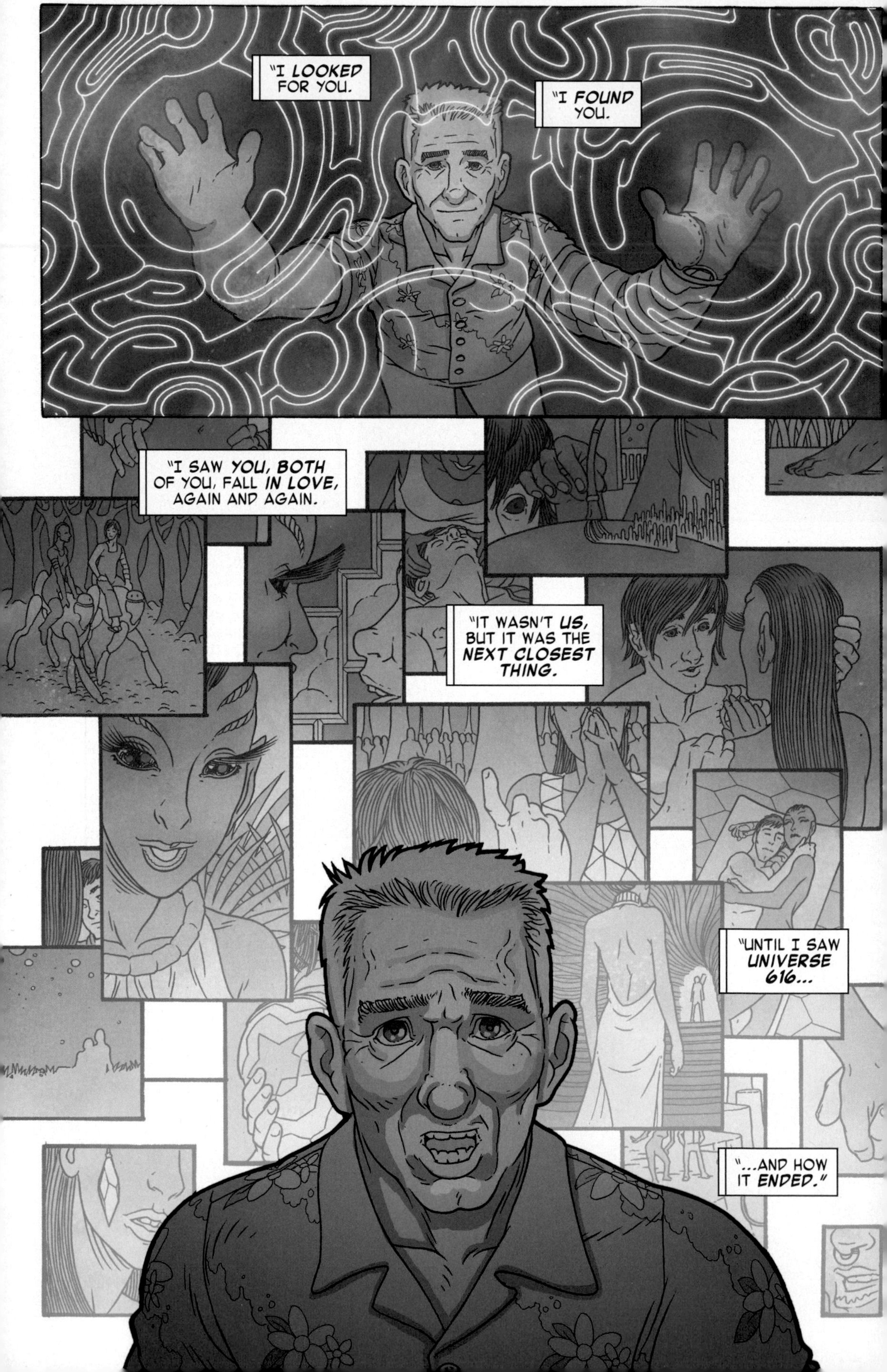
"I *LOOKED* FOR YOU.
"I *FOUND* YOU.
"I SAW *YOU, BOTH* OF YOU, FALL *IN LOVE*, AGAIN AND AGAIN.
"IT WASN'T *US*, BUT IT WAS THE *NEXT CLOSEST THING*.
"UNTIL I SAW *UNIVERSE 616*...
"...AND HOW IT *ENDED*."

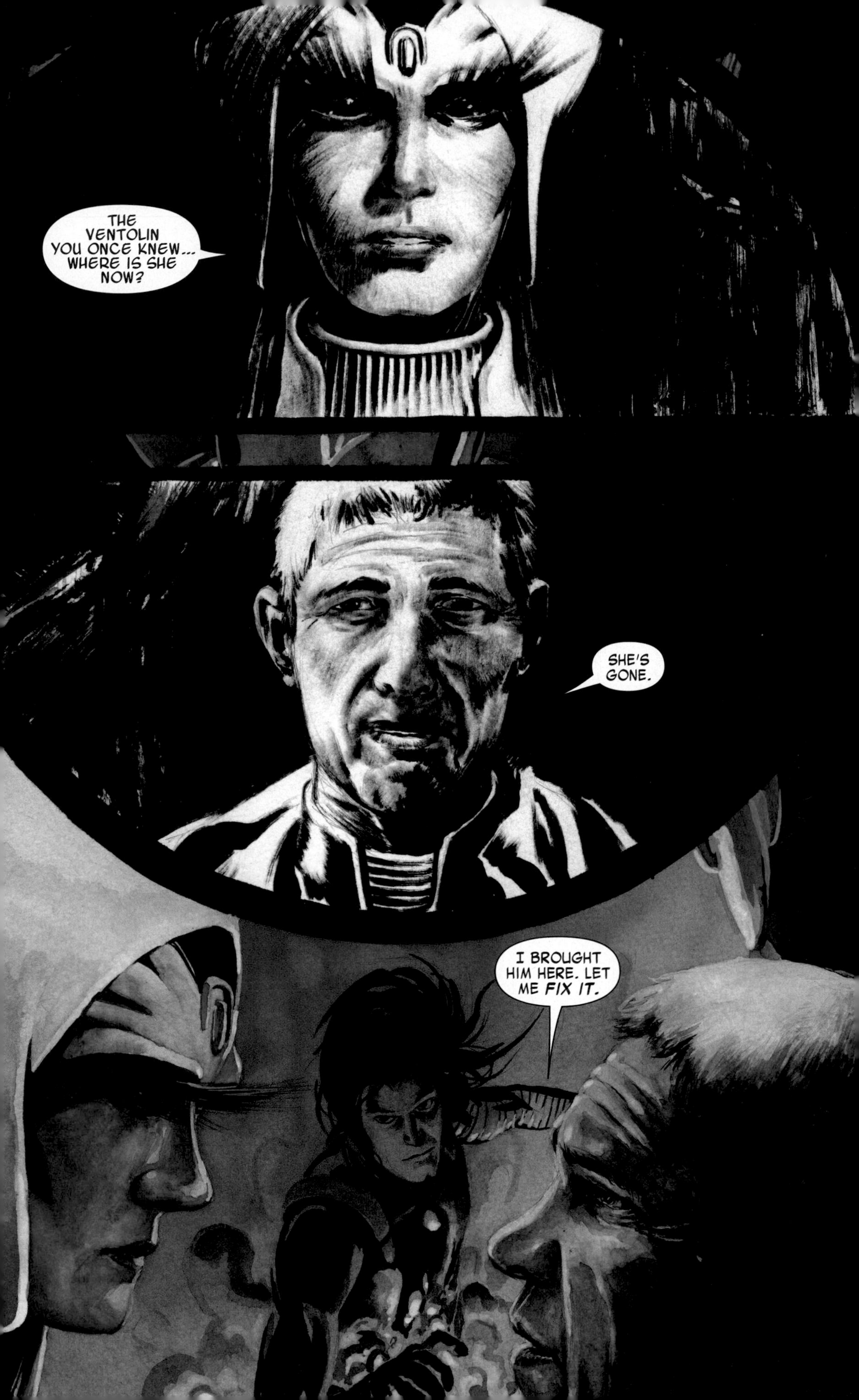
THE VENTOLIN YOU ONCE KNEW... WHERE IS SHE NOW?
SHE'S GONE.
I BROUGHT HIM HERE. LET ME *FIX IT.*

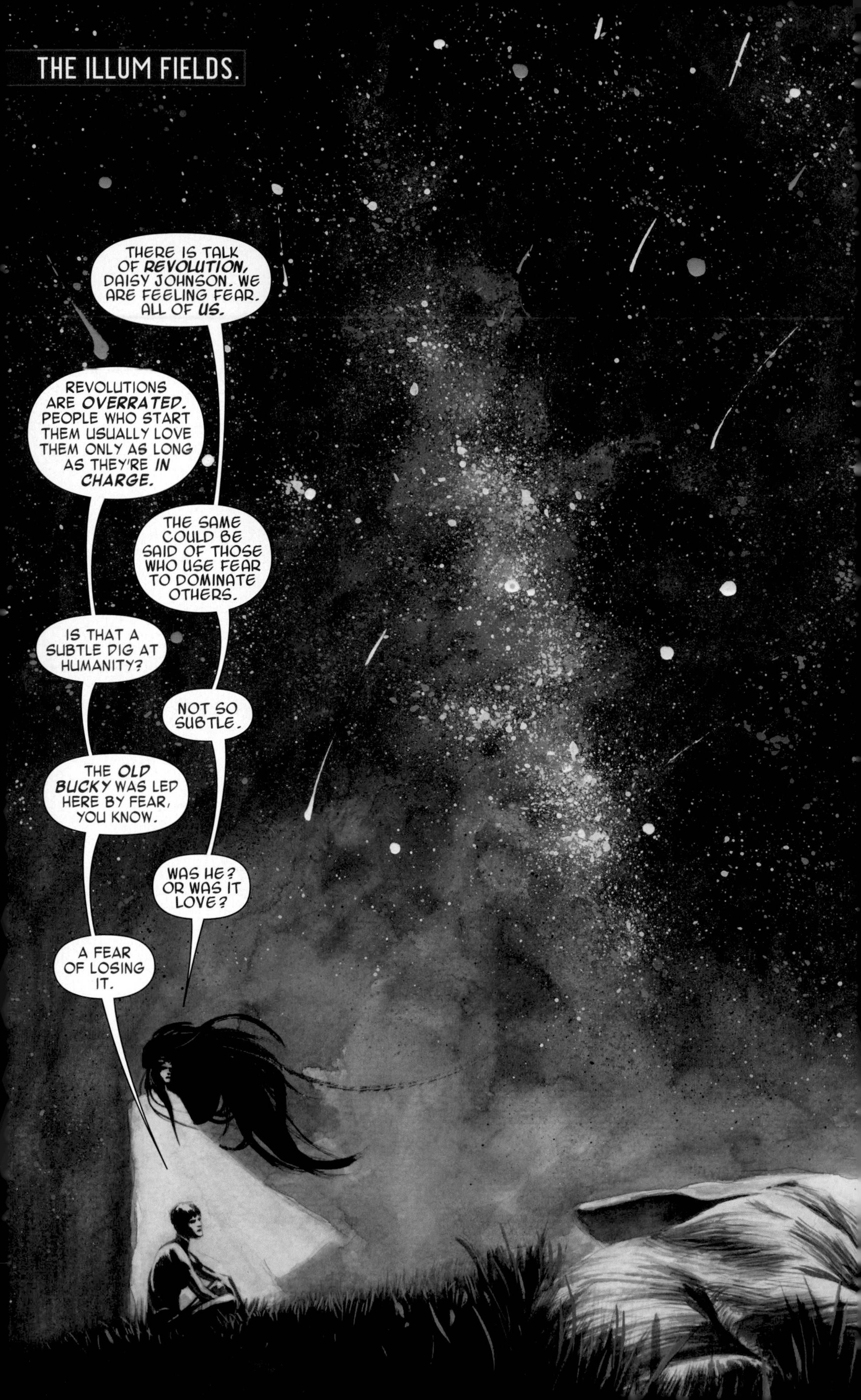
THE ILLUM FIELDS.
THERE IS TALK OF REVOLUTION, DAISY JOHNSON. WE ARE FEELING FEAR. ALL OF US.
REVOLUTIONS ARE OVERRATED. PEOPLE WHO START THEM USUALLY LOVE THEM ONLY AS LONG AS THEY'RE IN CHARGE.
THE SAME COULD BE SAID OF THOSE WHO USE FEAR TO DOMINATE OTHERS.
IS THAT A SUBTLE DIG AT HUMANITY?
NOT SO SUBTLE.
THE OLD BUCKY WAS LED HERE BY FEAR, YOU KNOW.
WAS HE? OR WAS IT LOVE?
A FEAR OF LOSING IT.

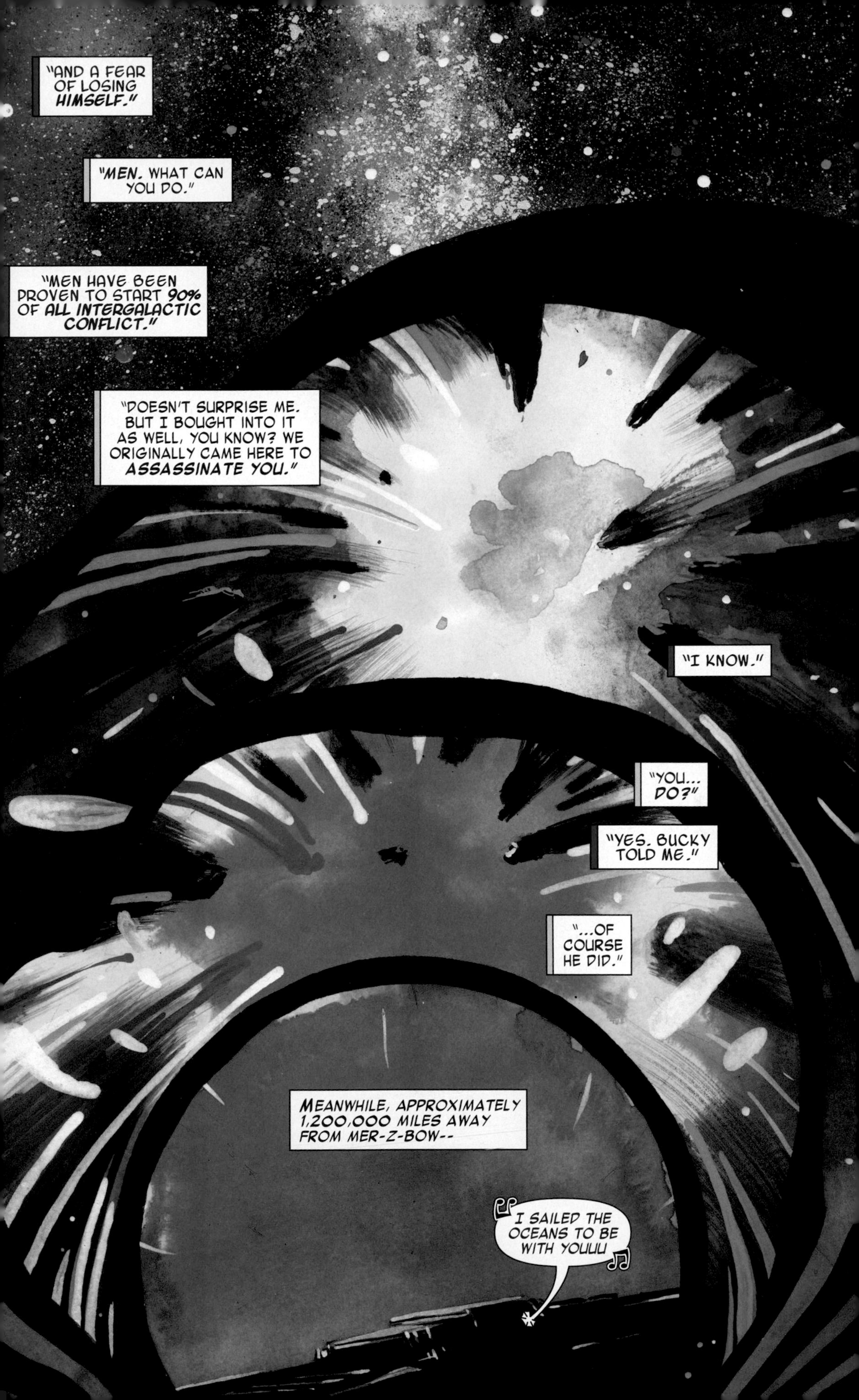
"AND A FEAR OF LOSING HIMSELF."
"MEN. WHAT CAN YOU DO."
"MEN HAVE BEEN PROVEN TO START 90% OF ALL INTERGALACTIC CONFLICT."
"DOESN'T SURPRISE ME. BUT I BOUGHT INTO IT AS WELL, YOU KNOW? WE ORIGINALLY CAME HERE TO ASSASSINATE YOU."
"I KNOW."
"YOU... DO?"
"YES. BUCKY TOLD ME."
"...OF COURSE HE DID."
MEANWHILE, APPROXIMATELY 1,200,000 MILES AWAY FROM MER-Z-BOW--
I SAILED THE OCEANS TO BE WITH YOUUU

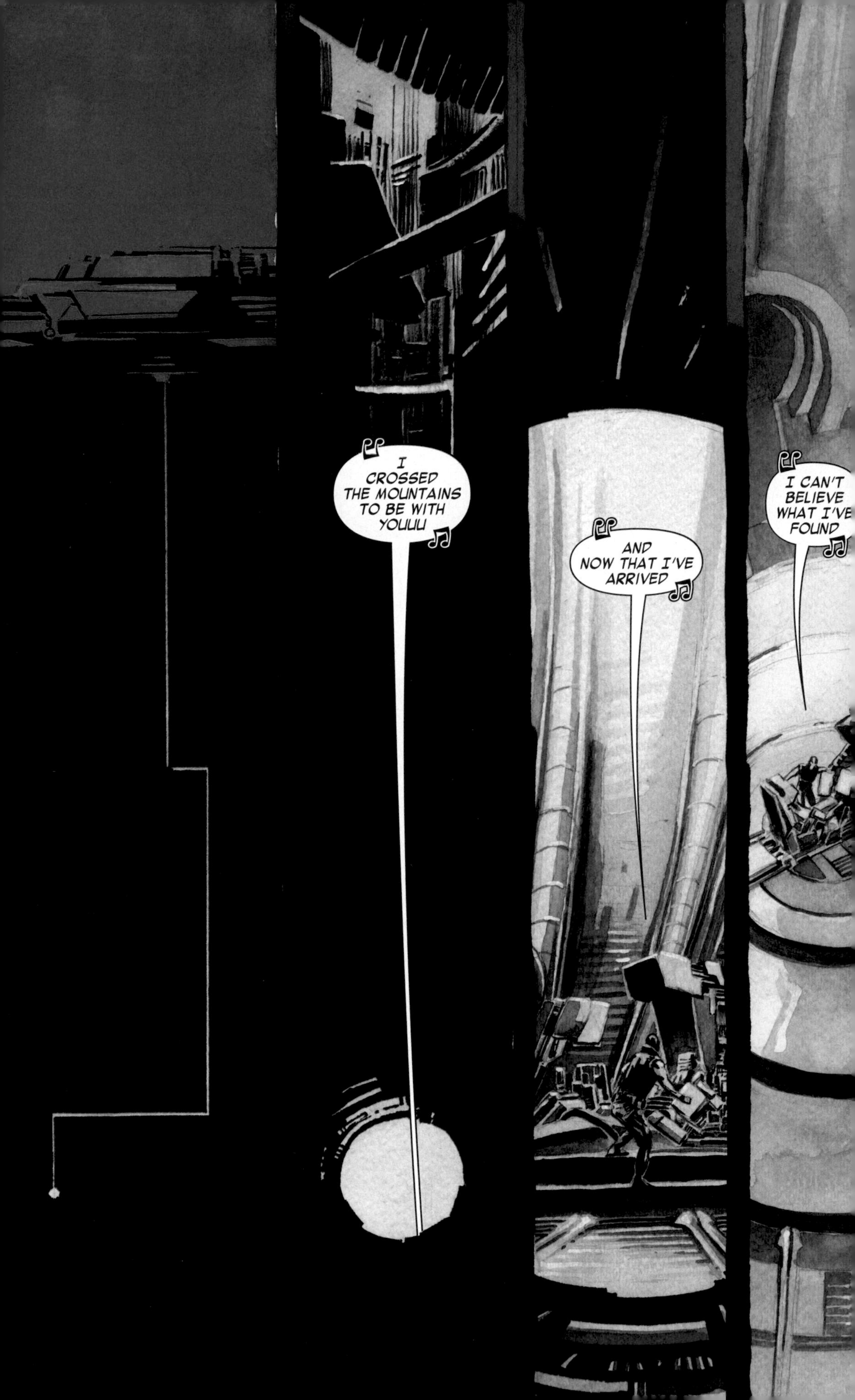
I CROSSED THE MOUNTAINS TO BE WITH YOUUU
AND NOW THAT I'VE ARRIVED
I CAN'T BELIEVE WHAT I'VE FOUND

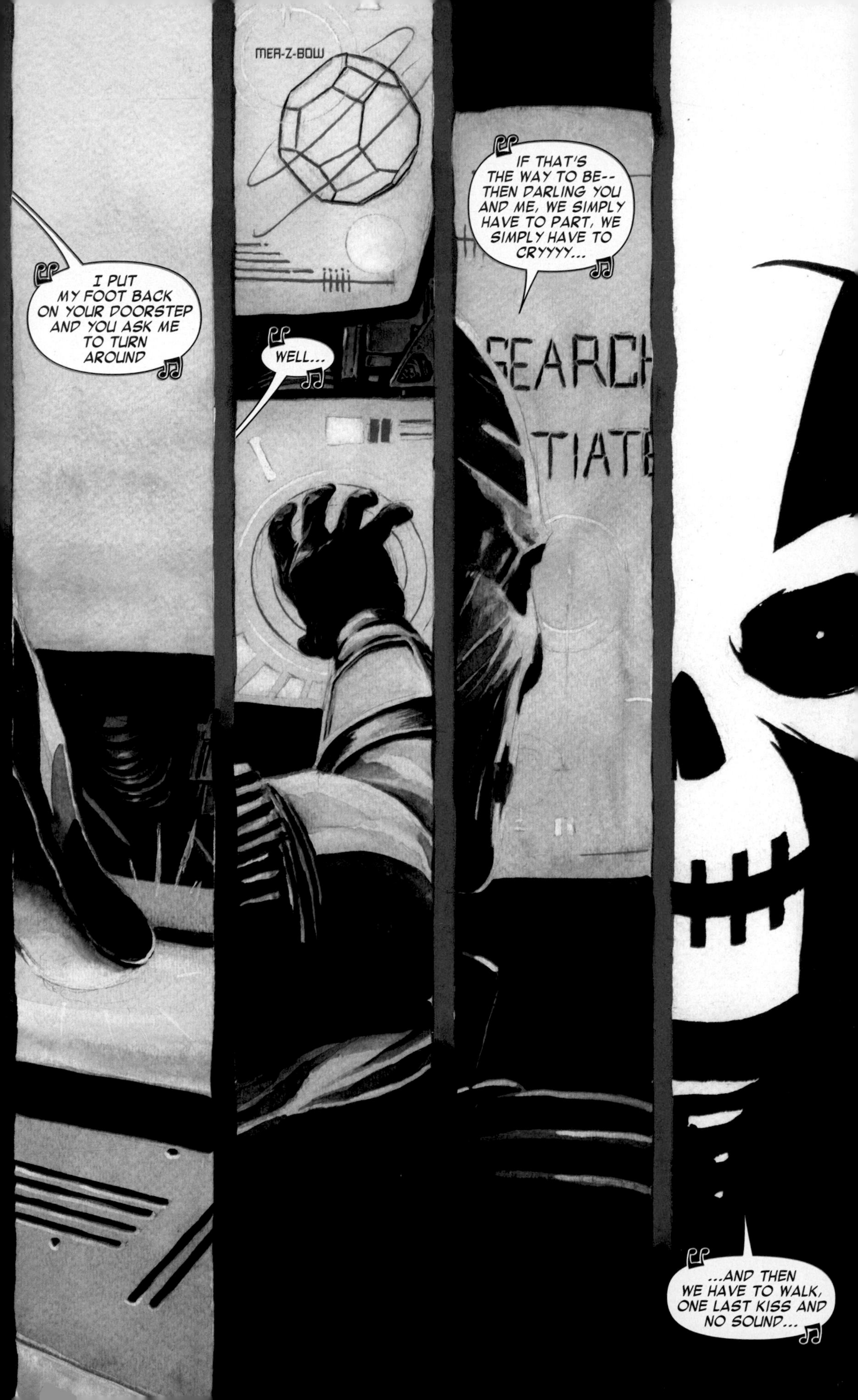
MER-Z-BOW
I PUT MY FOOT BACK ON YOUR DOORSTEP AND YOU ASK ME TO TURN AROUND
WELL...
IF THAT'S THE WAY TO BE-- THEN DARLING YOU AND ME, WE SIMPLY HAVE TO PART, WE SIMPLY HAVE TO CRYYYY...
SEARCH
TIATE
...AND THEN WE HAVE TO WALK, ONE LAST KISS AND NO SOUND...

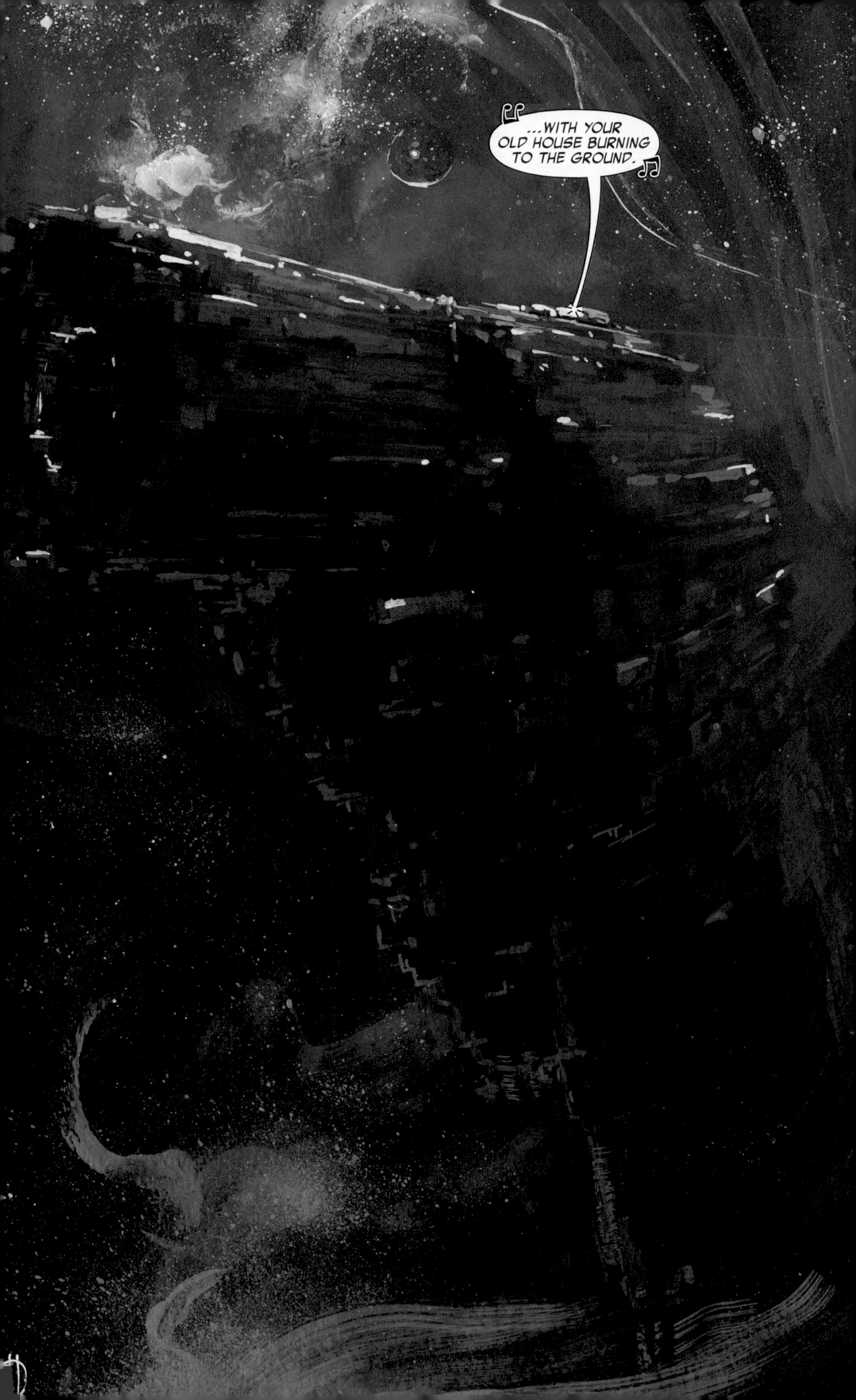
...WITH YOUR OLD HOUSE BURNING TO THE GROUND.

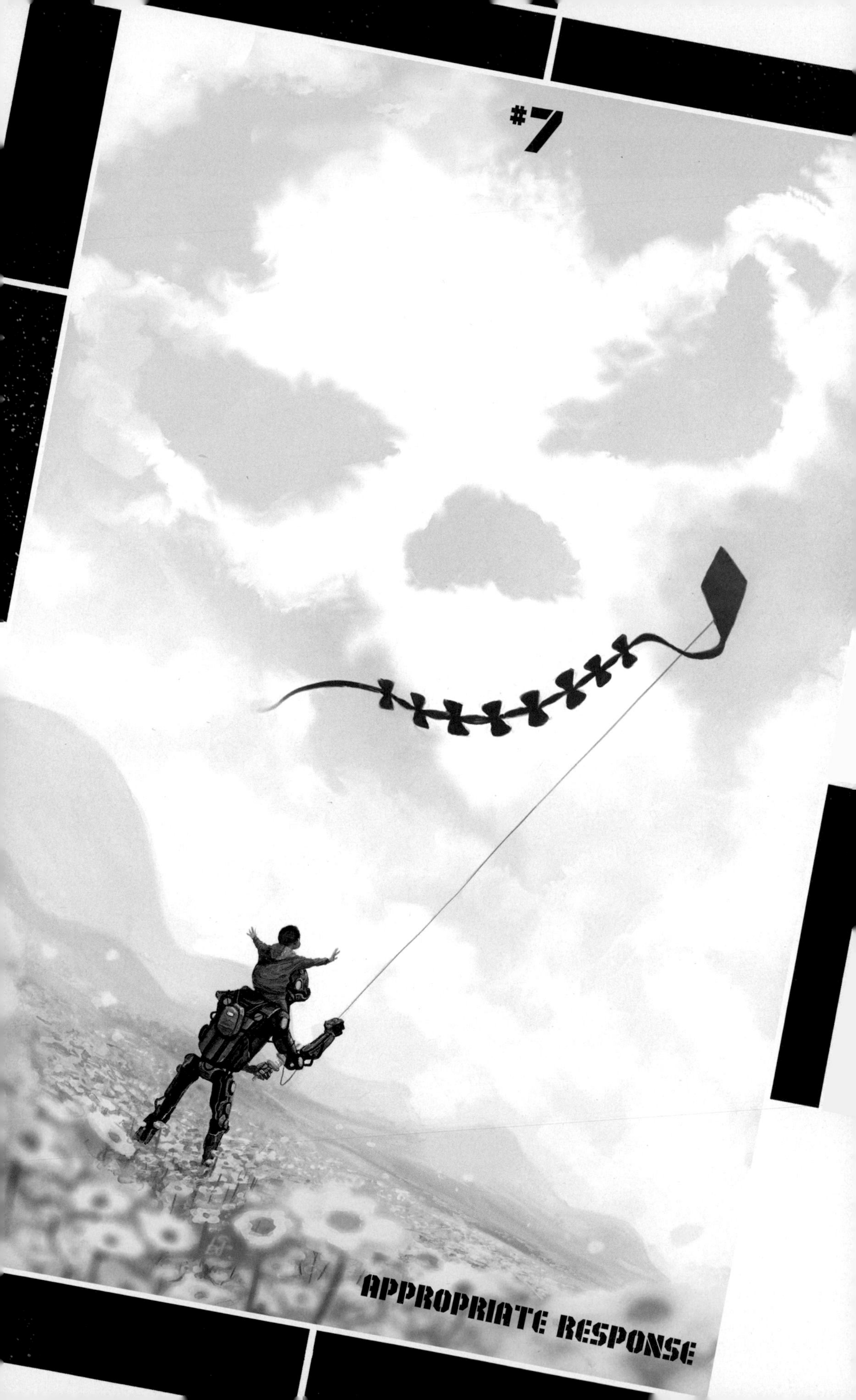
#7
APPROPRIATE RESPONSE

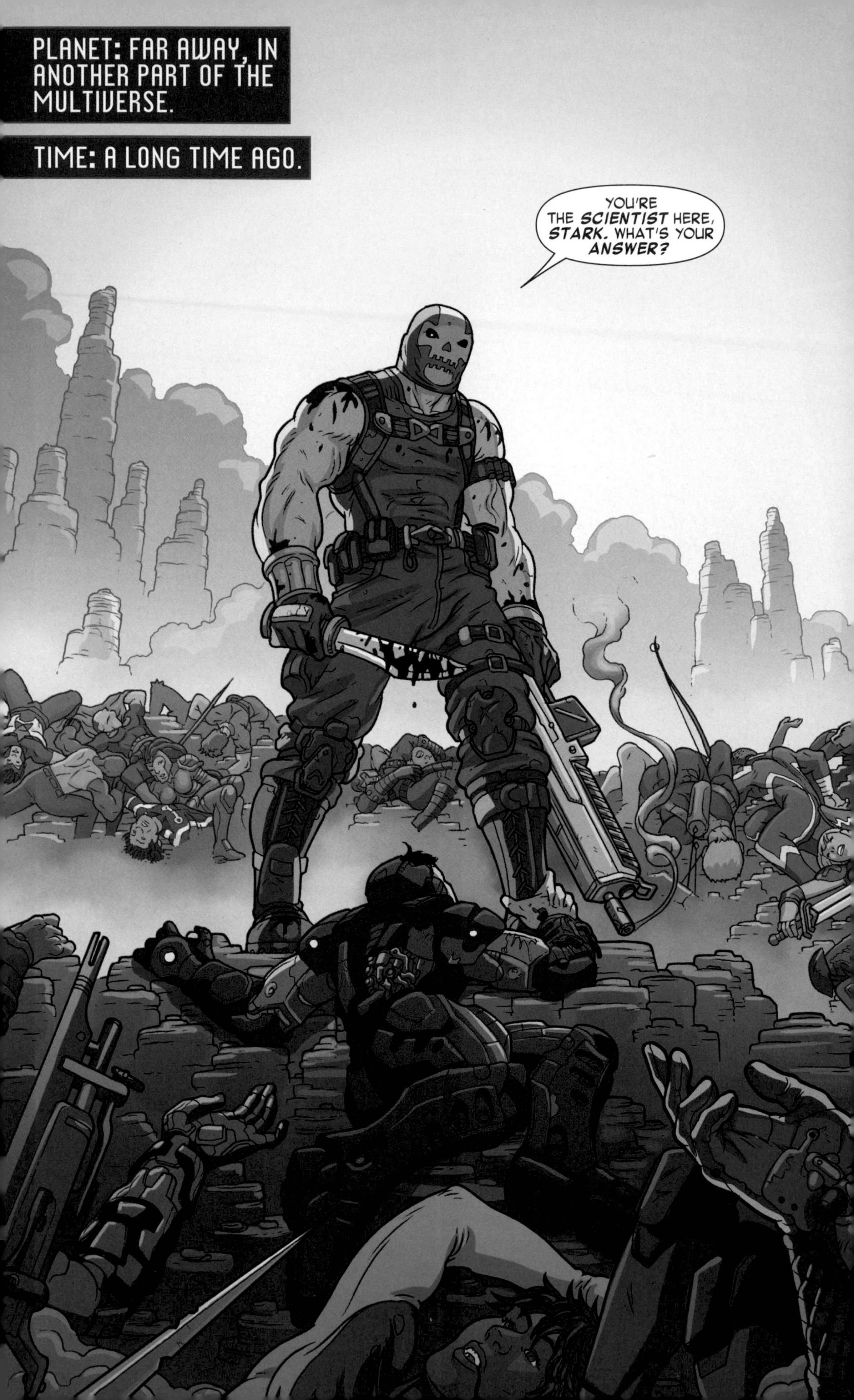
PLANET: FAR AWAY, IN ANOTHER PART OF THE MULTIVERSE.
TIME: A LONG TIME AGO.
YOU'RE THE SCIENTIST HERE, STARK. WHAT'S YOUR ANSWER?

THERE'S... THERE'S *NO ONE* PERFECTLY APPROPRIATE *RESPONSE* TO *REALITY.*

BUT... SOME THINGS ARE *WRONG* AND SOME THINGS ARE *RIGHT,* AND I *KNOW* THEM WHEN I *SEE* THEM.

SAY IT. GO ON.

MAKES ME *WRONG,* DON'T IT?

...MAKES YOU *INSANE.*

WELL, THAT'S THE THING, DON'TCHA KNOW...?

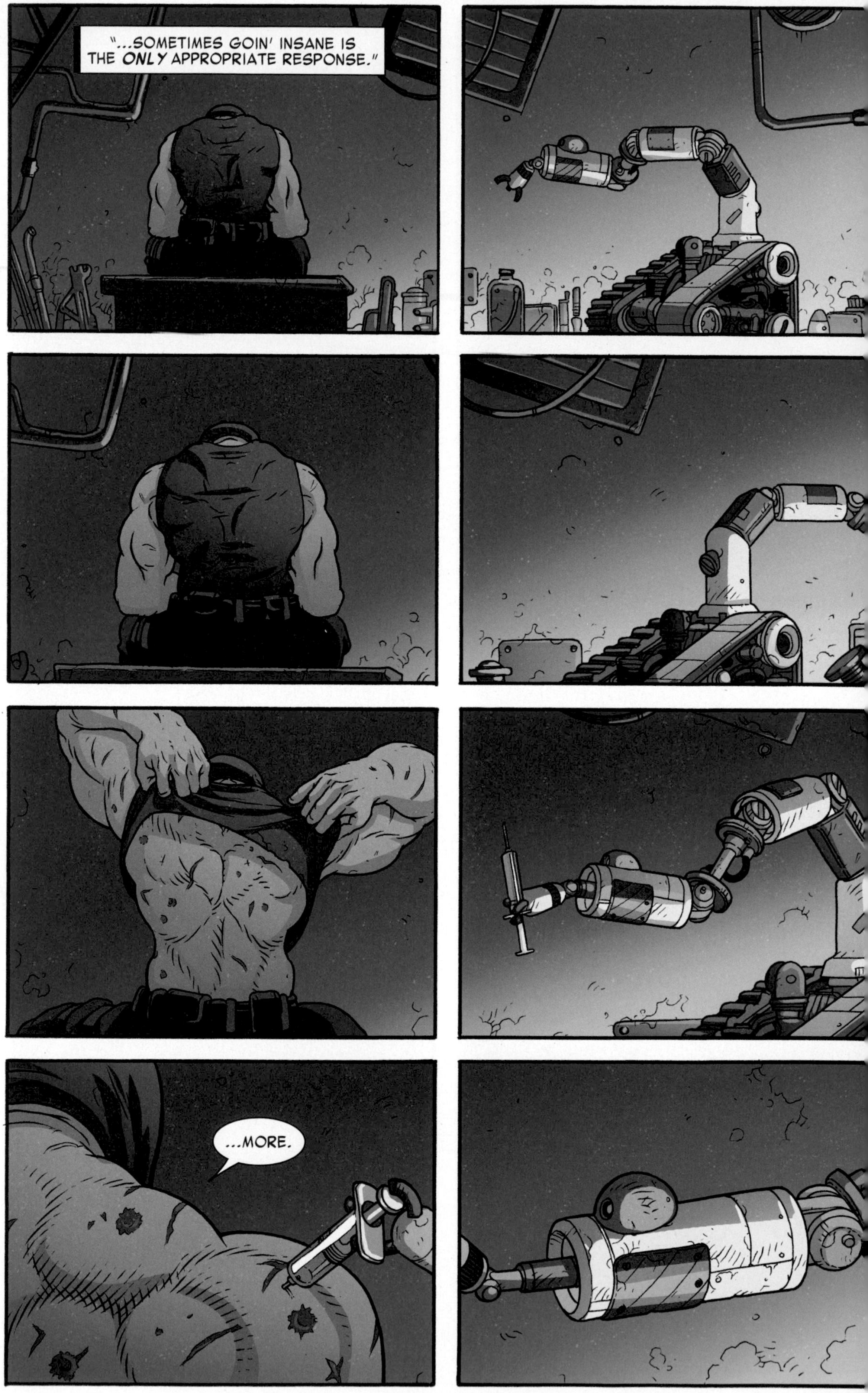
"...SOMETIMES GOIN' INSANE IS THE ONLY APPROPRIATE RESPONSE."
...MORE.

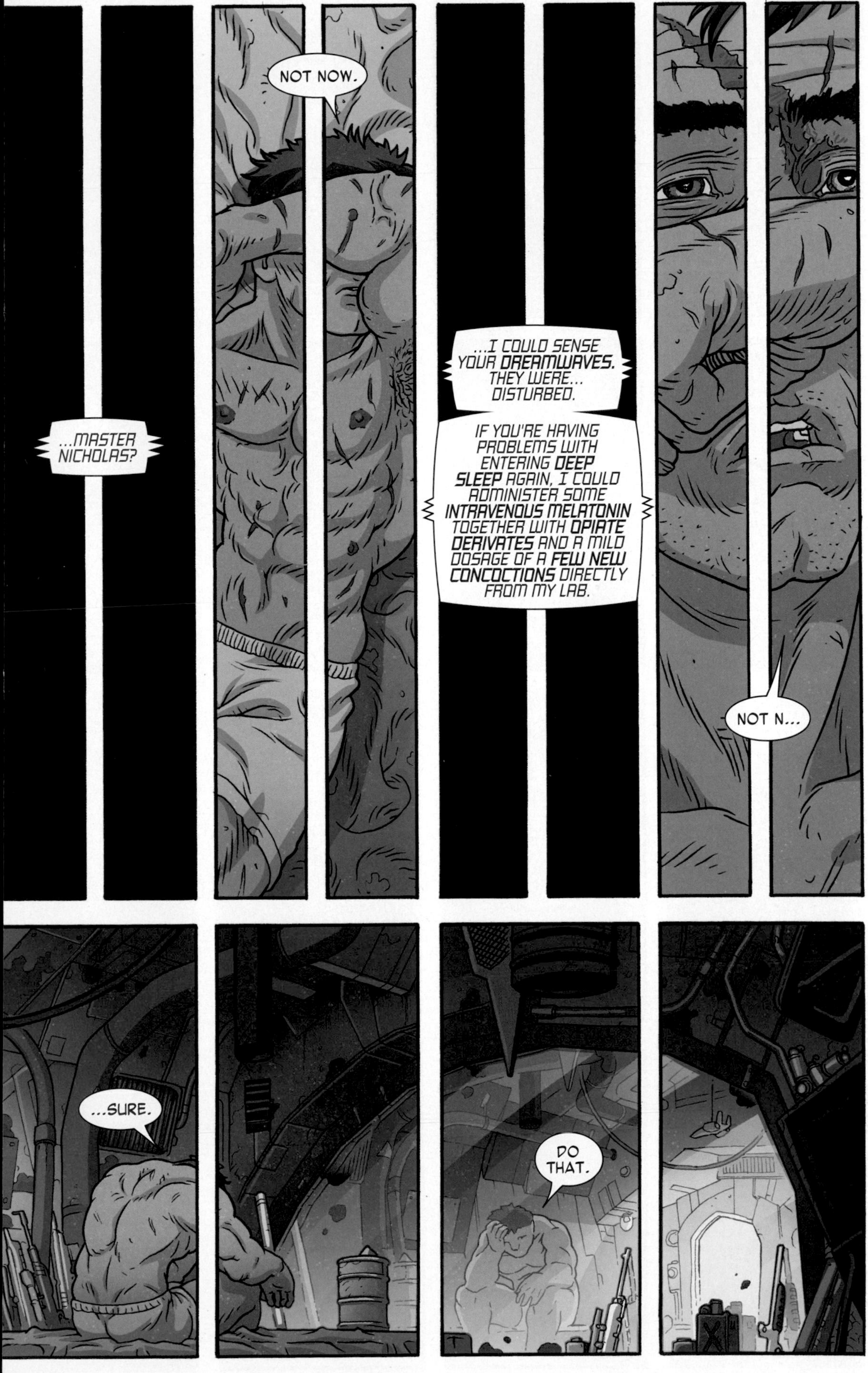

...MASTER NICHOLAS?
NOT NOW.
...I COULD SENSE YOUR **DREAMWAVES.** THEY WERE... DISTURBED.
IF YOU'RE HAVING PROBLEMS WITH ENTERING **DEEP SLEEP** AGAIN, I COULD ADMINISTER SOME **INTRAVENOUS MELATONIN** TOGETHER WITH **OPIATE DERIVATES** AND A MILD DOSAGE OF A **FEW NEW CONCOCTIONS** DIRECTLY FROM MY LAB.
NOT N...
...SURE.
DO THAT.

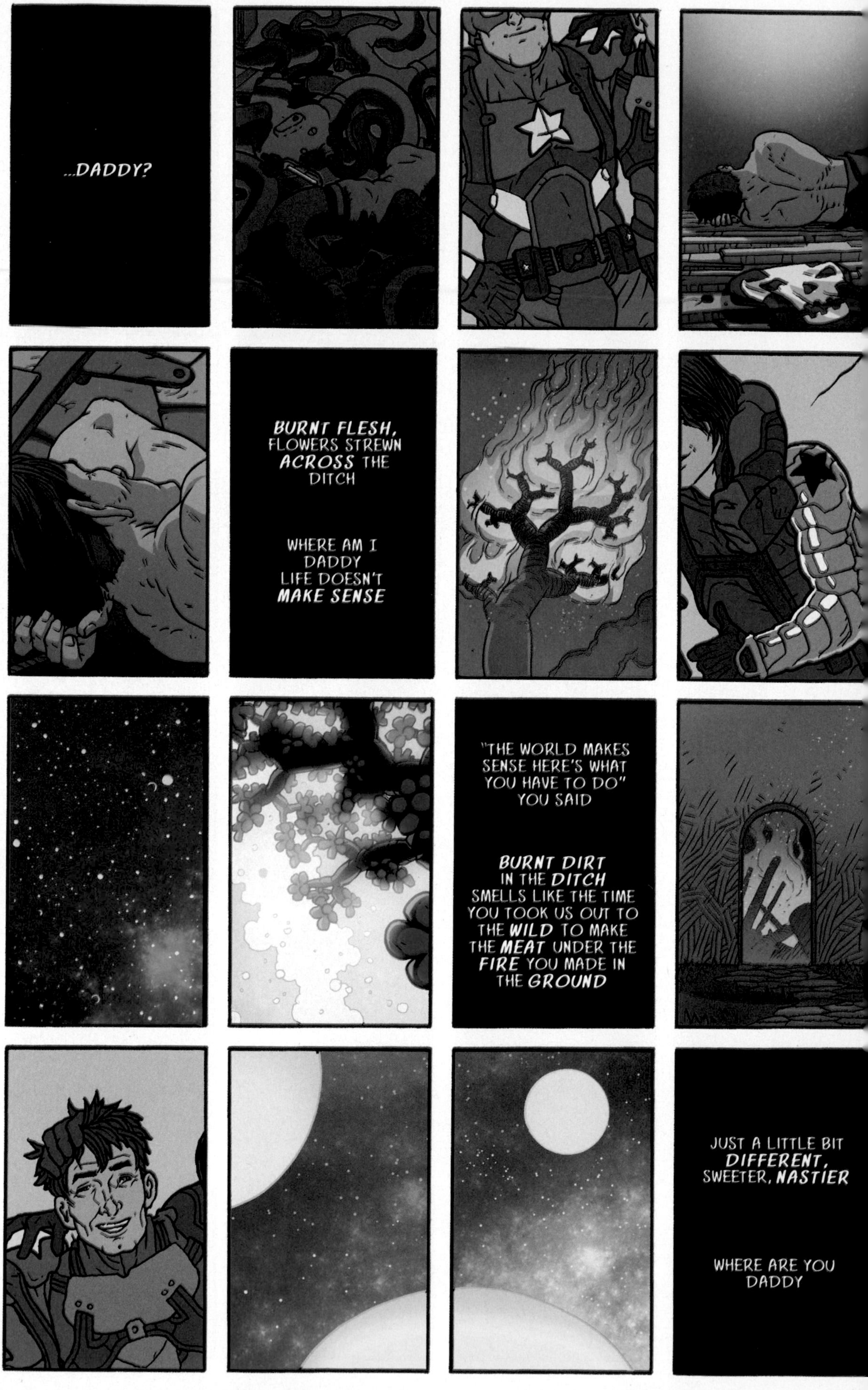

...DADDY?
BURNT FLESH, FLOWERS STREWN ACROSS THE DITCH
WHERE AM I DADDY LIFE DOESN'T MAKE SENSE
"THE WORLD MAKES SENSE HERE'S WHAT YOU HAVE TO DO" YOU SAID
BURNT DIRT IN THE DITCH SMELLS LIKE THE TIME YOU TOOK US OUT TO THE WILD TO MAKE THE MEAT UNDER THE FIRE YOU MADE IN THE GROUND
JUST A LITTLE BIT DIFFERENT, SWEETER, NASTIER
WHERE ARE YOU DADDY

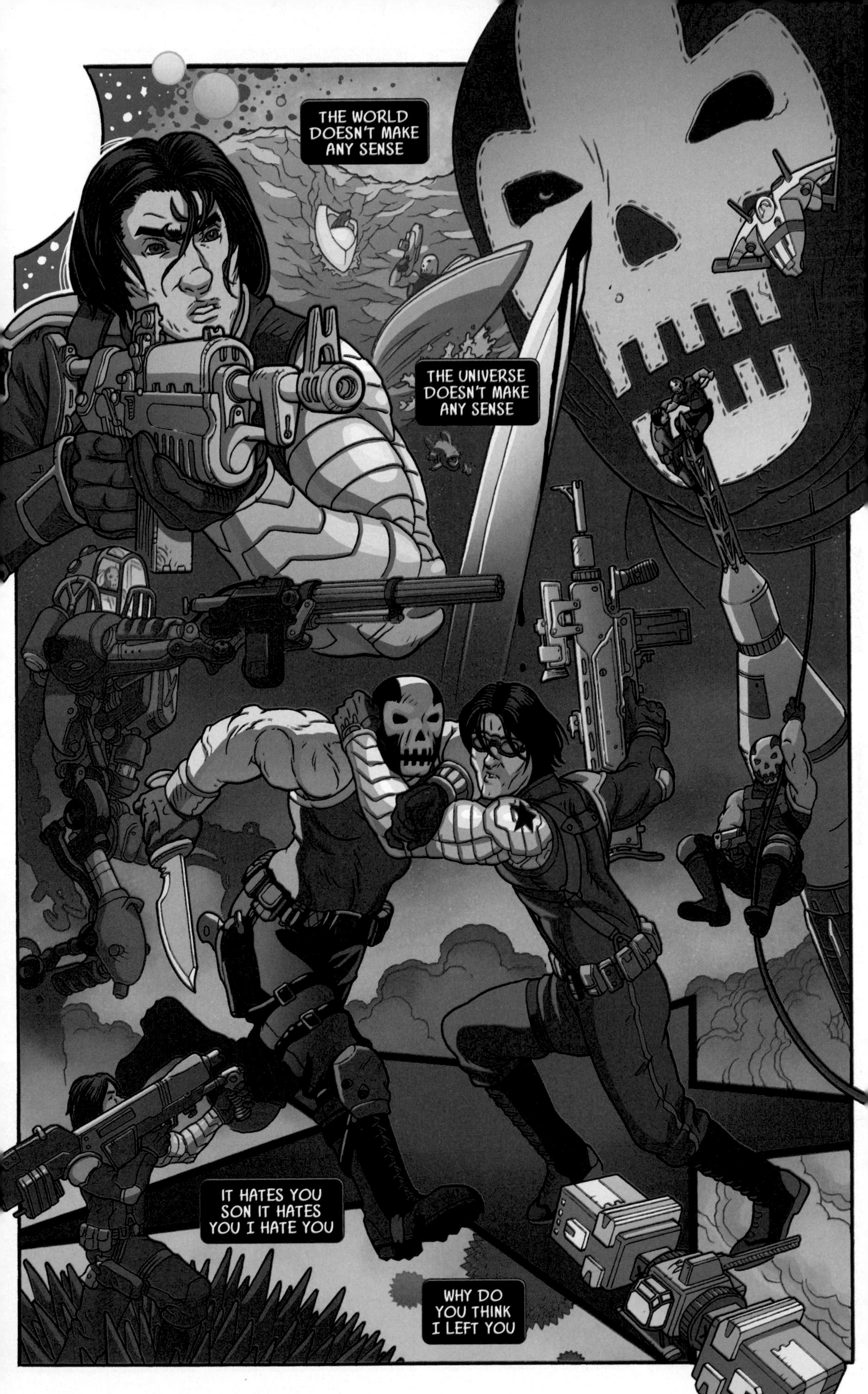
THE WORLD DOESN'T MAKE ANY SENSE
THE UNIVERSE DOESN'T MAKE ANY SENSE
IT HATES YOU SON IT HATES YOU I HATE YOU
WHY DO YOU THINK I LEFT YOU

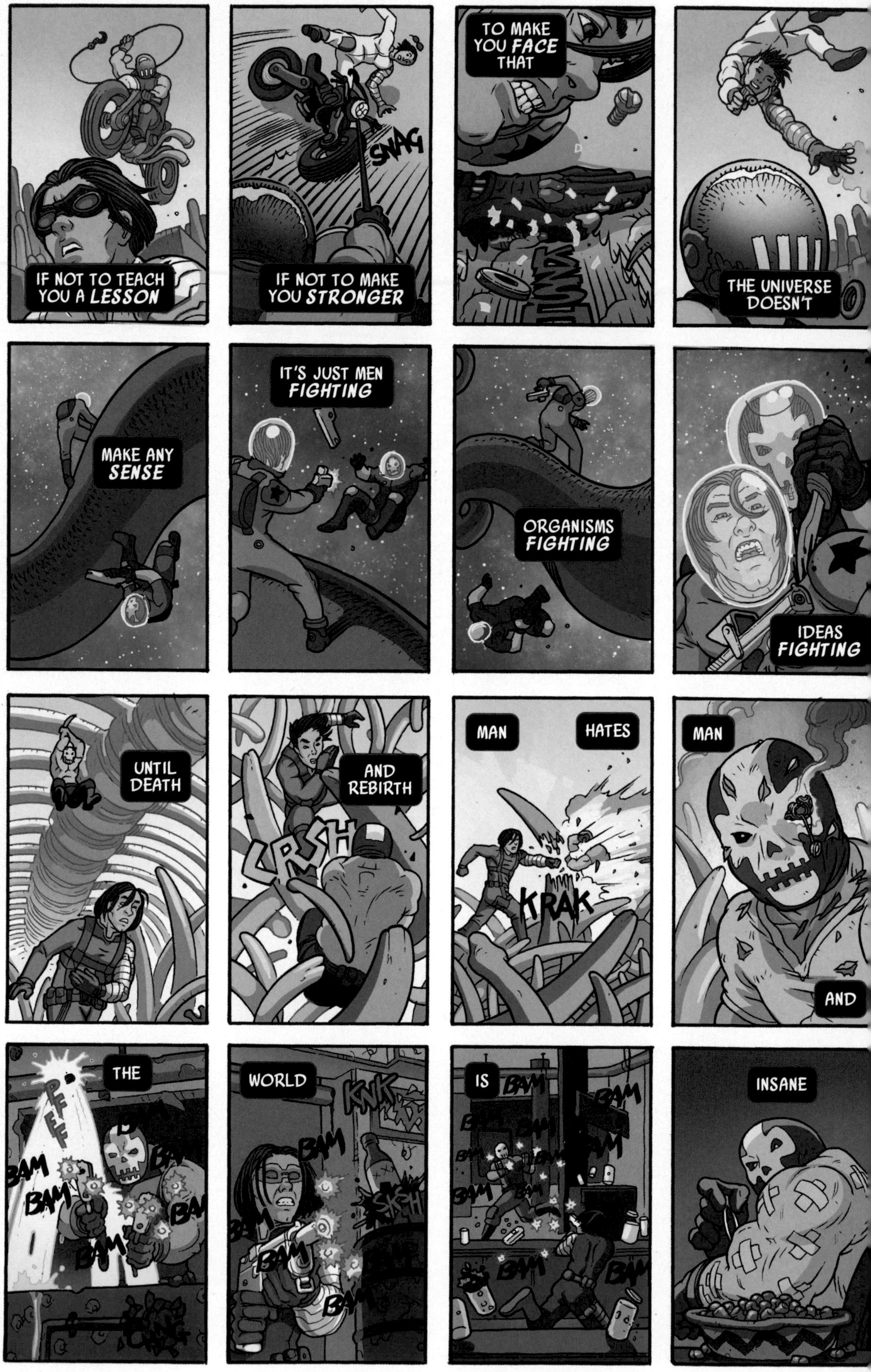
IF NOT TO TEACH YOU A LESSON
SNAG
IF NOT TO MAKE YOU STRONGER
TO MAKE YOU FACE THAT
THE UNIVERSE DOESN'T
MAKE ANY SENSE
IT'S JUST MEN FIGHTING
ORGANISMS FIGHTING
IDEAS FIGHTING
UNTIL DEATH
AND REBIRTH
CRSH
MAN
HATES
KRAK
MAN
AND
THE
PFFF
BAM
BAM
BAM
WORLD
KNK
BAM
BAM
SKSH
IS
BAM
BAM
INSANE

What is the point of marking this entry with a date?

The universe is a lie.

The war...

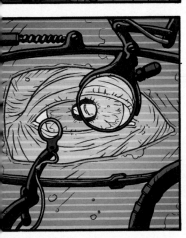

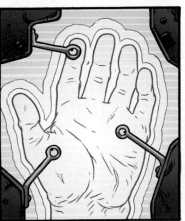

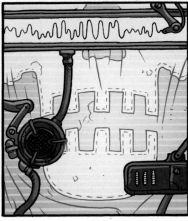

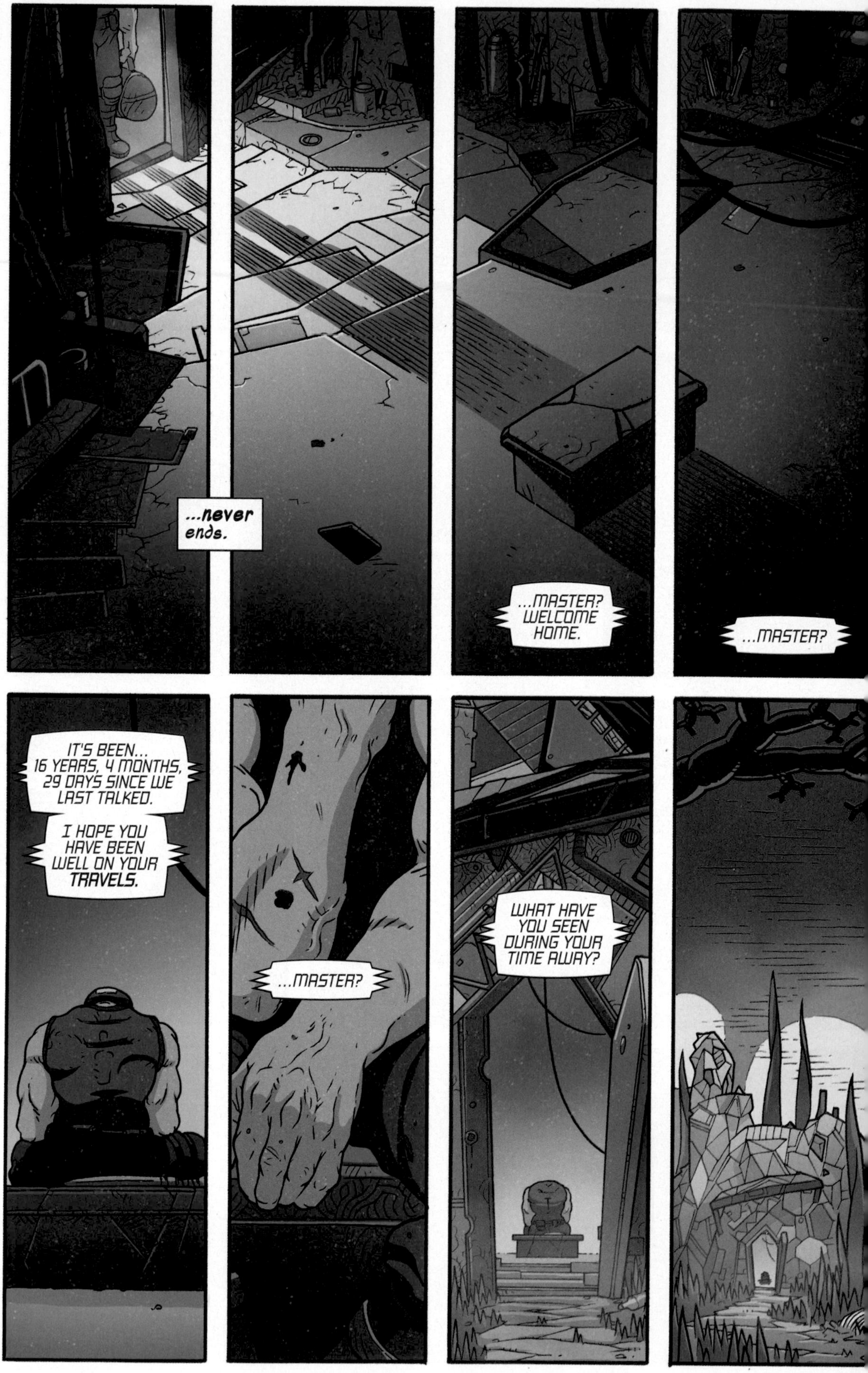
...never ends.
...MASTER? WELCOME HOME.
...MASTER?
IT'S BEEN... 16 YEARS, 4 MONTHS, 29 DAYS SINCE WE LAST TALKED.
I HOPE YOU HAVE BEEN WELL ON YOUR TRAVELS.
...MASTER?
WHAT HAVE YOU SEEN DURING YOUR TIME AWAY?

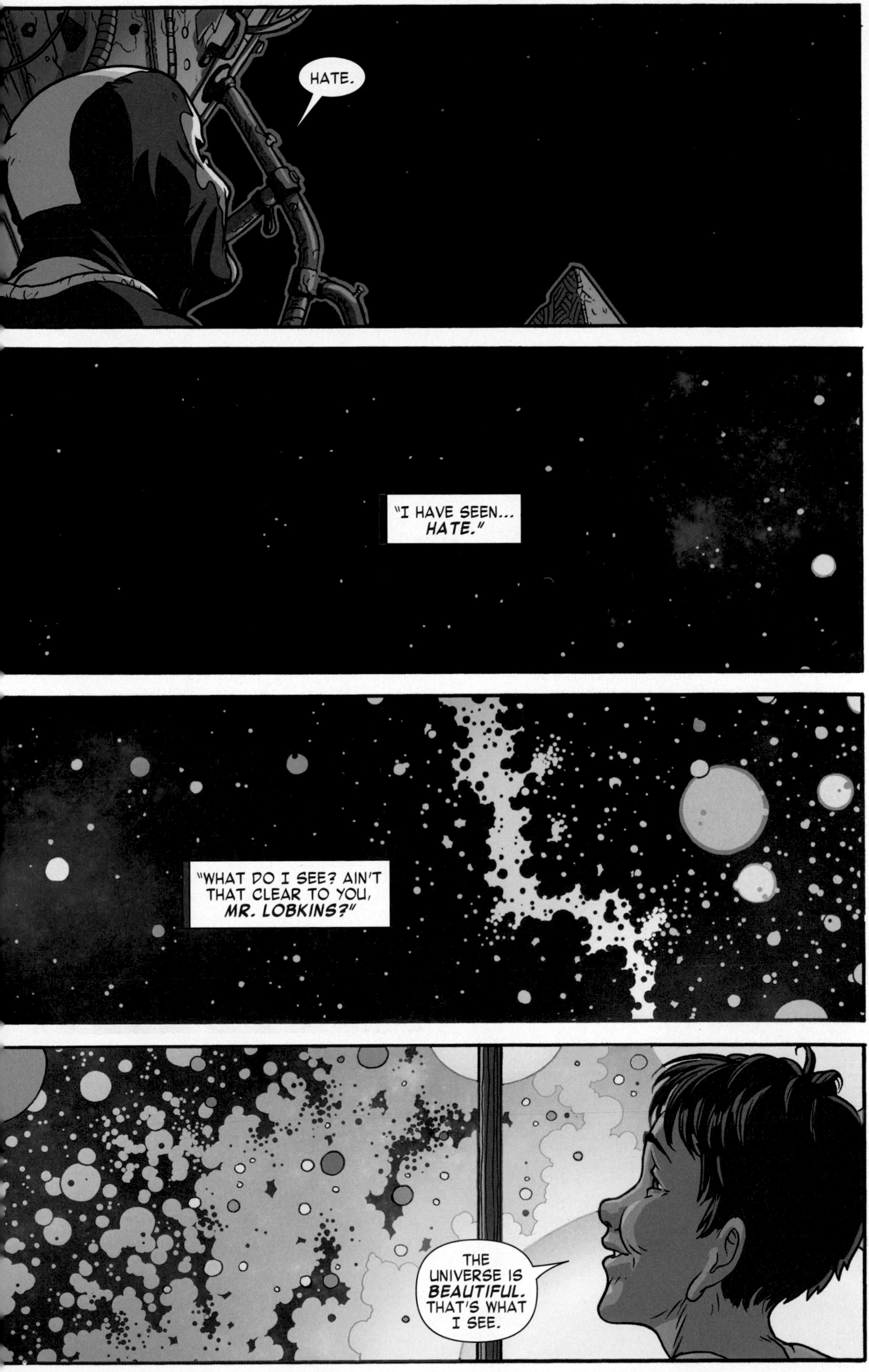
HATE.
"I HAVE SEEN... HATE."
"WHAT DO I SEE? AIN'T THAT CLEAR TO YOU, MR. LOBKINS?"
THE UNIVERSE IS BEAUTIFUL. THAT'S WHAT I SEE.

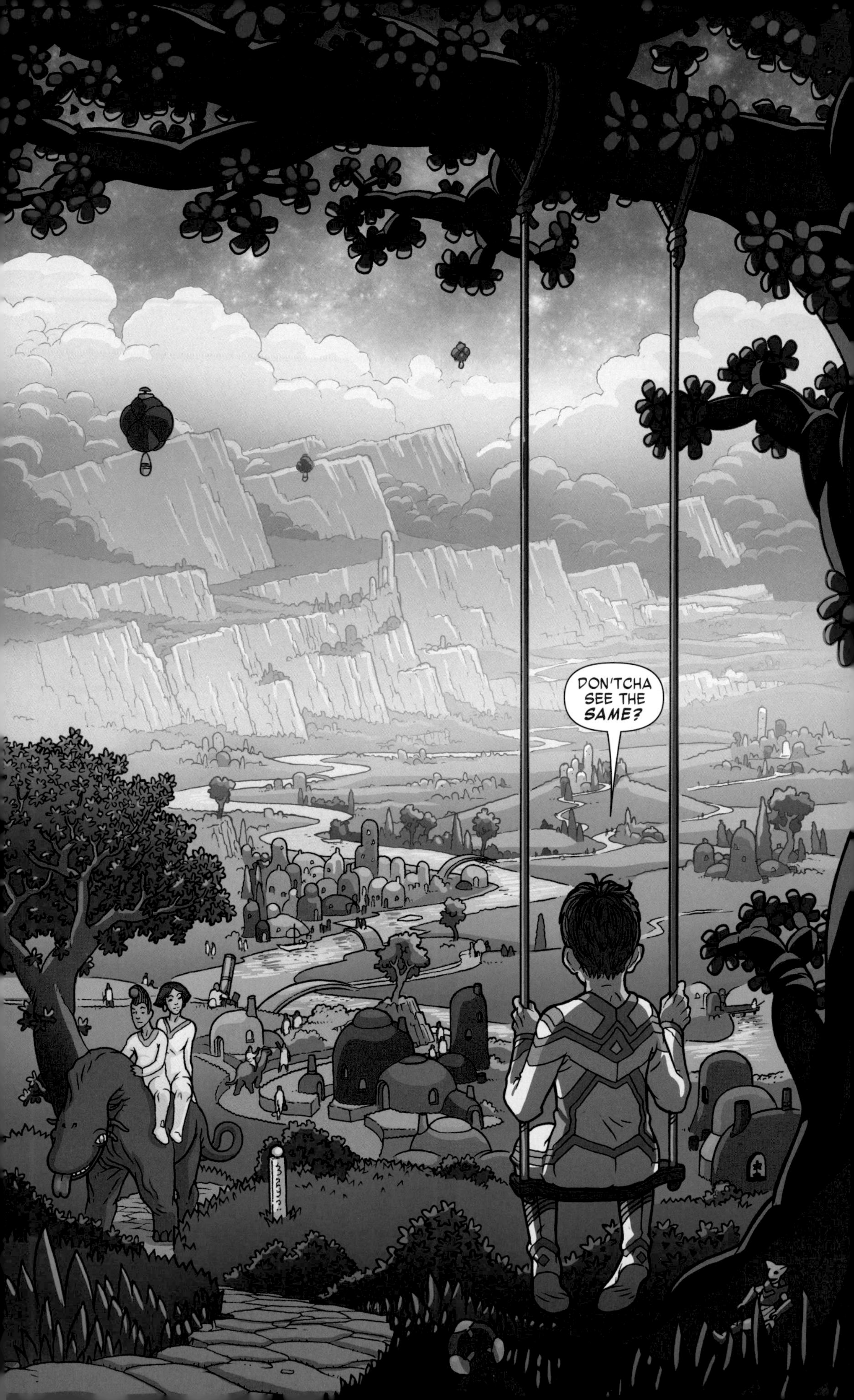
DON'TCHA SEE THE SAME?

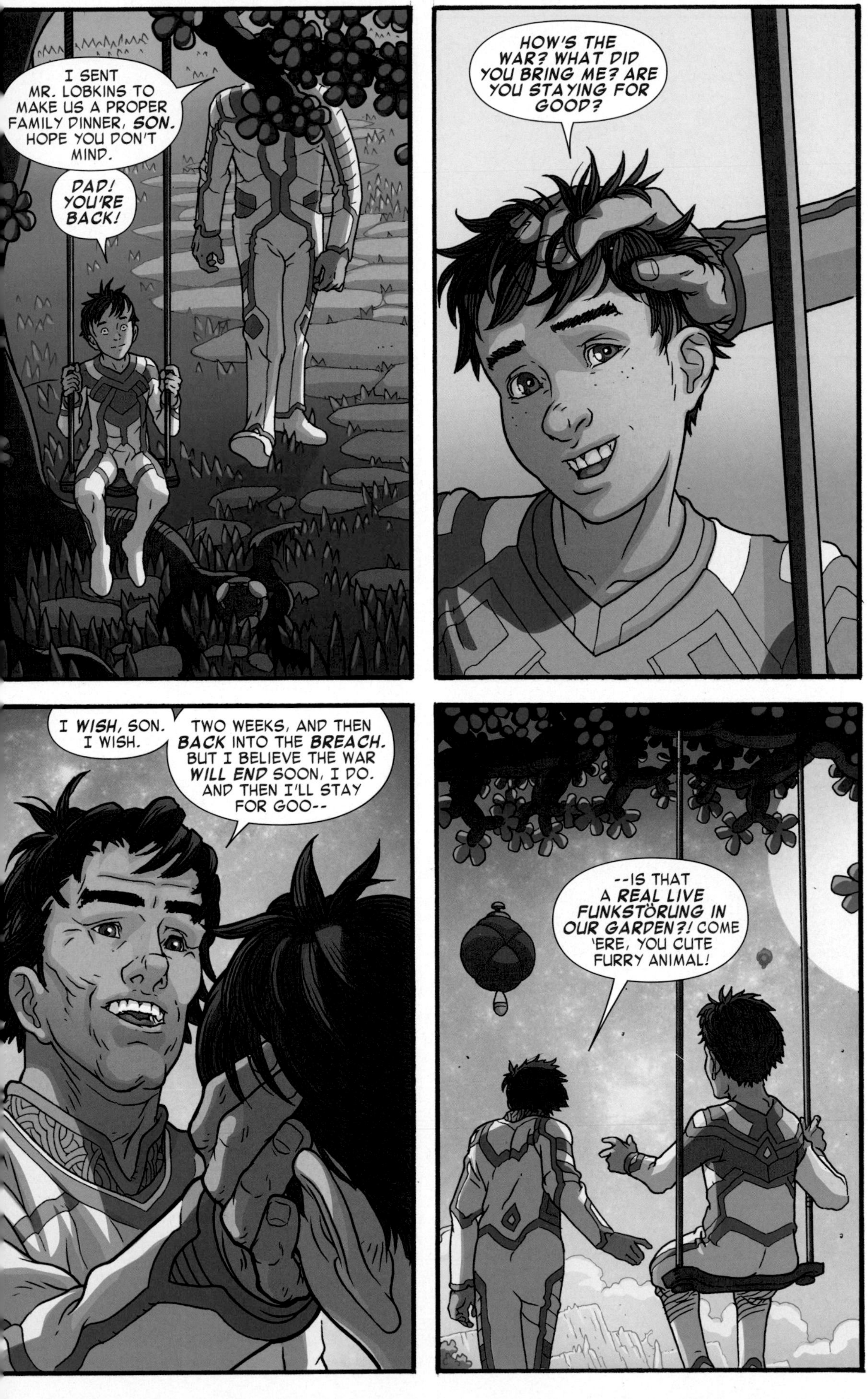
I SENT MR. LOBKINS TO MAKE US A PROPER FAMILY DINNER, SON. HOPE YOU DON'T MIND.
DAD! YOU'RE BACK!
HOW'S THE WAR? WHAT DID YOU BRING ME? ARE YOU STAYING FOR GOOD?
I WISH, SON. I WISH.
TWO WEEKS, AND THEN BACK INTO THE BREACH. BUT I BELIEVE THE WAR WILL END SOON, I DO. AND THEN I'LL STAY FOR GOO--
--IS THAT A REAL LIVE FUNKSTÖRUNG IN OUR GARDEN?! COME 'ERE, YOU CUTE FURRY ANIMAL!

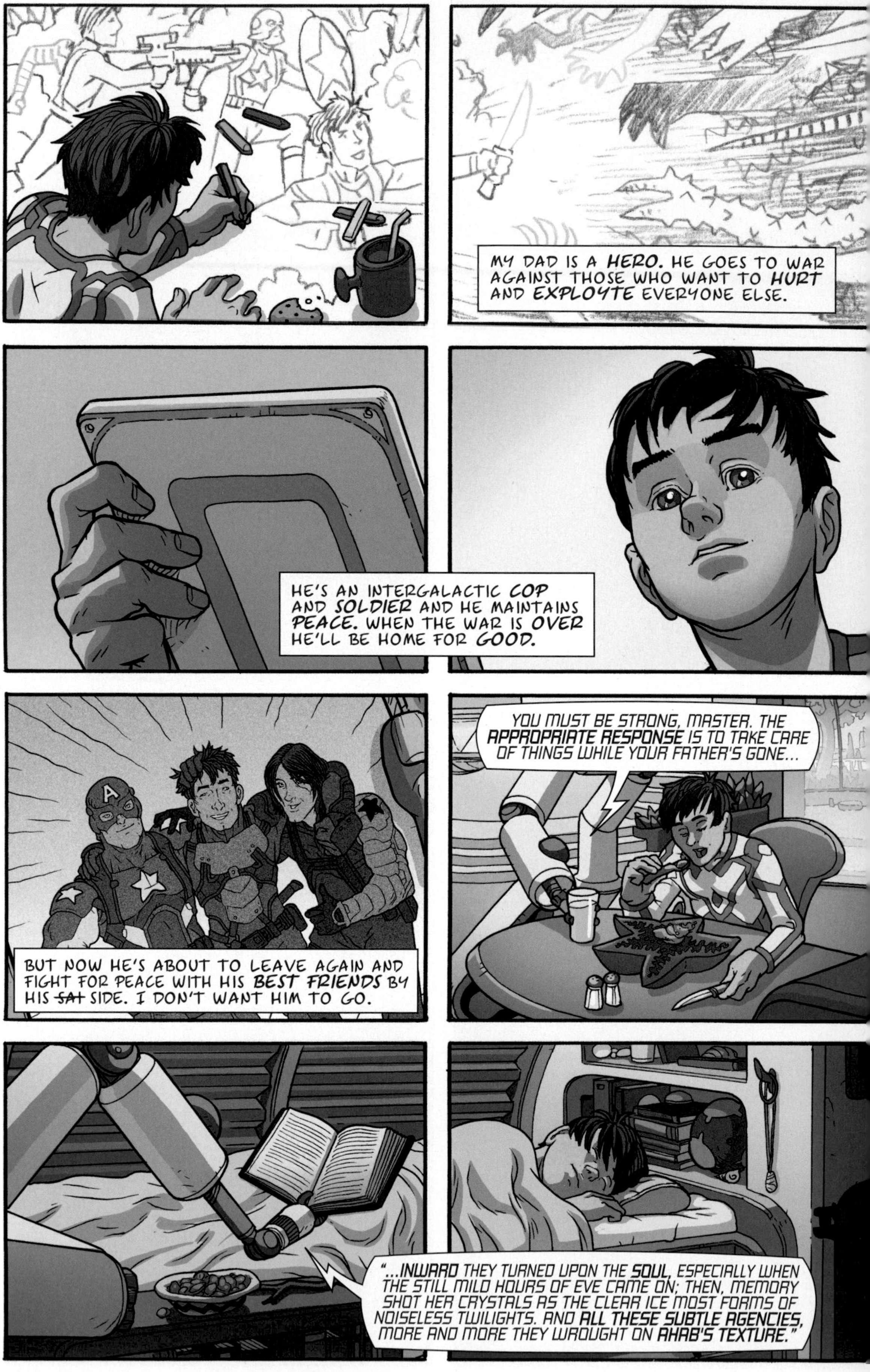
MY DAD IS A HERO. HE GOES TO WAR AGAINST THOSE WHO WANT TO HURT AND EXPLOYTE EVERYONE ELSE.
HE'S AN INTERGALACTIC COP AND SOLDIER AND HE MAINTAINS PEACE. WHEN THE WAR IS OVER HE'LL BE HOME FOR GOOD.
BUT NOW HE'S ABOUT TO LEAVE AGAIN AND FIGHT FOR PEACE WITH HIS BEST FRIENDS BY HIS SAI SIDE. I DON'T WANT HIM TO GO.
YOU MUST BE STRONG, MASTER. THE APPROPRIATE RESPONSE IS TO TAKE CARE OF THINGS WHILE YOUR FATHER'S GONE...
"...INWARD THEY TURNED UPON THE SOUL, ESPECIALLY WHEN THE STILL MILD HOURS OF EVE CAME ON; THEN, MEMORY SHOT HER CRYSTALS AS THE CLEAR ICE MOST FORMS OF NOISELESS TWILIGHTS. AND ALL THESE SUBTLE AGENCIES, MORE AND MORE THEY WROUGHT ON AHAB'S TEXTURE."

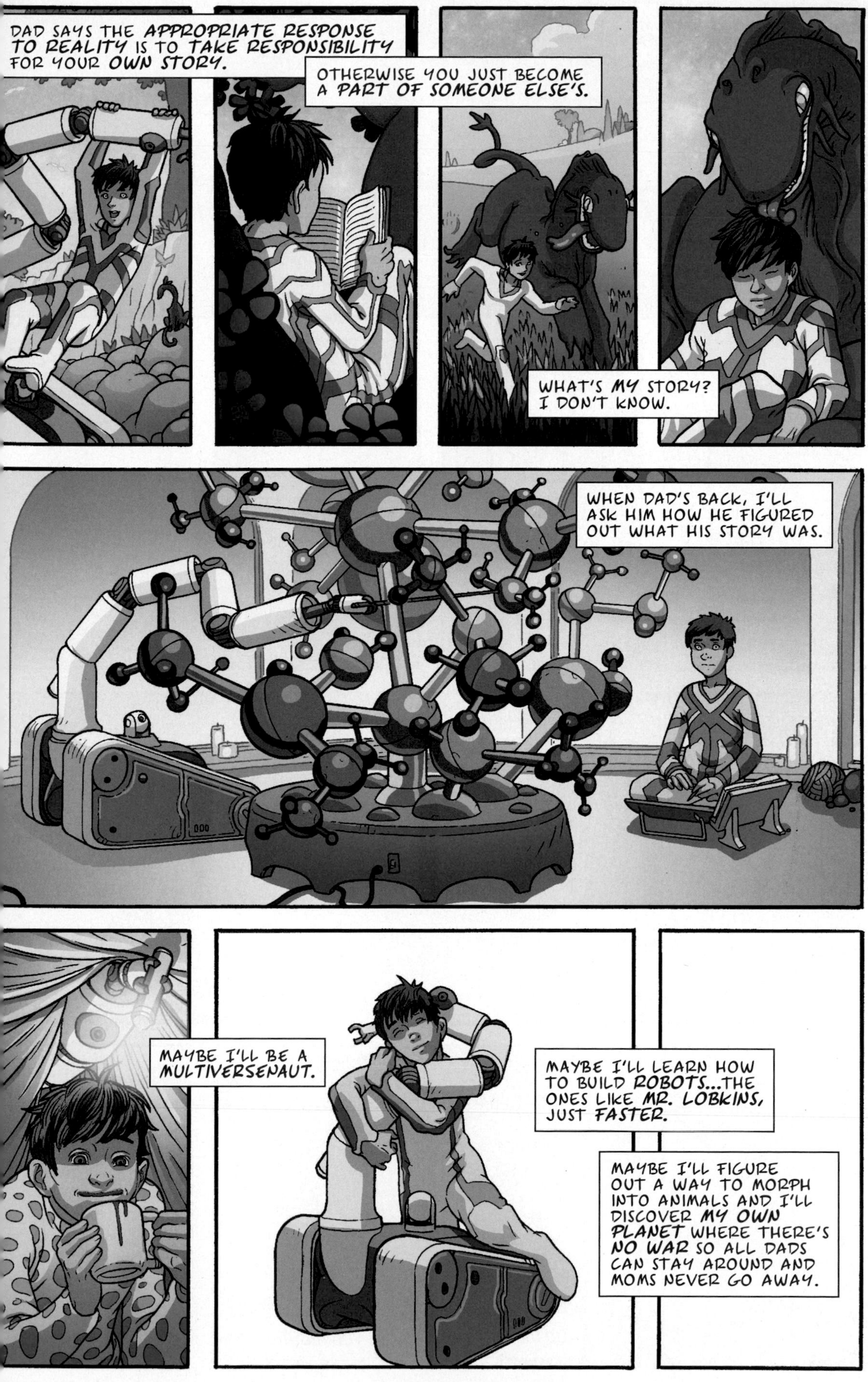
DAD SAYS THE APPROPRIATE RESPONSE TO REALITY IS TO TAKE RESPONSIBILITY FOR YOUR OWN STORY.
OTHERWISE YOU JUST BECOME A PART OF SOMEONE ELSE'S.
WHAT'S MY STORY? I DON'T KNOW.
WHEN DAD'S BACK, I'LL ASK HIM HOW HE FIGURED OUT WHAT HIS STORY WAS.
MAYBE I'LL BE A MULTIVERSENAUT.
MAYBE I'LL LEARN HOW TO BUILD ROBOTS...THE ONES LIKE MR. LOBKINS, JUST FASTER.
MAYBE I'LL FIGURE OUT A WAY TO MORPH INTO ANIMALS AND I'LL DISCOVER MY OWN PLANET WHERE THERE'S NO WAR SO ALL DADS CAN STAY AROUND AND MOMS NEVER GO AWAY.

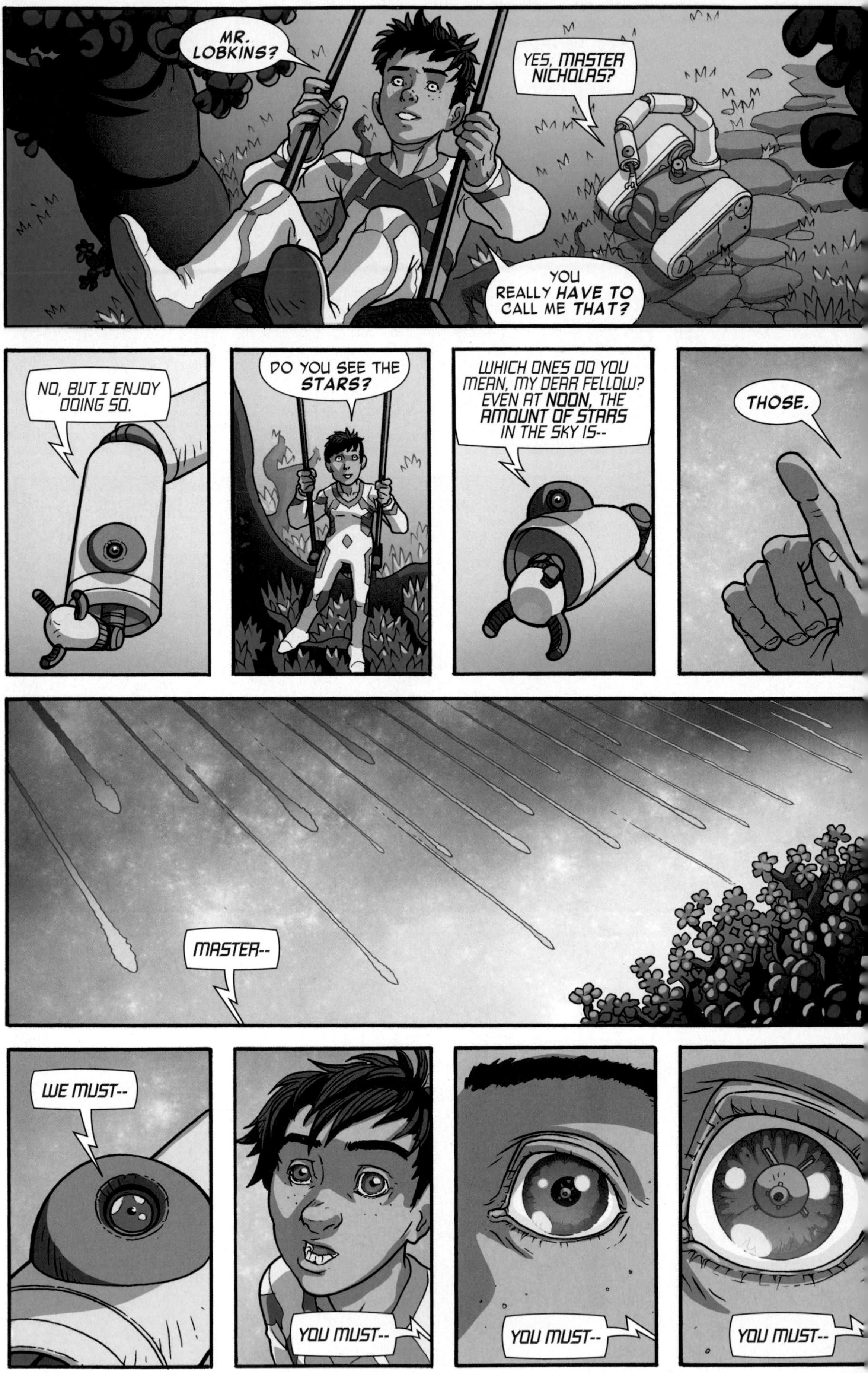
MR. LOBKINS?
YES, MASTER NICHOLAS?
YOU REALLY HAVE TO CALL ME THAT?
NO, BUT I ENJOY DOING SO.
DO YOU SEE THE STARS?
WHICH ONES DO YOU MEAN, MY DEAR FELLOW? EVEN AT NOON, THE AMOUNT OF STARS IN THE SKY IS--
THOSE.
MASTER--
WE MUST--
YOU MUST--
YOU MUST--
YOU MUST--

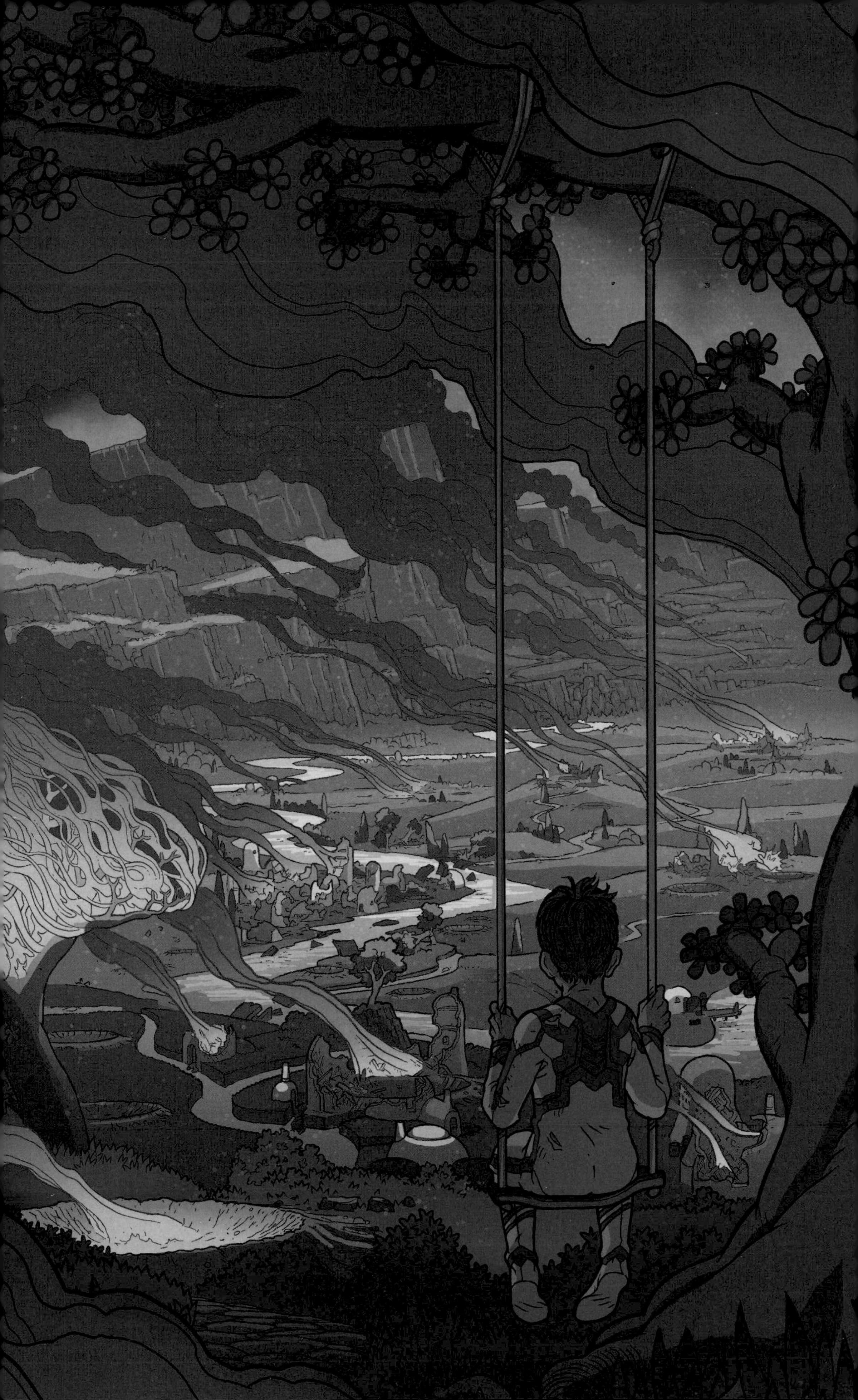

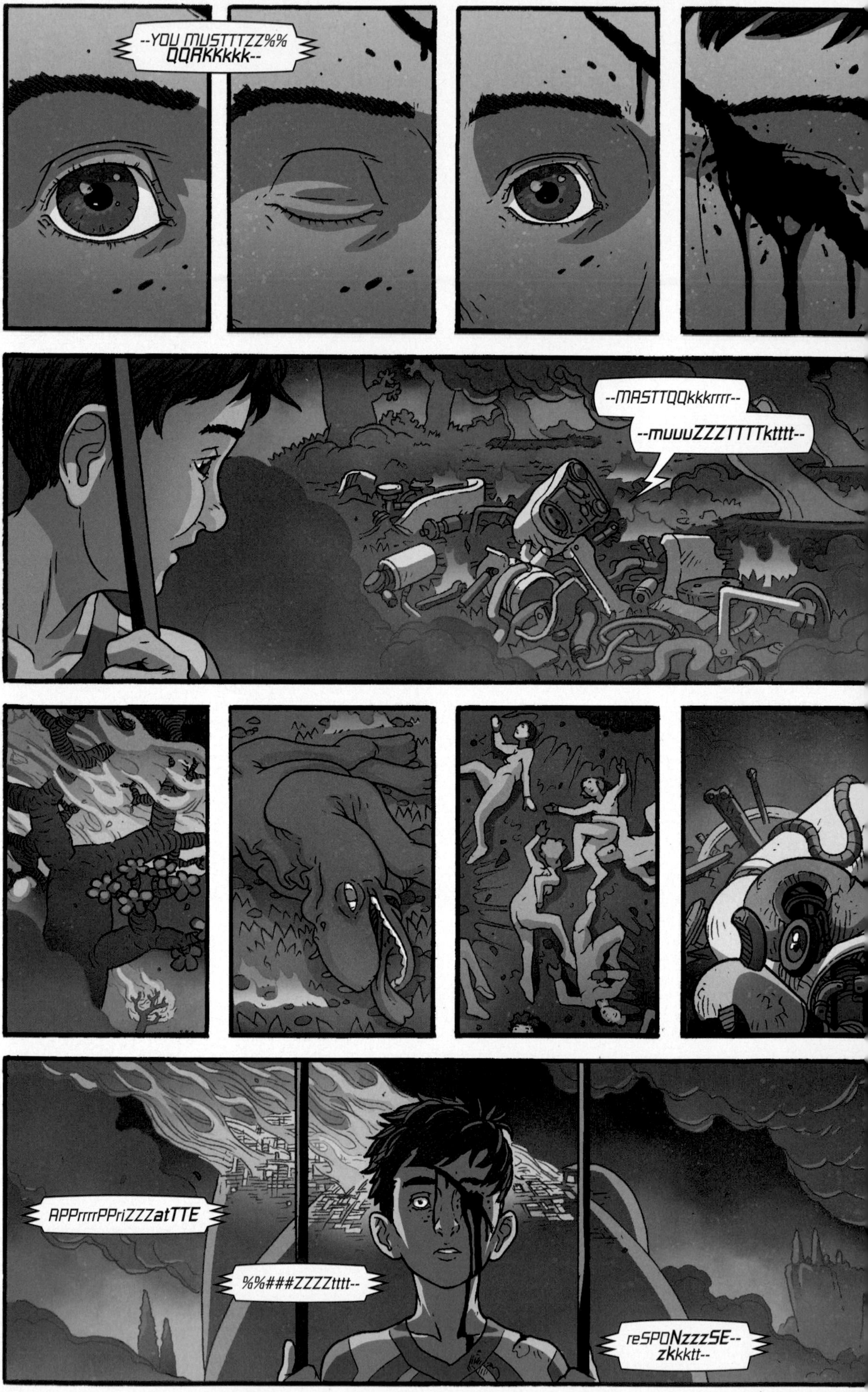
--YOU MUSTTTZZ%%
QQRKKkkk--
--MASTTQQkkkrrrr--
--muuuZZZTTTTktttt--
APPrrrrPPriZZZatTTE
%%###ZZZZtttt--
reSPONzzzSE--
zkkktt--

YOU KNOW WHAT TODAY IS, LOBKINS?

...MASTER? ARE YOU TALKING TO ME AGAIN? I AM SO--

TODAY'S THE DAY I KILLED MOST OF THE SO-CALLED "HEROES" OF THIS UNIVERSE. JUST TO PROVE A POINT.

...

IS THIS...

...WHAT?

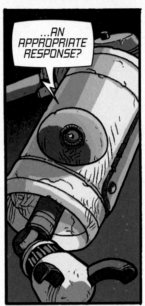

...AN APPROPRIATE RESPONSE?

THE APPROPRIATE RESPONSE IS TO TEACH THE WINTER SOLDIER THE LESSON HE'D BEEN AVOIDING ALL THIS TIME.

LIFE IS HATE.

ALL IS WAR.

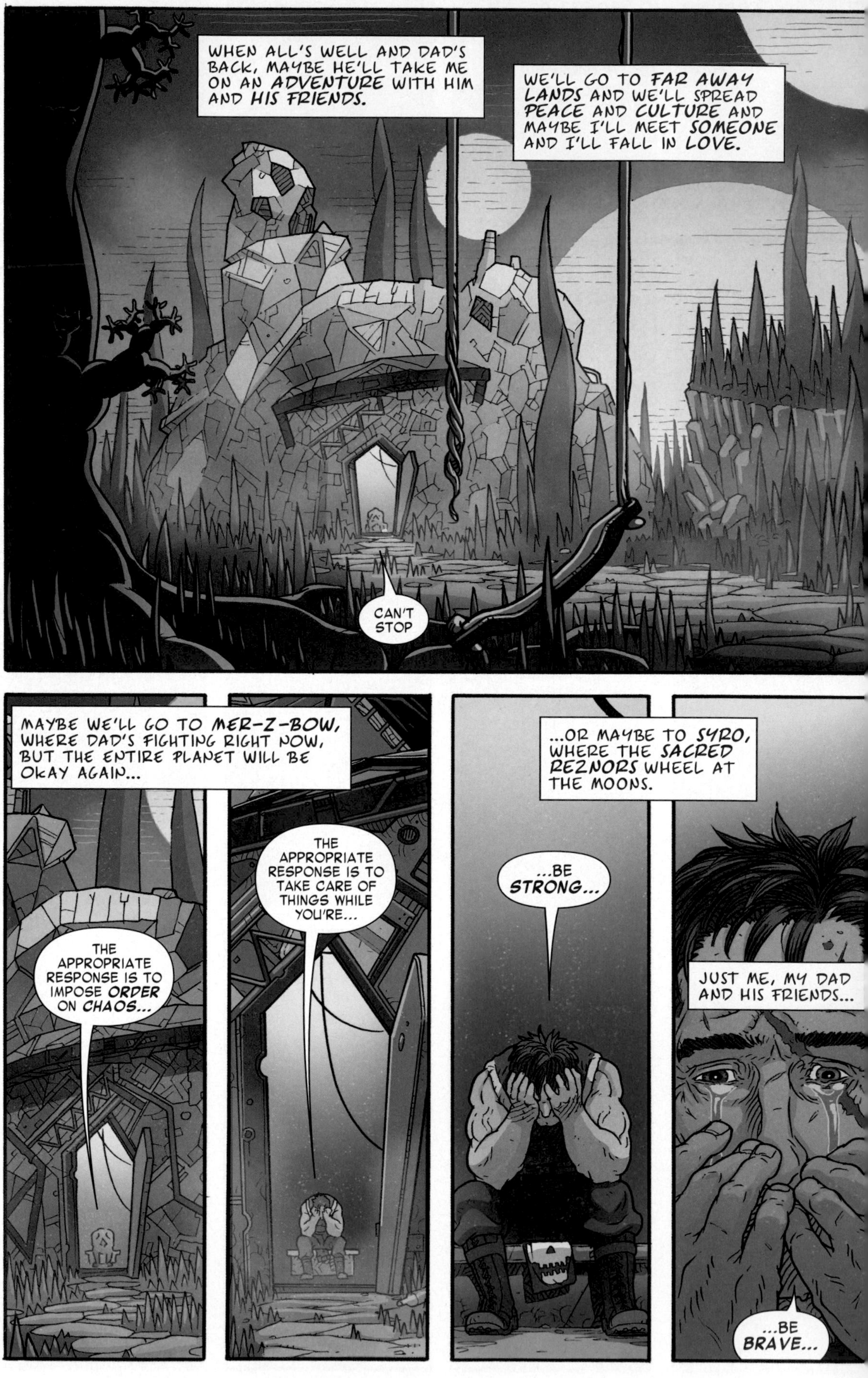
WHEN ALL'S WELL AND DAD'S BACK, MAYBE HE'LL TAKE ME ON AN ADVENTURE WITH HIM AND HIS FRIENDS.
WE'LL GO TO FAR AWAY LANDS AND WE'LL SPREAD PEACE AND CULTURE AND MAYBE I'LL MEET SOMEONE AND I'LL FALL IN LOVE.
CAN'T STOP
MAYBE WE'LL GO TO MER-Z-BOW, WHERE DAD'S FIGHTING RIGHT NOW, BUT THE ENTIRE PLANET WILL BE OKAY AGAIN...
THE APPROPRIATE RESPONSE IS TO IMPOSE ORDER ON CHAOS...
THE APPROPRIATE RESPONSE IS TO TAKE CARE OF THINGS WHILE YOU'RE...
...OR MAYBE TO SYRO, WHERE THE SACRED REZNORS WHEEL AT THE MOONS.
...BE STRONG...
JUST ME, MY DAD AND HIS FRIENDS...
...BE BRAVE...

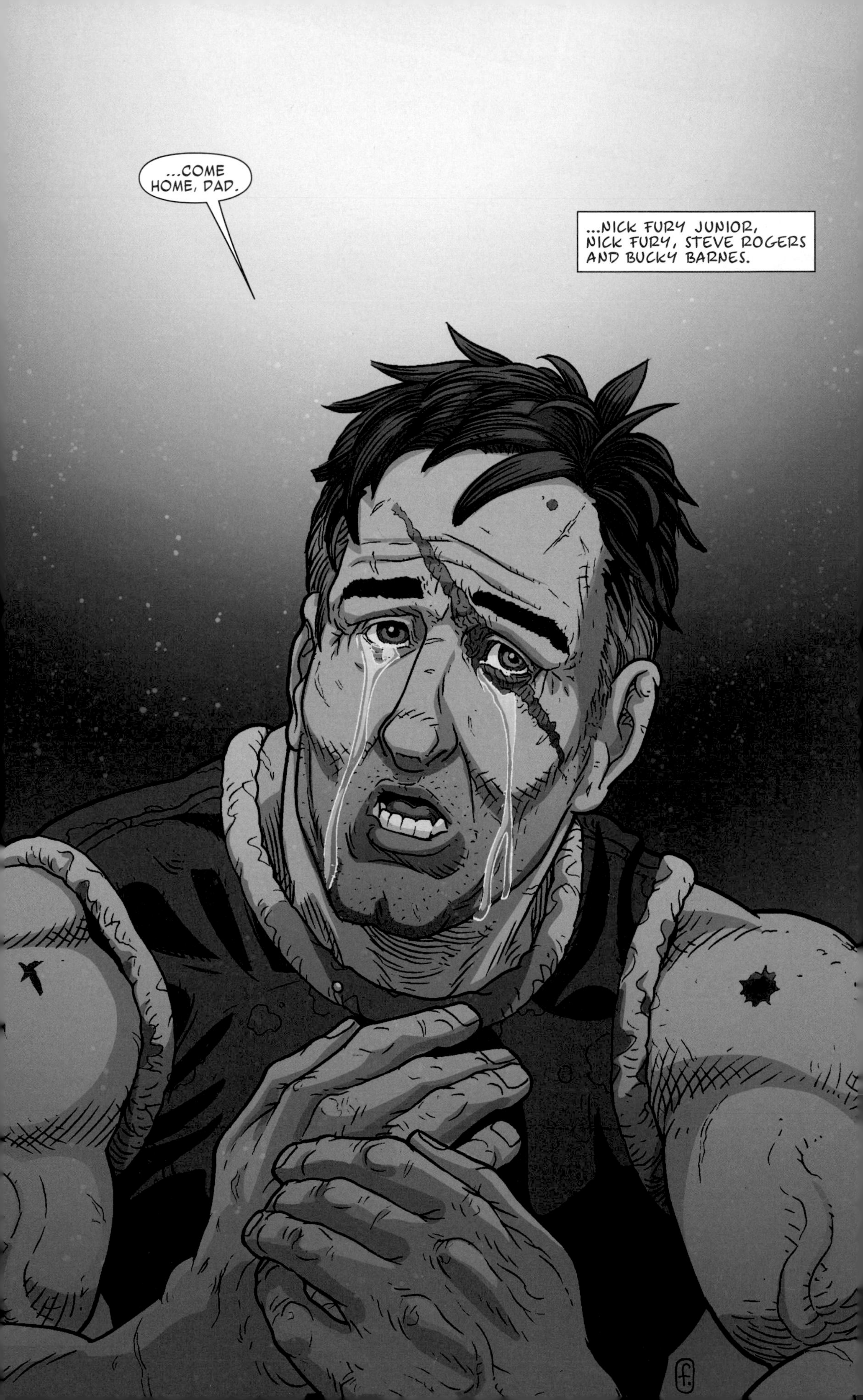
...COME HOME, DAD.
...NICK FURY JUNIOR, NICK FURY, STEVE ROGERS AND BUCKY BARNES.

## 8

TARGET: MER-Z-BOW

**Interplanetary Space-Rifle Association**
**OFFICIAL GUN-PLANET TARGET**
For use in all Solar Systems.

| NAME | DISTANCE |
| BUCKY | 93,000,000 |
| DATE | SCORE |
| 05/13/15 | PENDIN |

KILL A PLANET, SAVE A UNIVERSE!
KILL A UNIVERSE, SAVE A MULTIVERSE!
FASTER, BUCKY BARNES! KILL KILL KILL!
(DON'T TRY THIS AT HOME. FICTIONAL ADVICE DOES NOT
NECESSARILY APPLY TO YOUR PARTICULAR REALITY.)

A NIGHT FLIGHT OVER YOUR HEART

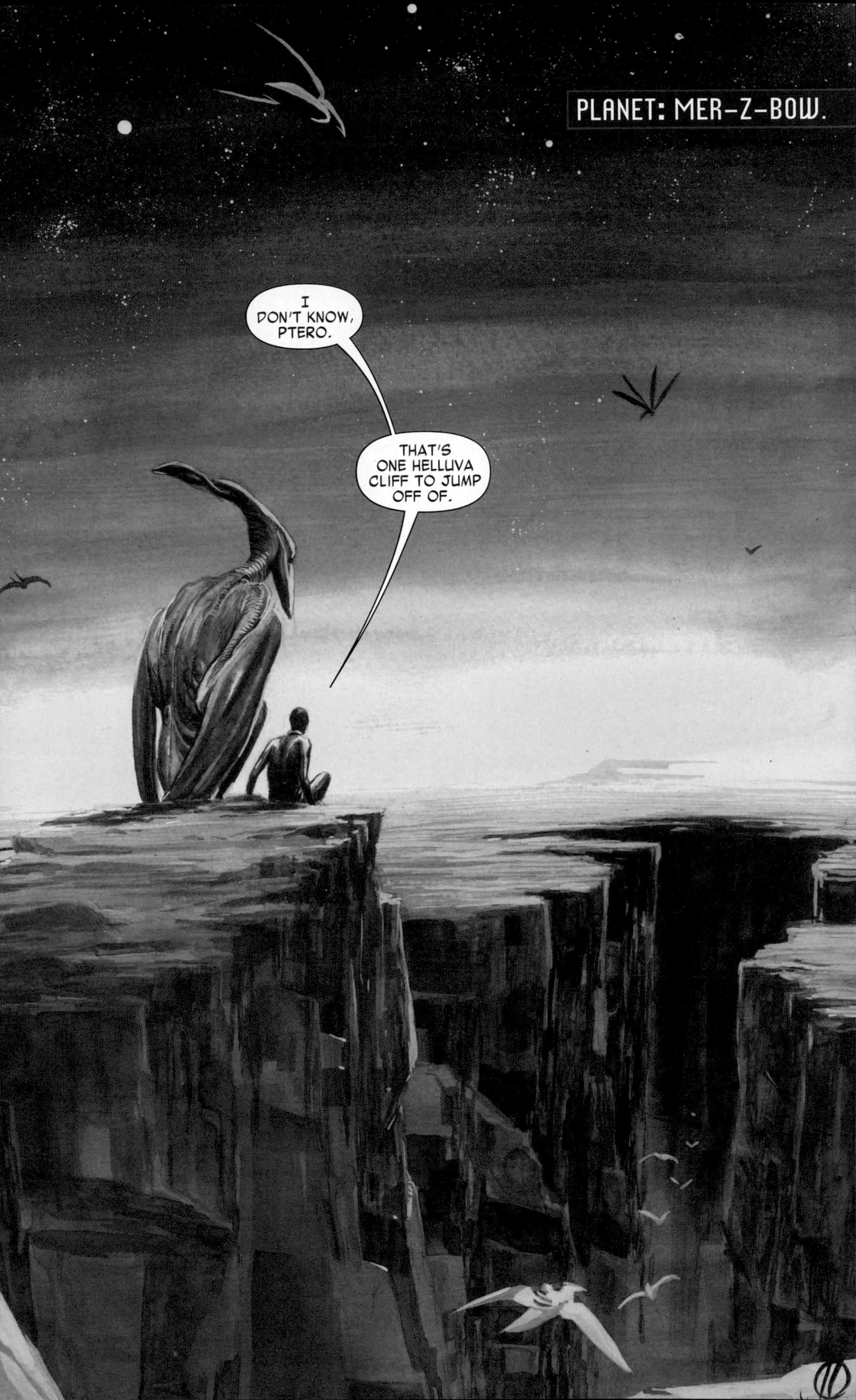
PLANET: MER-Z-BOW.
I DON'T KNOW, PTERO.
THAT'S ONE HELLUVA CLIFF TO JUMP OFF OF.

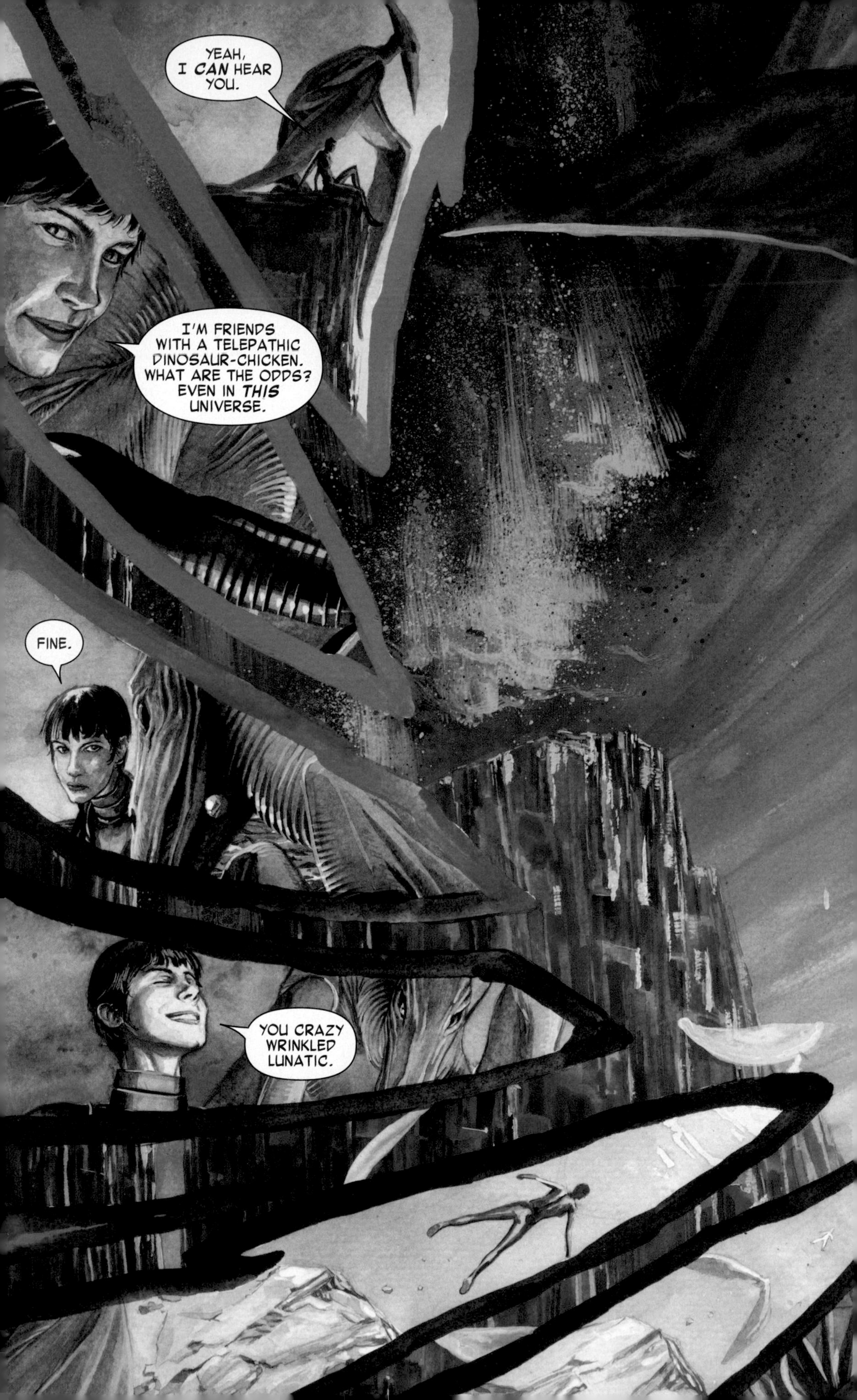
YEAH, I CAN HEAR YOU.
I'M FRIENDS WITH A TELEPATHIC DINOSAUR-CHICKEN. WHAT ARE THE ODDS? EVEN IN THIS UNIVERSE.
FINE.
YOU CRAZY WRINKLED LUNATIC.

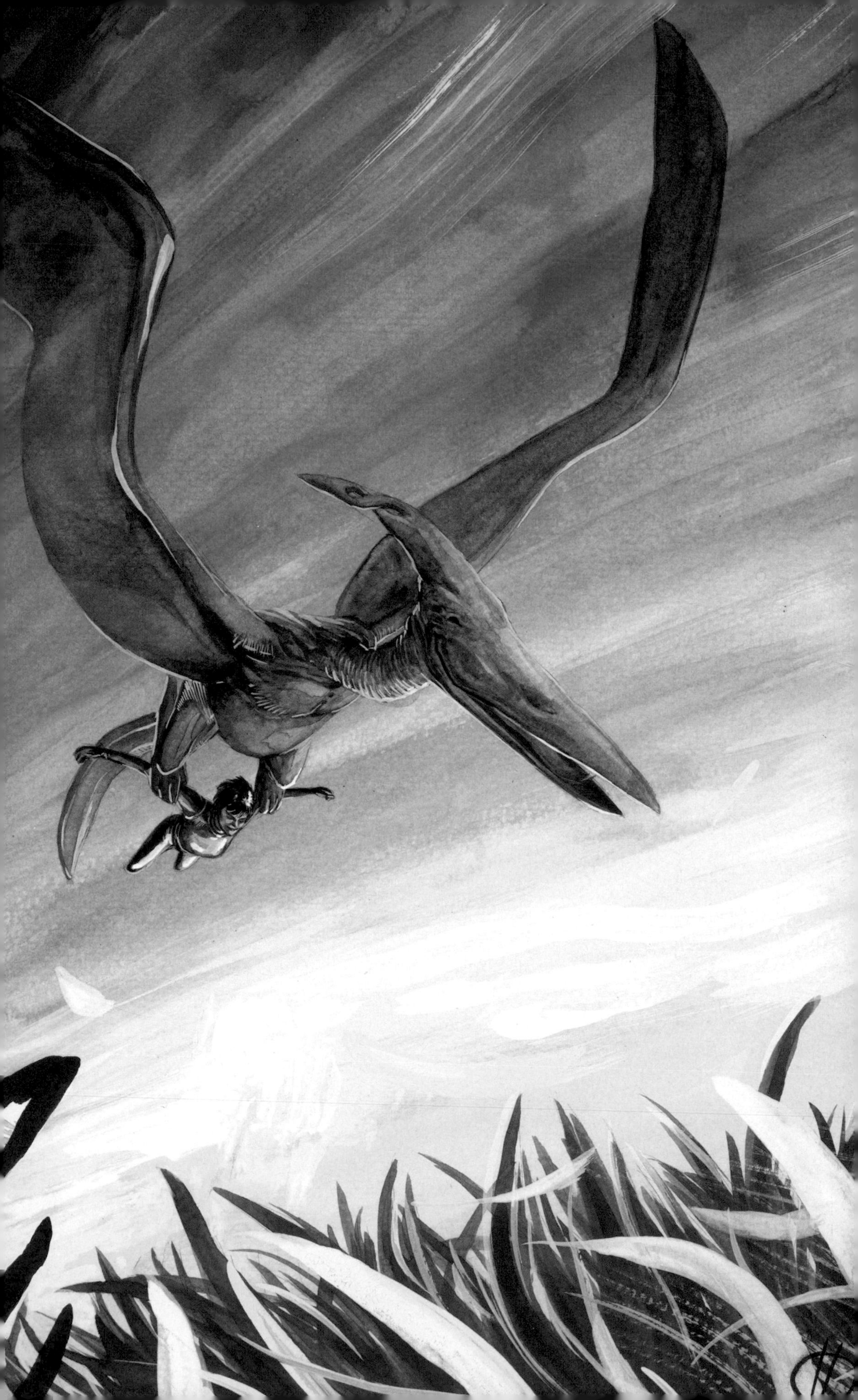

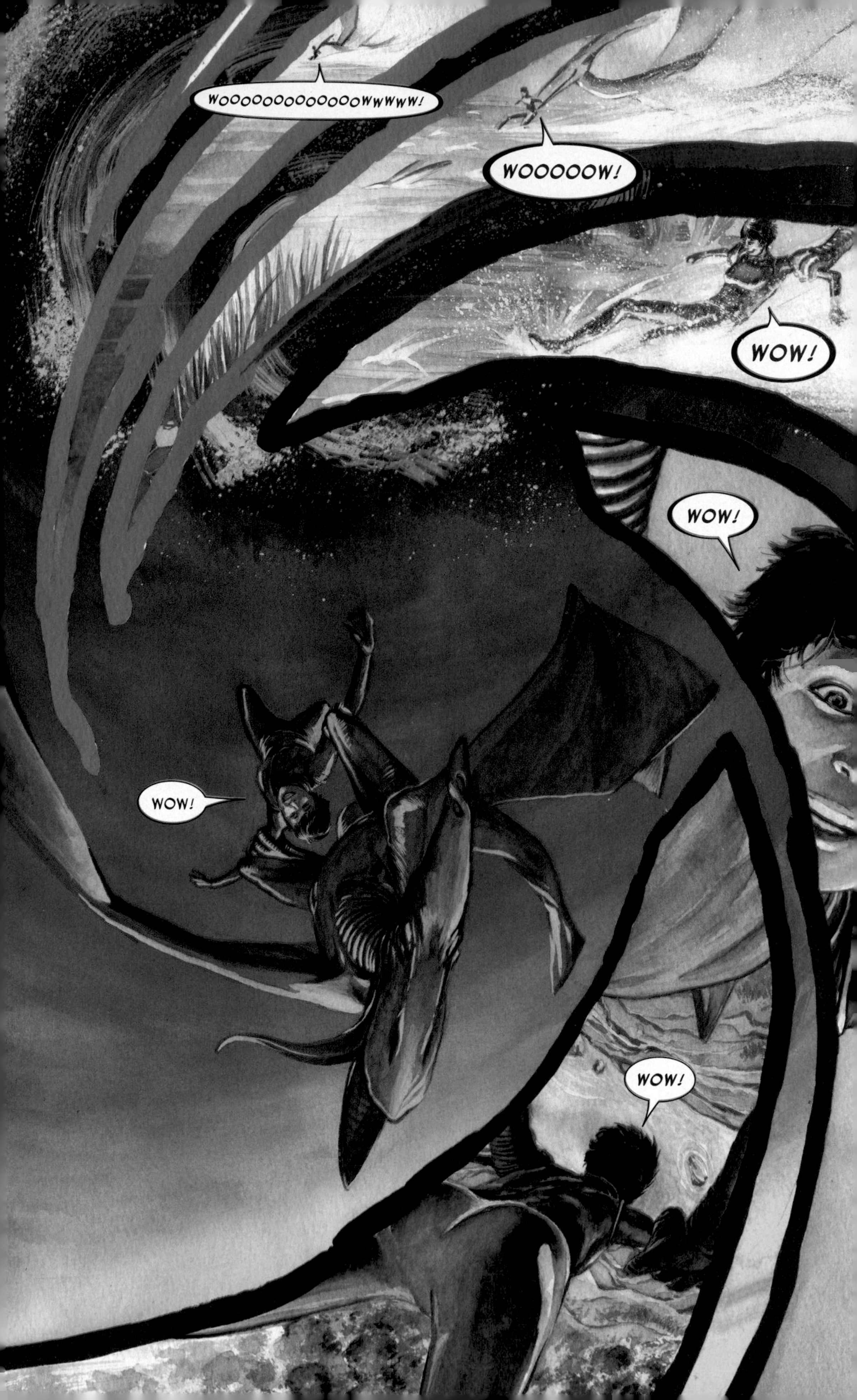
WOOOOOOOOOOOOOWWWWW!
WOOOOOW!
WOW!
WOW!
WOW!
WOW!

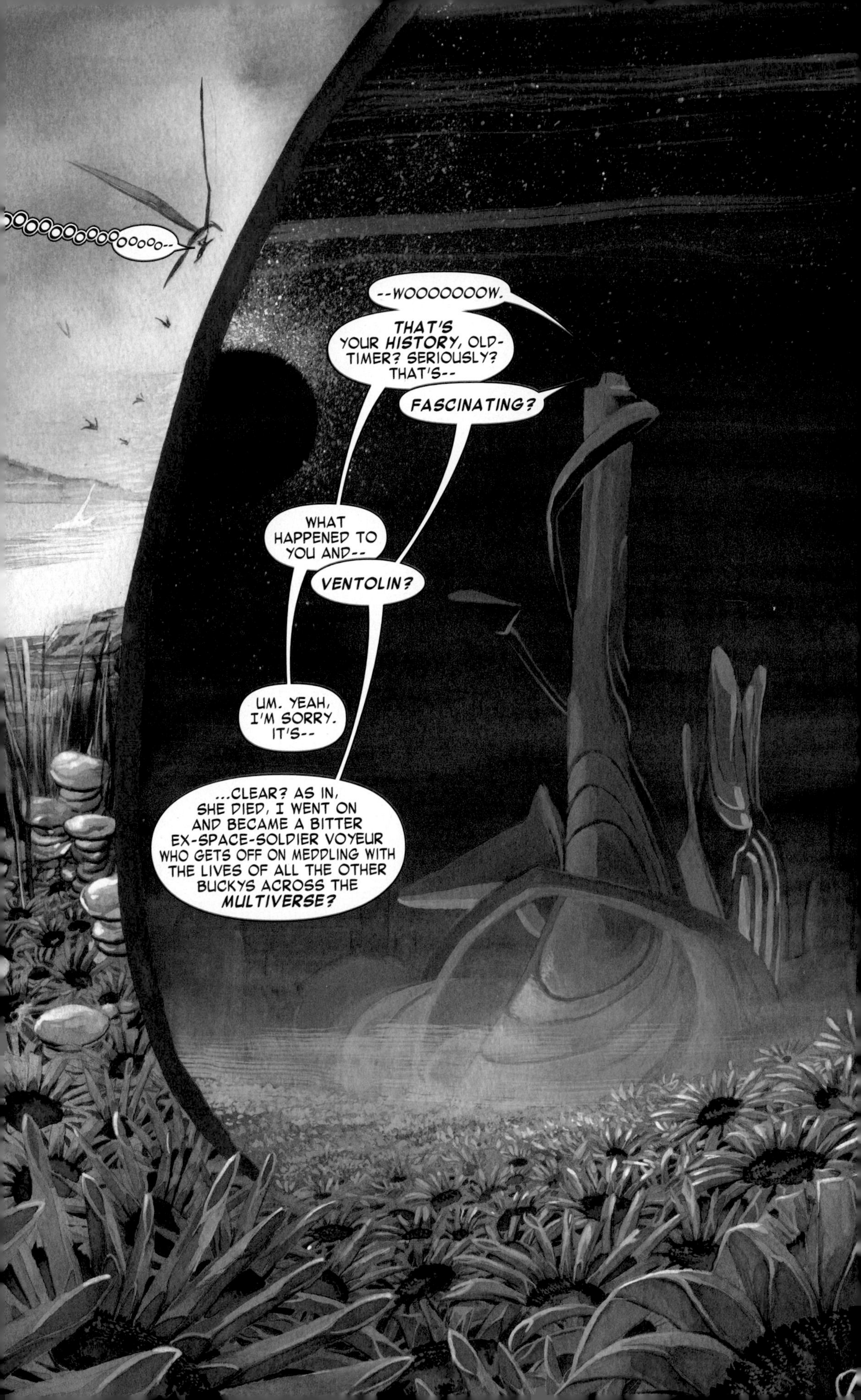
oOOOOOOOOOOoooo--
--WOOOOOOOW.
THAT'S YOUR HISTORY, OLD-TIMER? SERIOUSLY? THAT'S--
FASCINATING?
WHAT HAPPENED TO YOU AND--
VENTOLIN?
UM. YEAH, I'M SORRY. IT'S--
...CLEAR? AS IN, SHE DIED, I WENT ON AND BECAME A BITTER EX-SPACE-SOLDIER VOYEUR WHO GETS OFF ON MEDDLING WITH THE LIVES OF ALL THE OTHER BUCKYS ACROSS THE MULTIVERSE?

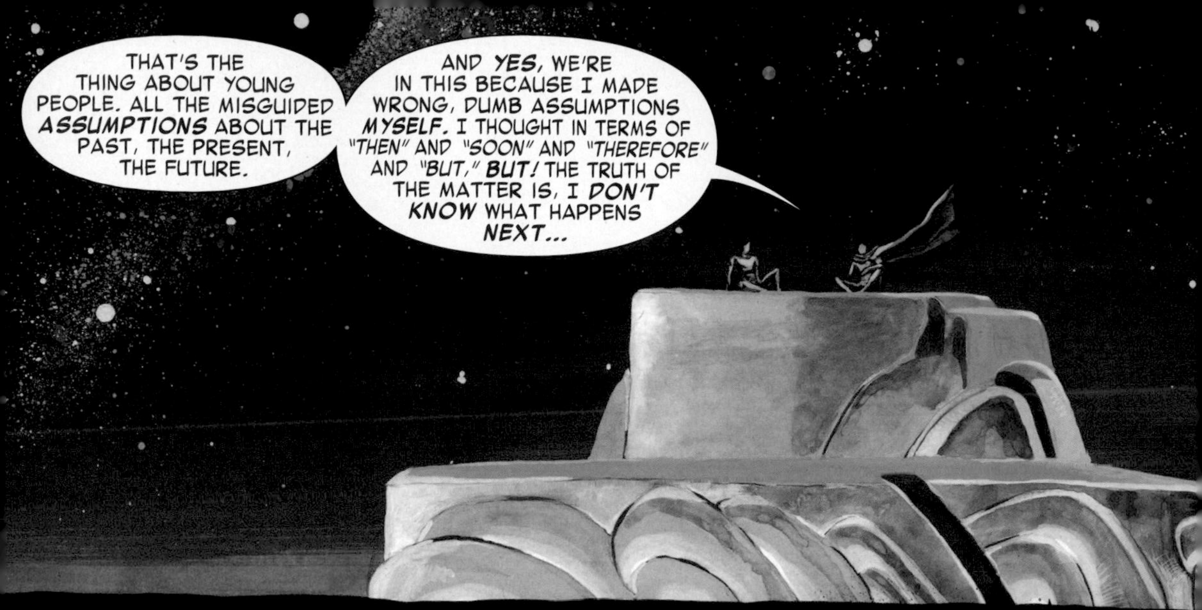
THAT'S THE THING ABOUT YOUNG PEOPLE. ALL THE MISGUIDED ASSUMPTIONS ABOUT THE PAST, THE PRESENT, THE FUTURE.
AND YES, WE'RE IN THIS BECAUSE I MADE WRONG, DUMB ASSUMPTIONS MYSELF. I THOUGHT IN TERMS OF "THEN" AND "SOON" AND "THEREFORE" AND "BUT," BUT! THE TRUTH OF THE MATTER IS, I DON'T KNOW WHAT HAPPENS NEXT...

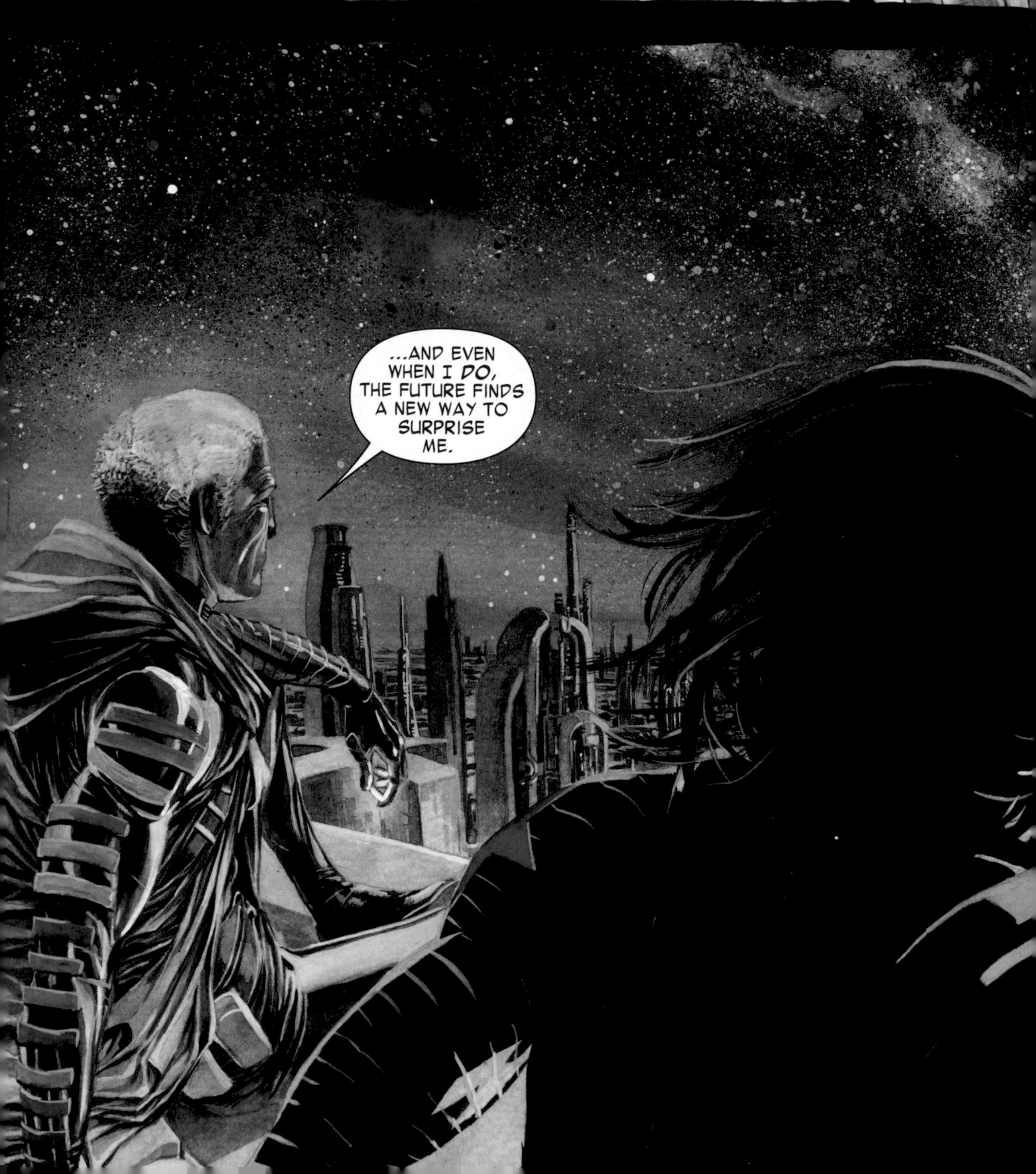
...AND EVEN WHEN I DO, THE FUTURE FINDS A NEW WAY TO SURPRISE ME.

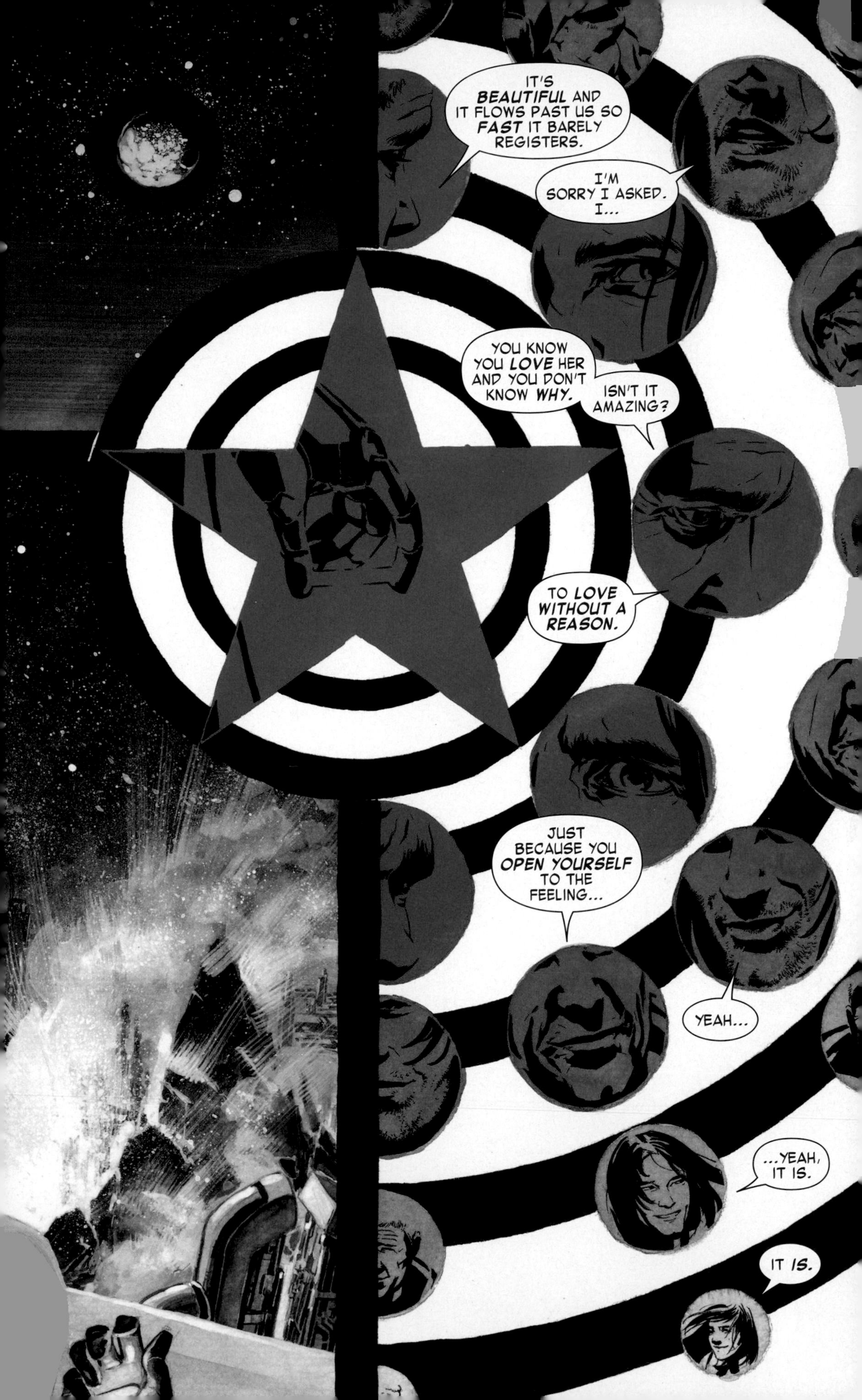
IT'S BEAUTIFUL AND IT FLOWS PAST US SO FAST IT BARELY REGISTERS.
I'M SORRY I ASKED. I...
YOU KNOW YOU LOVE HER AND YOU DON'T KNOW WHY.
ISN'T IT AMAZING?
TO LOVE WITHOUT A REASON.
JUST BECAUSE YOU OPEN YOURSELF TO THE FEELING...
YEAH...
...YEAH, IT IS.
IT IS.

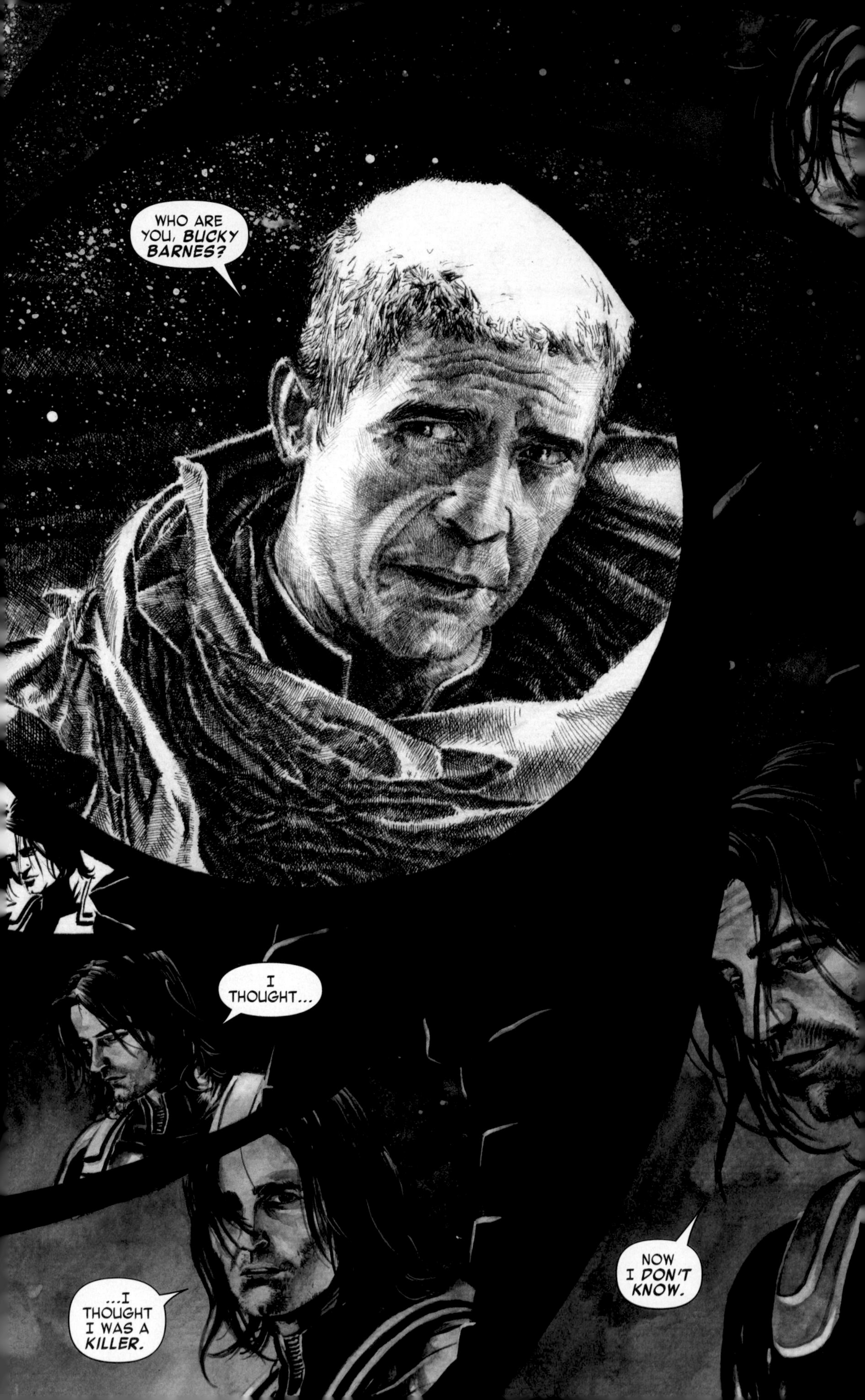
WHO ARE YOU, BUCKY BARNES?
I THOUGHT...
...I THOUGHT I WAS A KILLER.
NOW I DON'T KNOW.

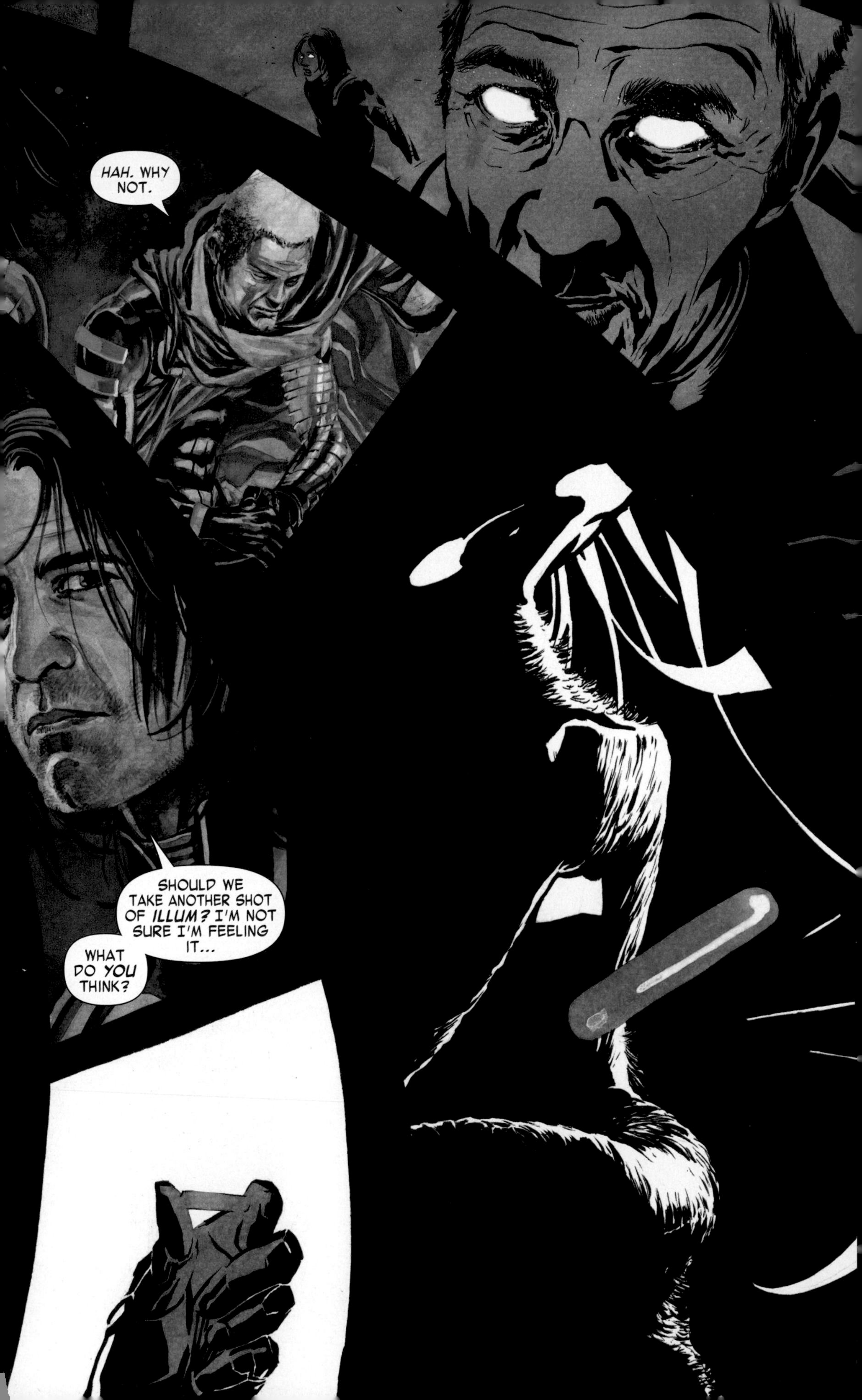
HAH. WHY NOT.
SHOULD WE TAKE ANOTHER SHOT OF ILLUM? I'M NOT SURE I'M FEELING IT...
WHAT DO YOU THINK?

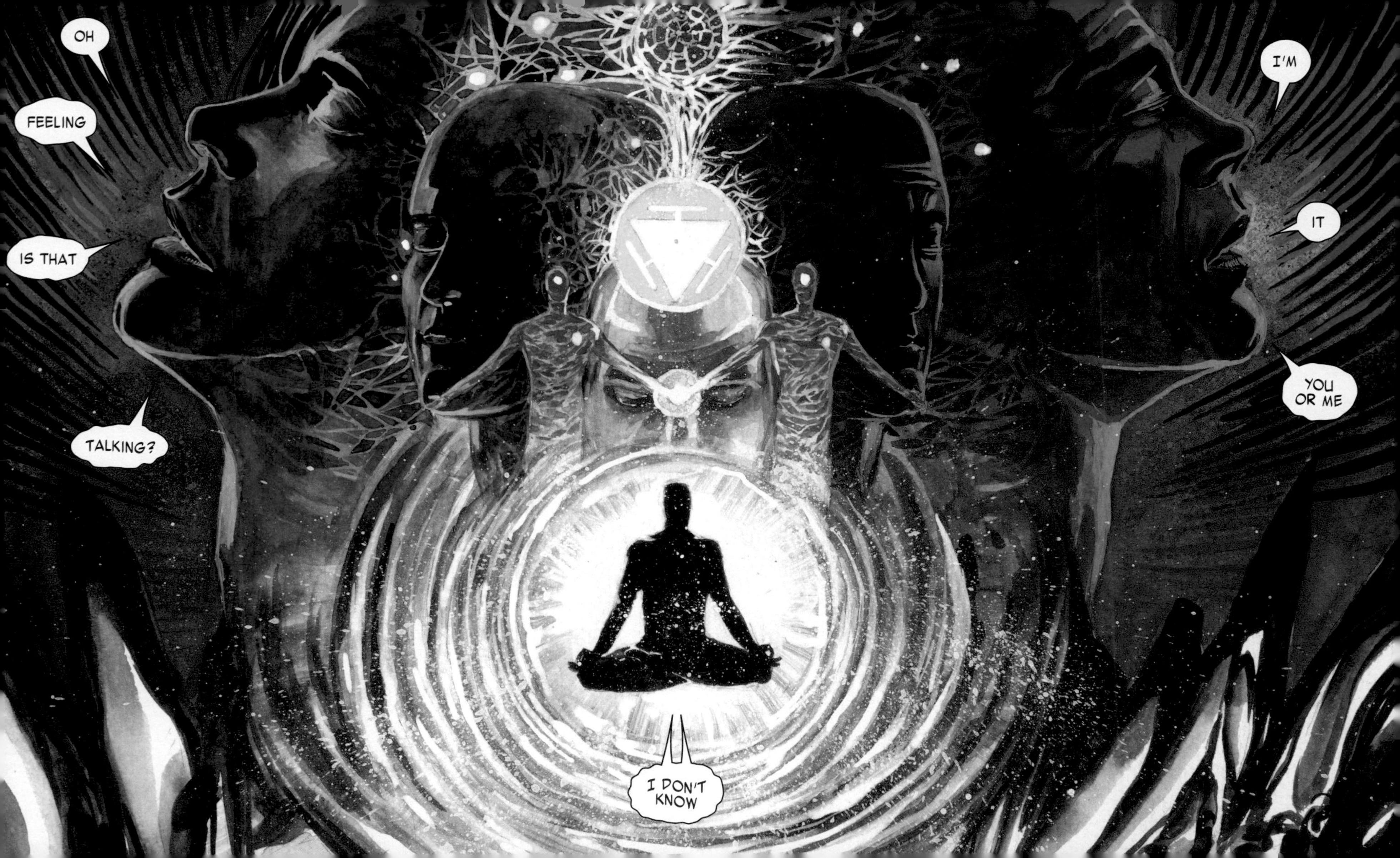

OH
FEELING
IS THAT
TALKING?
I'M
IT
YOU OR ME
I DON'T KNOW

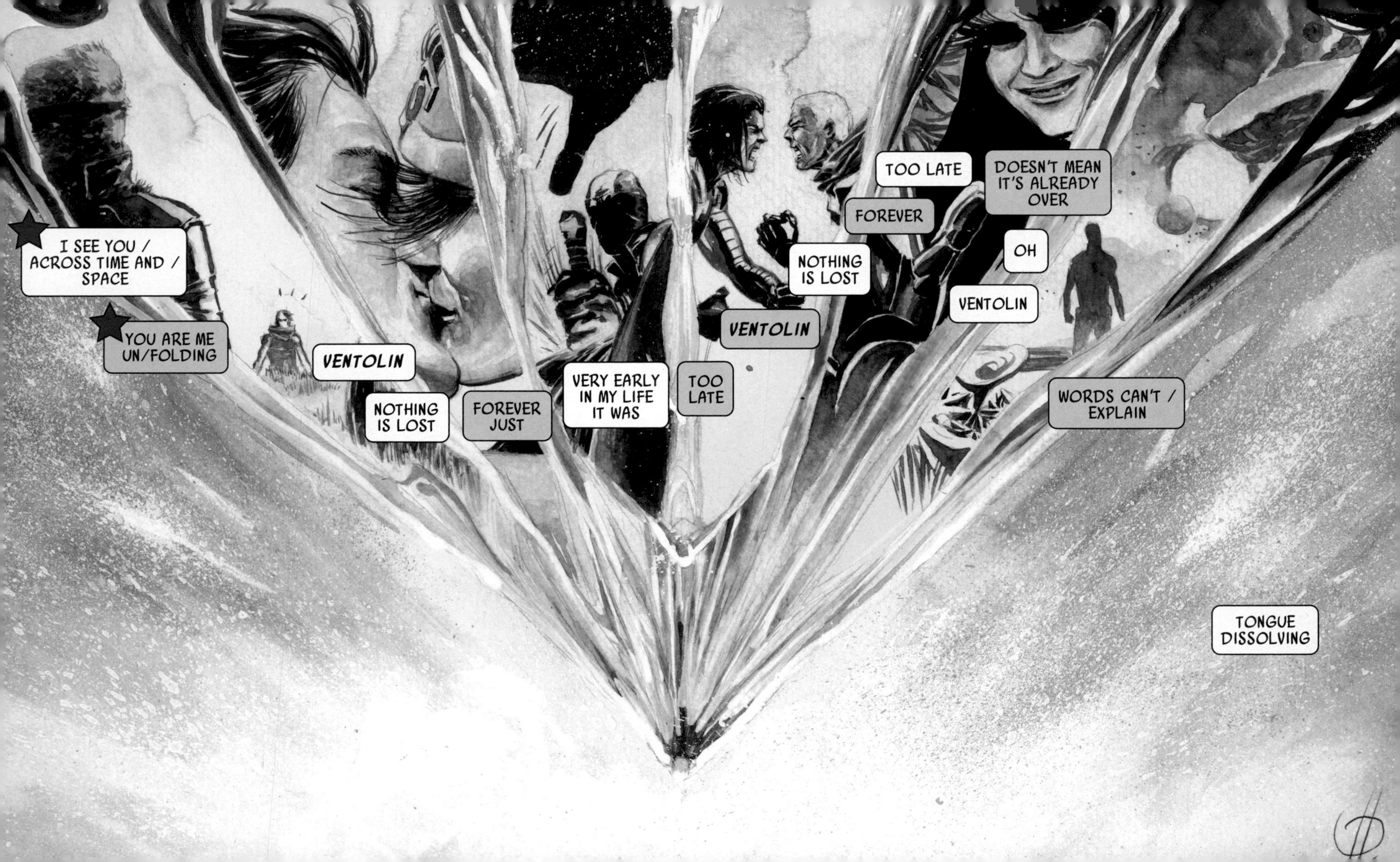
I SEE YOU / ACROSS TIME AND / SPACE
YOU ARE ME UN/FOLDING
VENTOLIN
NOTHING IS LOST
FOREVER JUST
VERY EARLY IN MY LIFE IT WAS
TOO LATE
VENTOLIN
NOTHING IS LOST
FOREVER
TOO LATE
DOESN'T MEAN IT'S ALREADY OVER
OH
VENTOLIN
WORDS CAN'T / EXPLAIN
TONGUE DISSOLVING

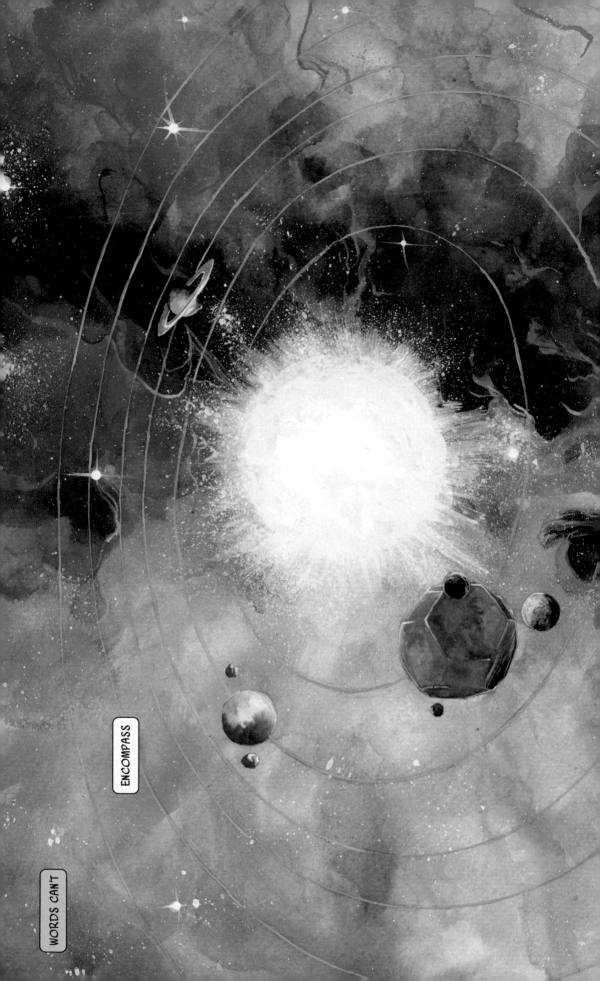

WORDS CAN'T

ENCOMPASS

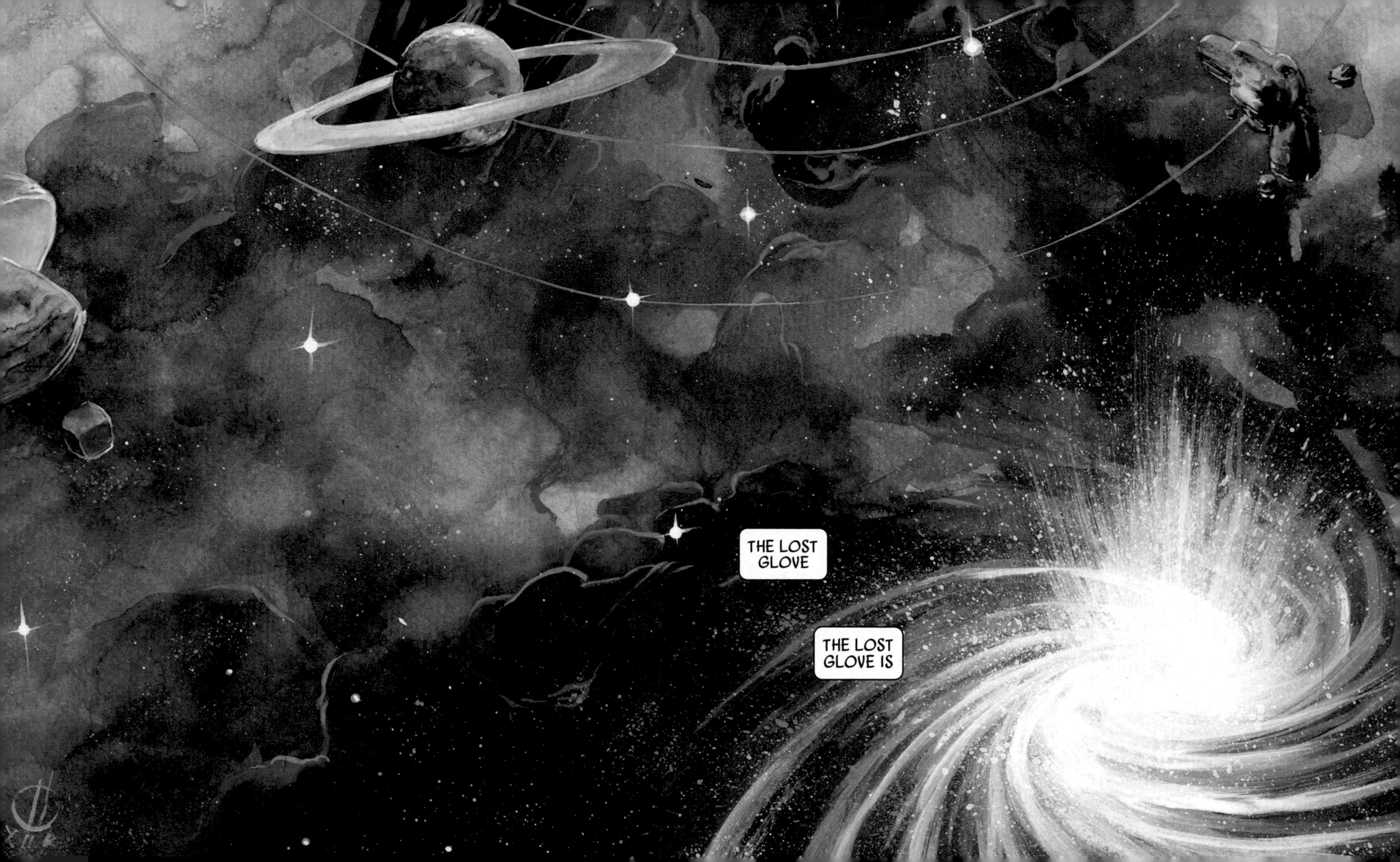
THE LOST GLOVE
THE LOST GLOVE IS

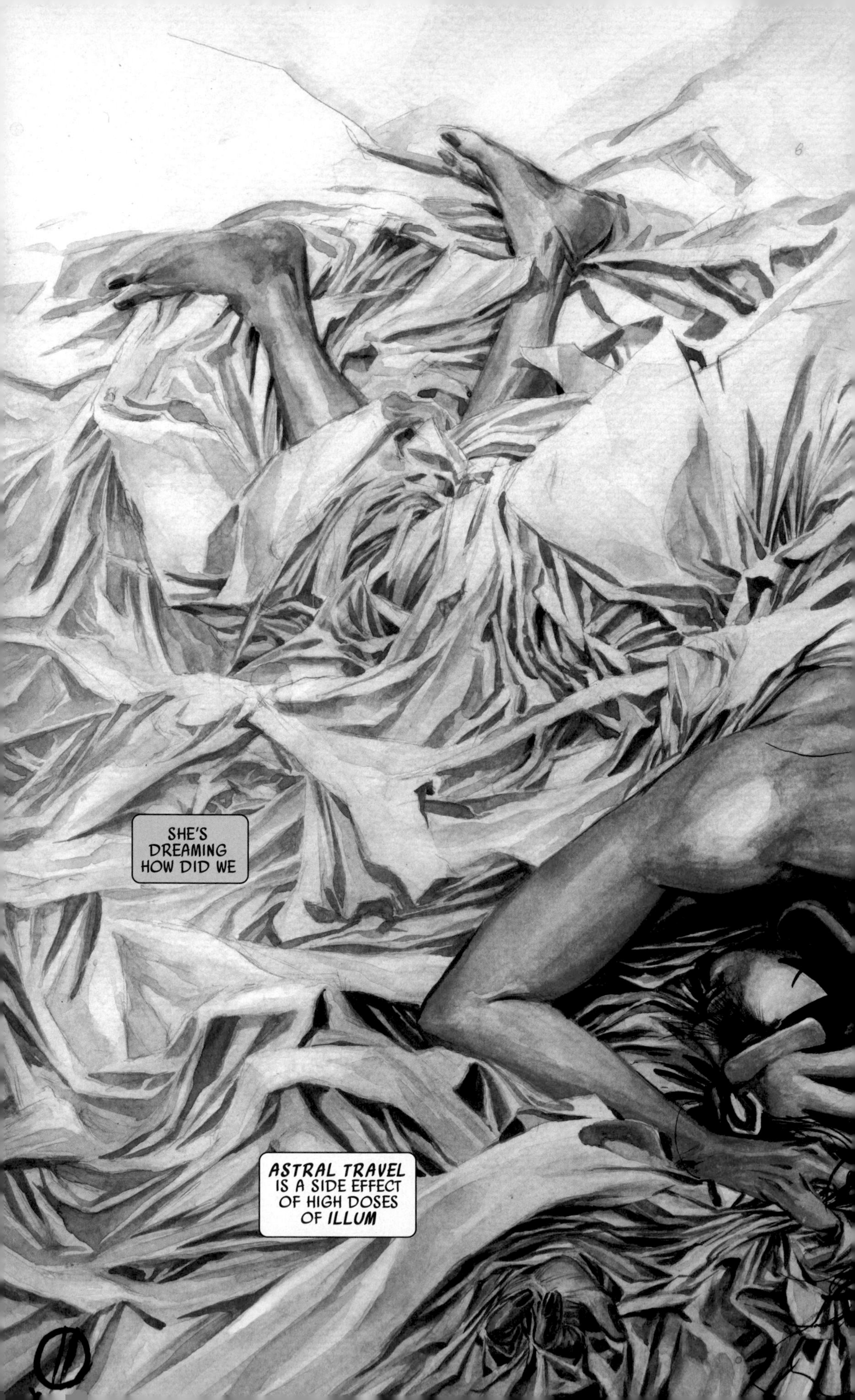
SHE'S DREAMING HOW DID WE
ASTRAL TRAVEL IS A SIDE EFFECT OF HIGH DOSES OF ILLUM

DREAMING ABOUT HER PAST
AND THE PAST OF HER ANCESTORS
ARE YOU MY ANCESTOR
HOW DOES THIS MULTIVERSE STUFF WORK
I CAN'T REALLY TELL I NEVER QUITE GOT THE HANG OF IT
WE'RE SEEING HER DREAMS IS THIS UNETHICAL
NO IT'S NOT
I LET YOU IN
AND SOFT-PINGED YOUR ASTRAL SELVES TO COME FORTH
I'M THE EXPERIENCED ONE HERE, BOYS
I AM DREAMING / MEDITATING / WAKING ACROSS THE BOUNDS OF THE DESERT OF THE SELF

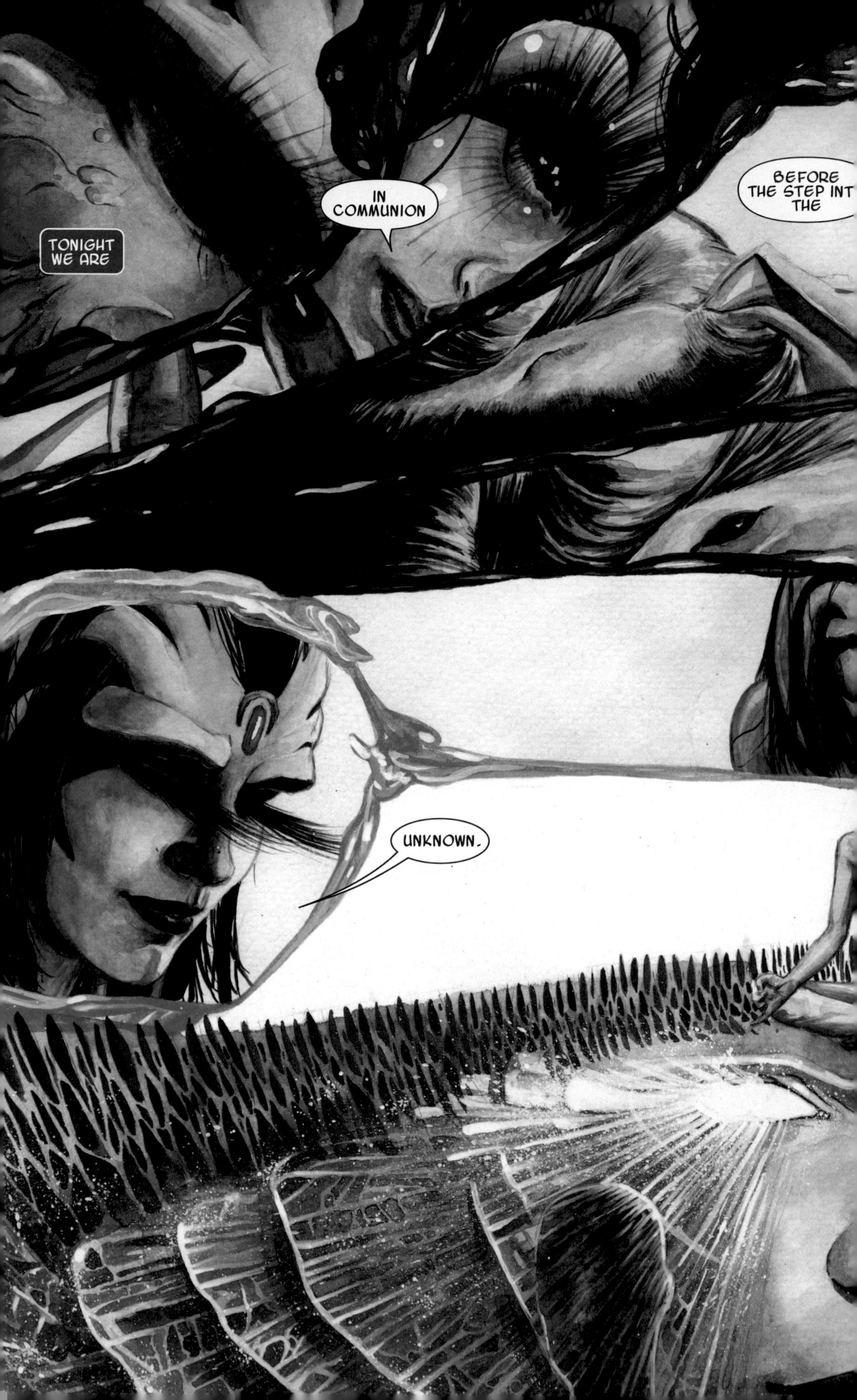
TONIGHT WE ARE
IN COMMUNION
BEFORE THE STEP INT THE
UNKNOWN.

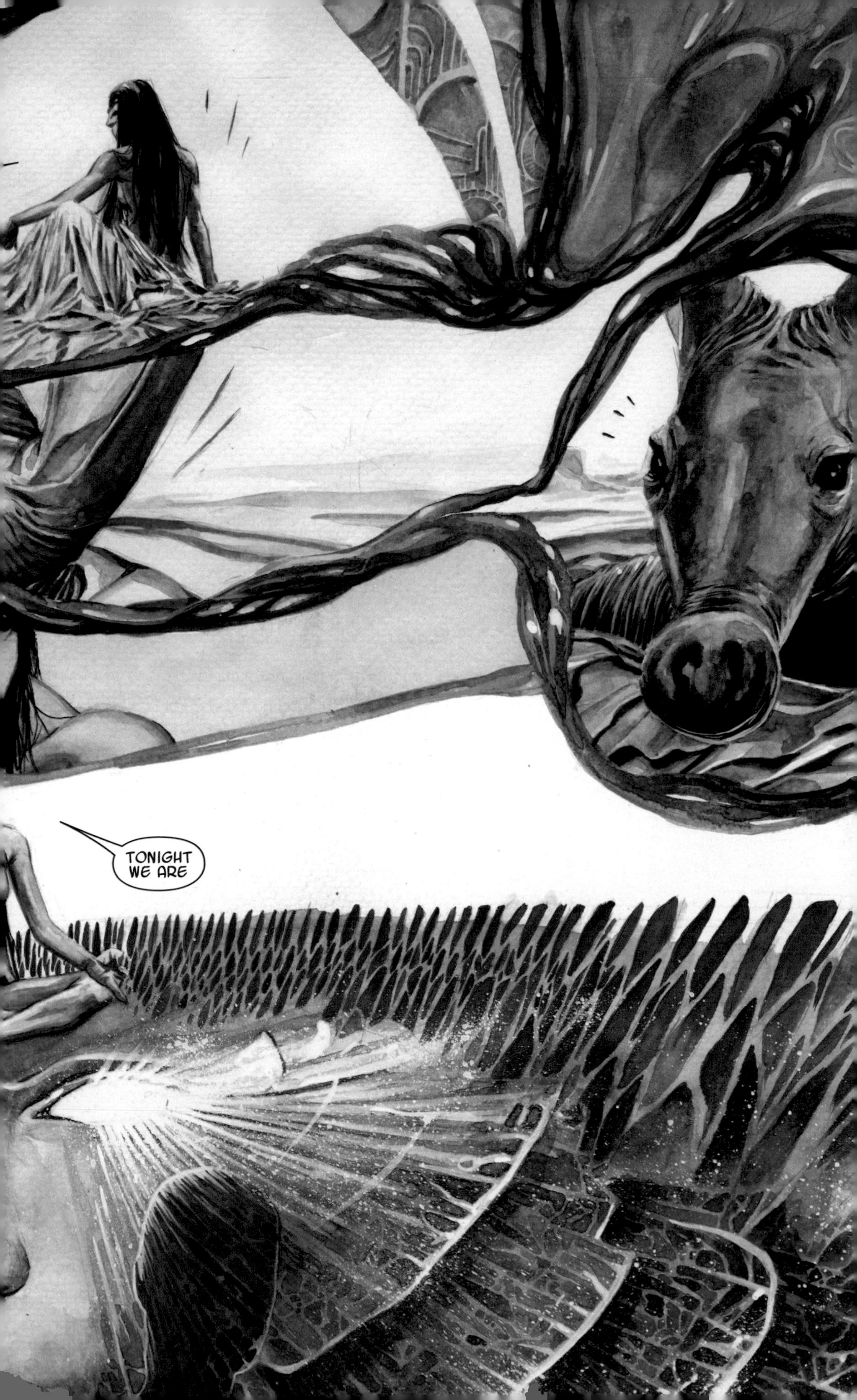
TONIGHT WE ARE

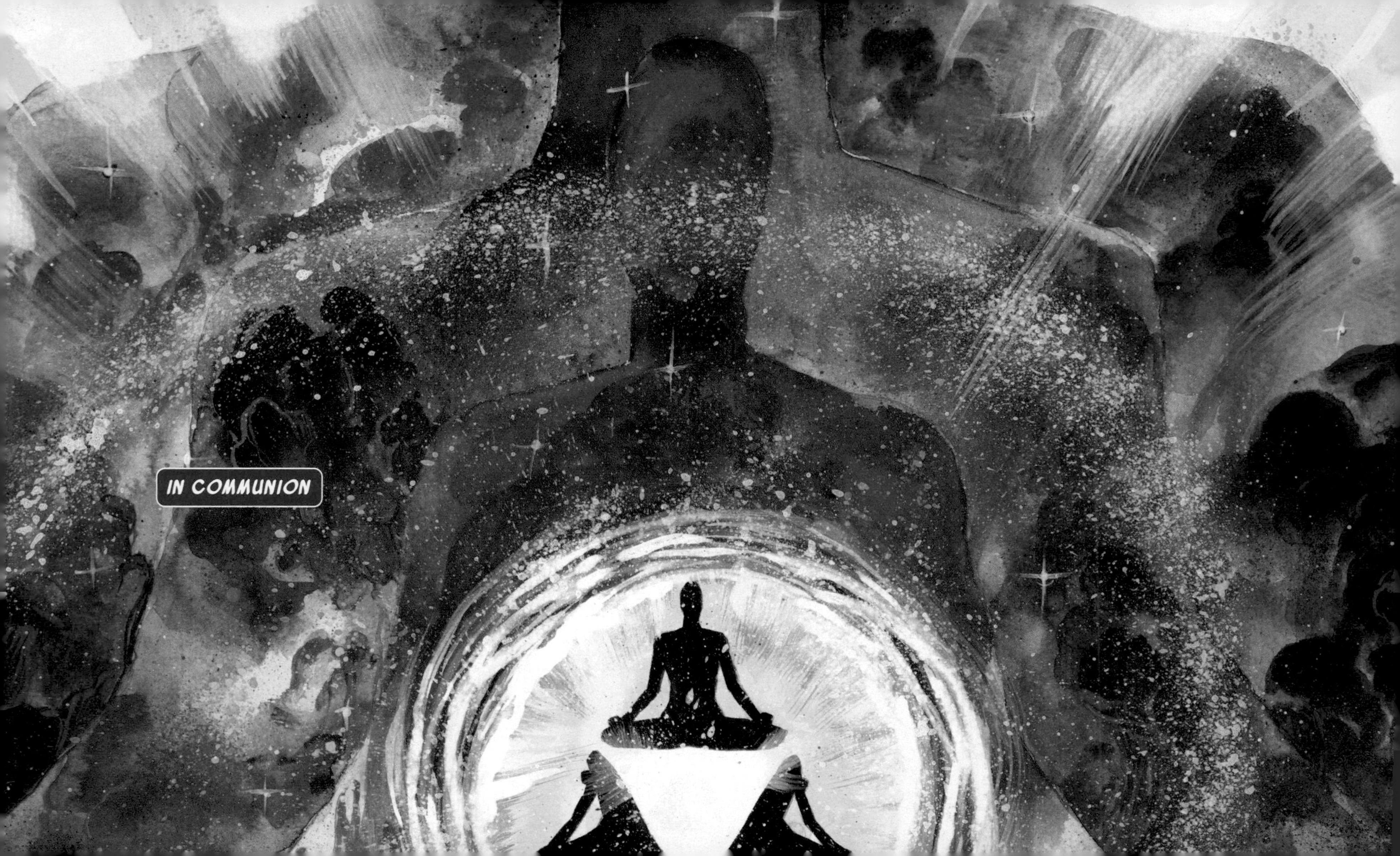
IN COMMUNION

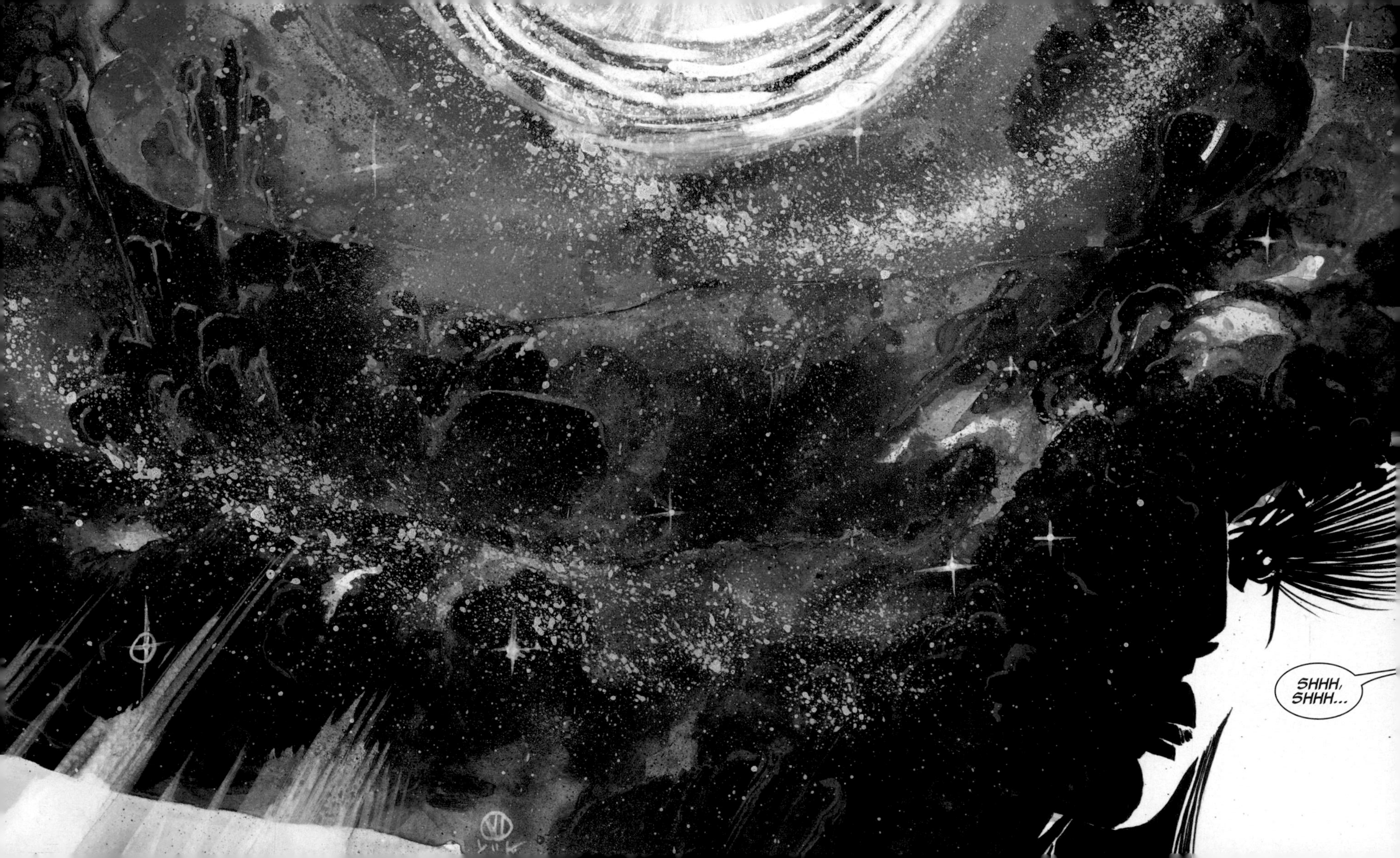
SHHH, SHHH...

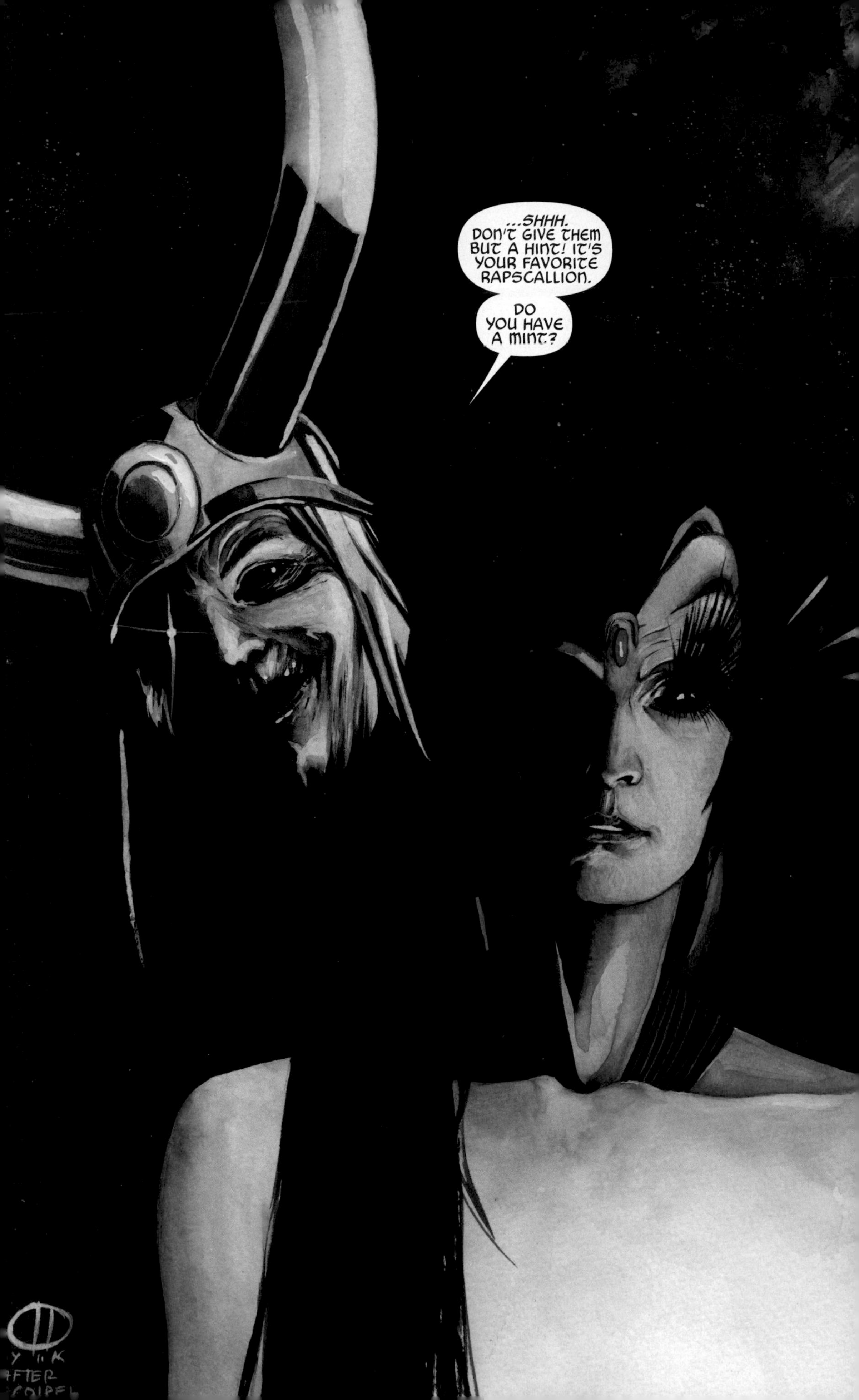
...SHHH. DON'T GIVE THEM BUT A HINT! IT'S YOUR FAVORITE RAPSCALLION.
DO YOU HAVE A MINT?

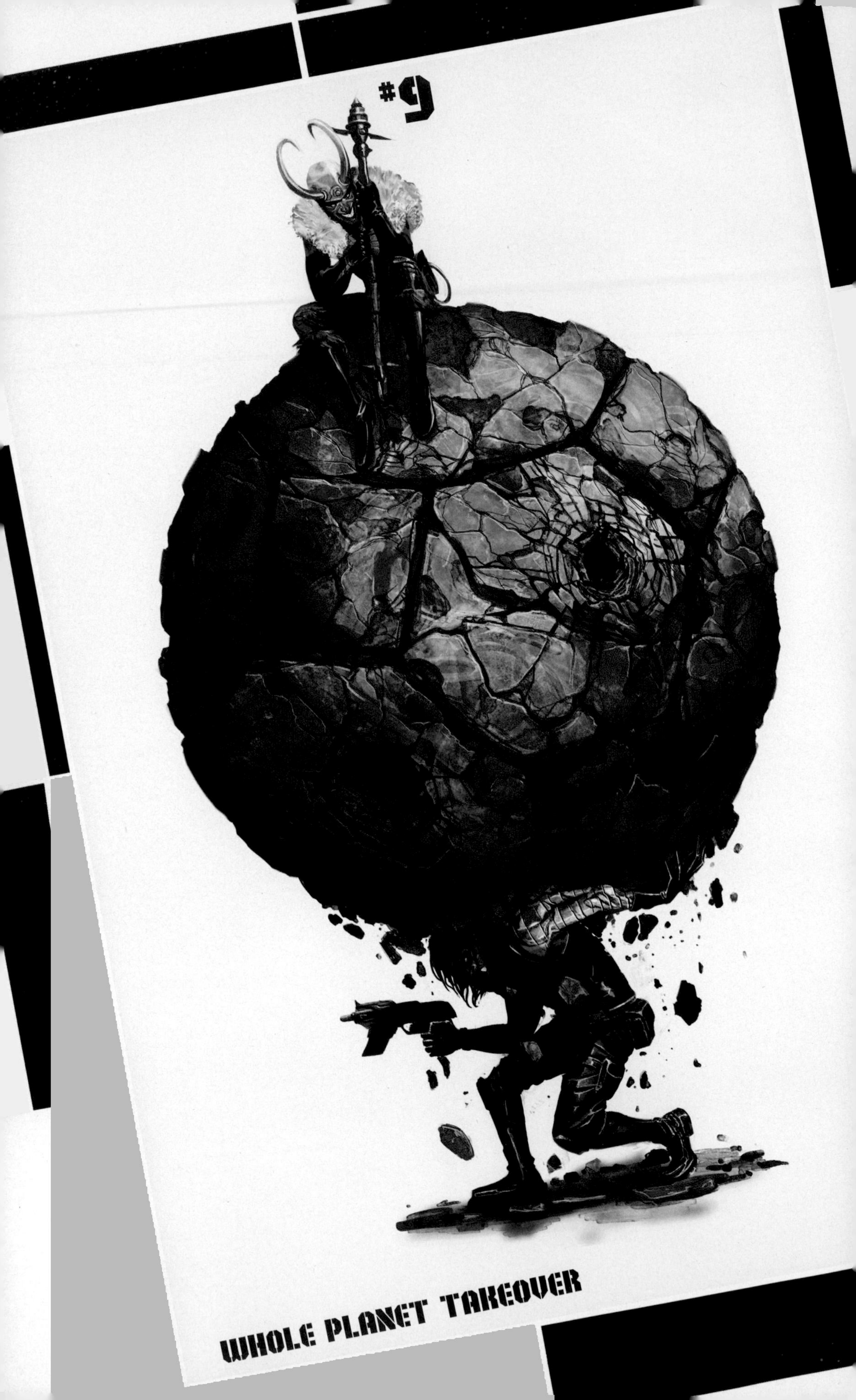
#9
WHOLE PLANET TAKEOVER

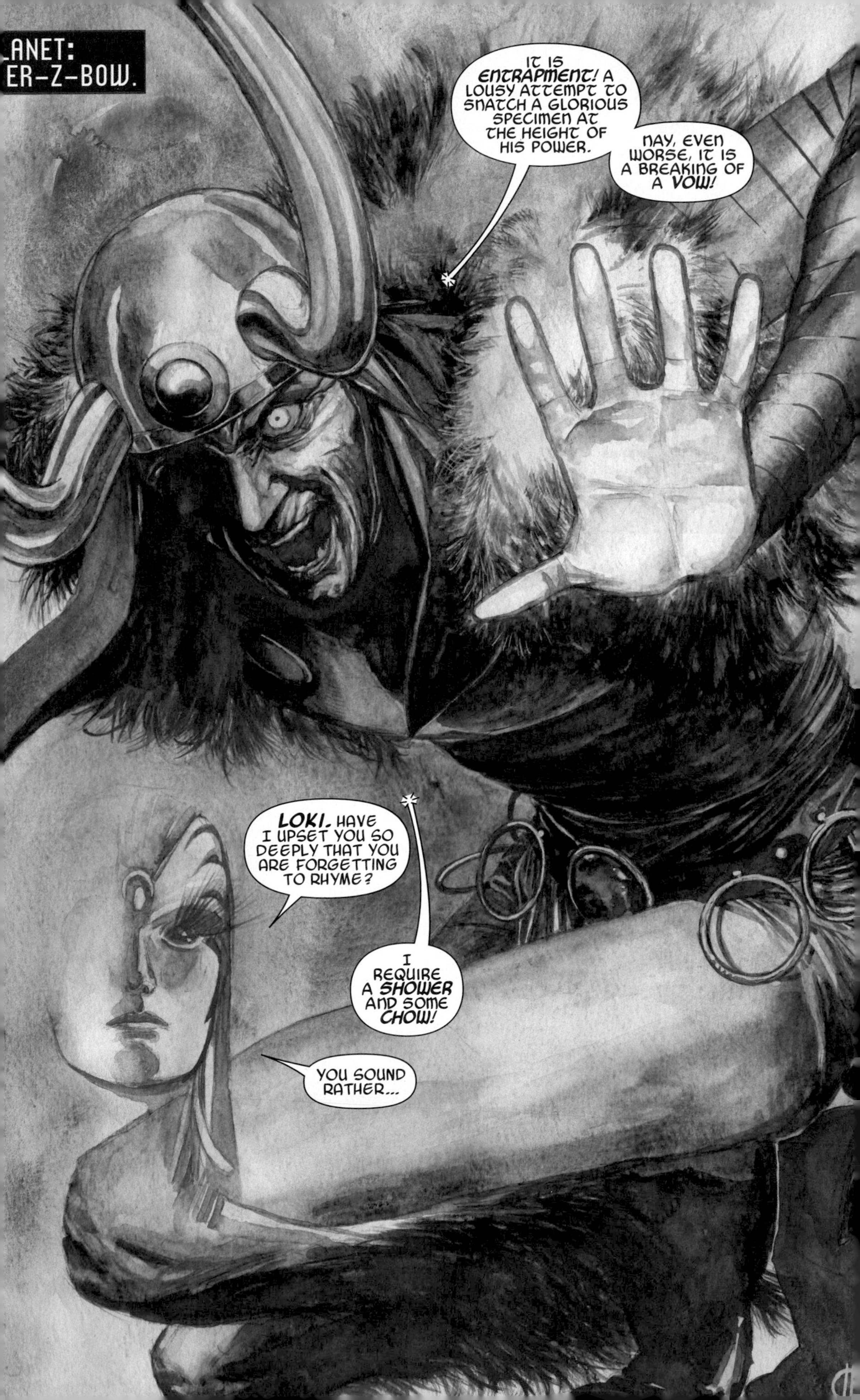

LANET:
ER-Z-BOW.
IT IS ENTRAPMENT! A LOUSY ATTEMPT TO SNATCH A GLORIOUS SPECIMEN AT THE HEIGHT OF HIS POWER.
NAY, EVEN WORSE, IT IS A BREAKING OF A VOW!
LOKI. HAVE I UPSET YOU SO DEEPLY THAT YOU ARE FORGETTING TO RHYME?
I REQUIRE A SHOWER AND SOME CHOW!
YOU SOUND RATHER...

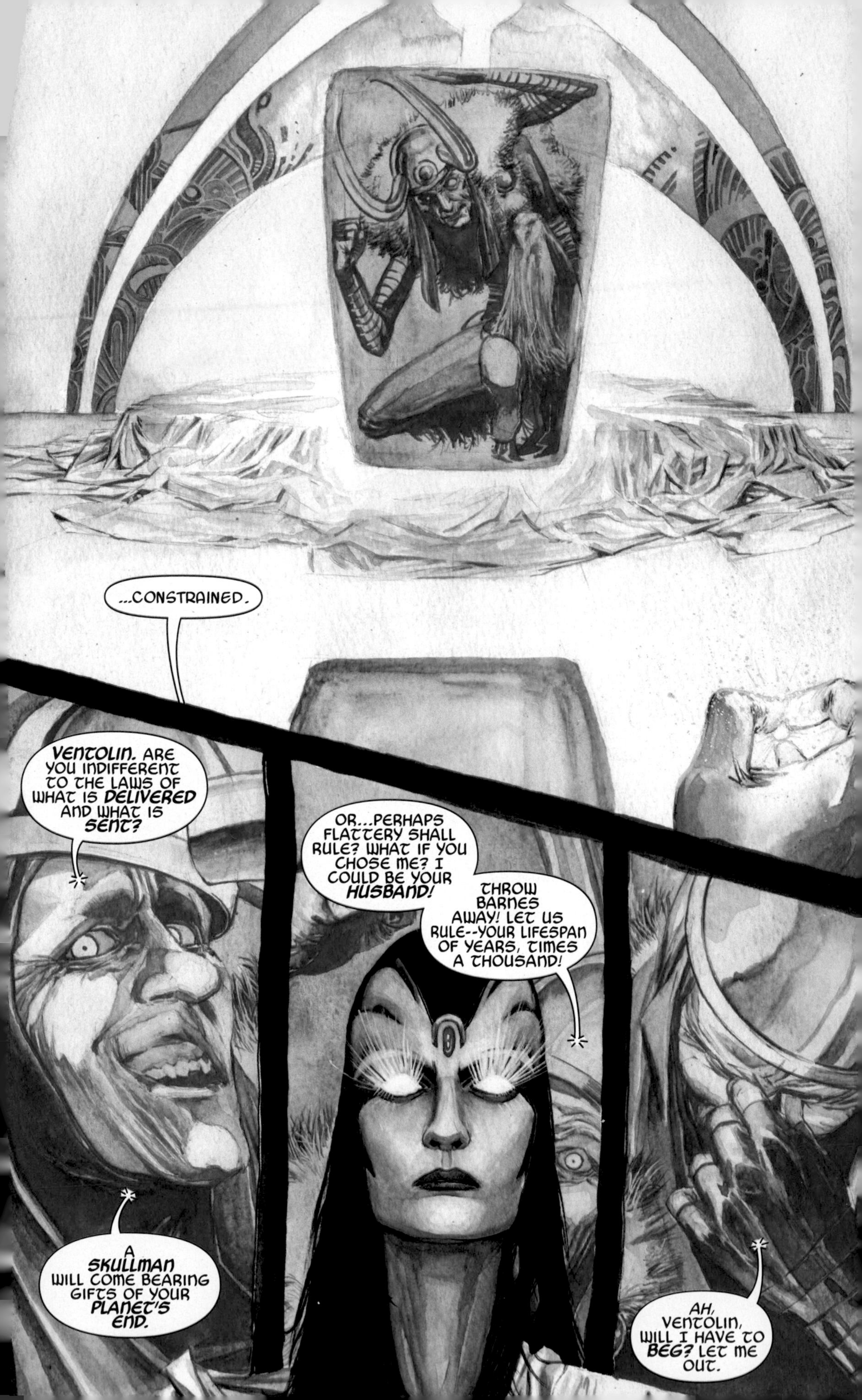
...CONSTRAINED.
VENTOLIN. ARE YOU INDIFFERENT TO THE LAWS OF WHAT IS DELIVERED AND WHAT IS SENT?
OR...PERHAPS FLATTERY SHALL RULE? WHAT IF YOU CHOSE ME? I COULD BE YOUR HUSBAND!
THROW BARNES AWAY! LET US RULE--YOUR LIFESPAN OF YEARS, TIMES A THOUSAND!
A SKULLMAN WILL COME BEARING GIFTS OF YOUR PLANET'S END.
AH, VENTOLIN, WILL I HAVE TO BEG? LET ME OUT.

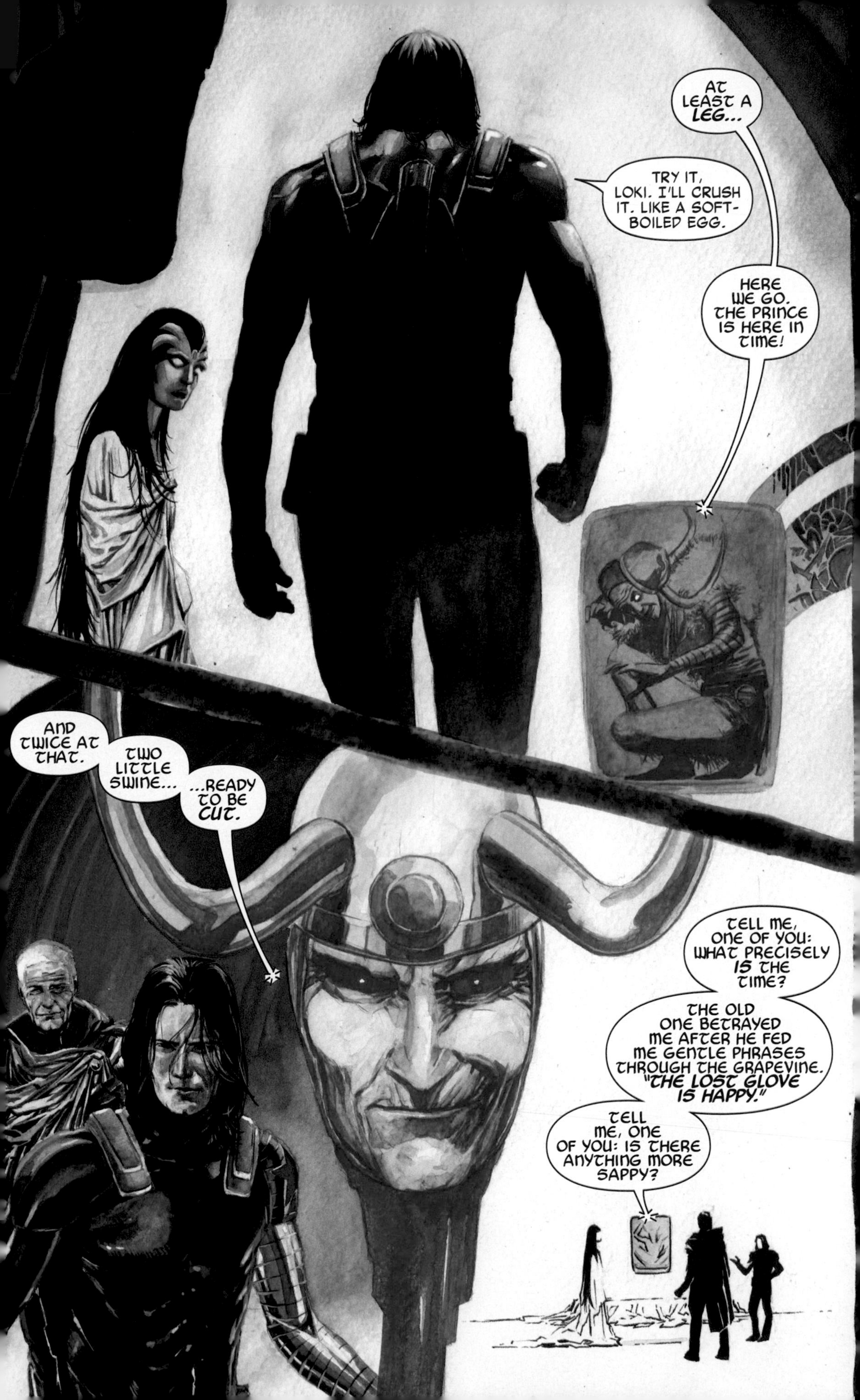
AT LEAST A LEG...
TRY IT, LOKI. I'LL CRUSH IT. LIKE A SOFT-BOILED EGG.
HERE WE GO. THE PRINCE IS HERE IN TIME!
AND TWICE AT THAT.
TWO LITTLE SWINE...
...READY TO BE CUT.
TELL ME, ONE OF YOU: WHAT PRECISELY IS THE TIME?
THE OLD ONE BETRAYED ME AFTER HE FED ME GENTLE PHRASES THROUGH THE GRAPEVINE. "THE LOST GLOVE IS HAPPY."
TELL ME, ONE OF YOU: IS THERE ANYTHING MORE SAPPY?

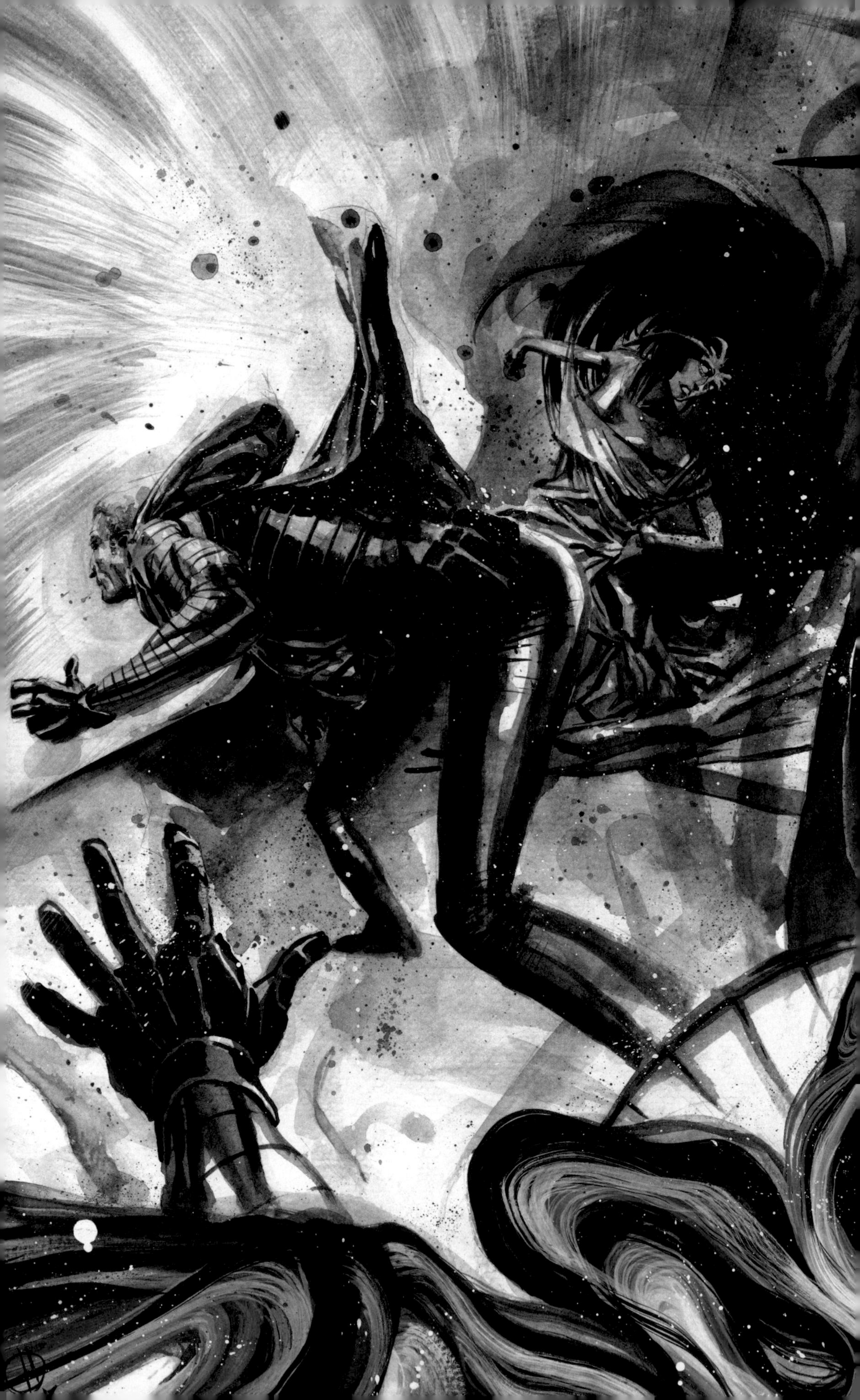

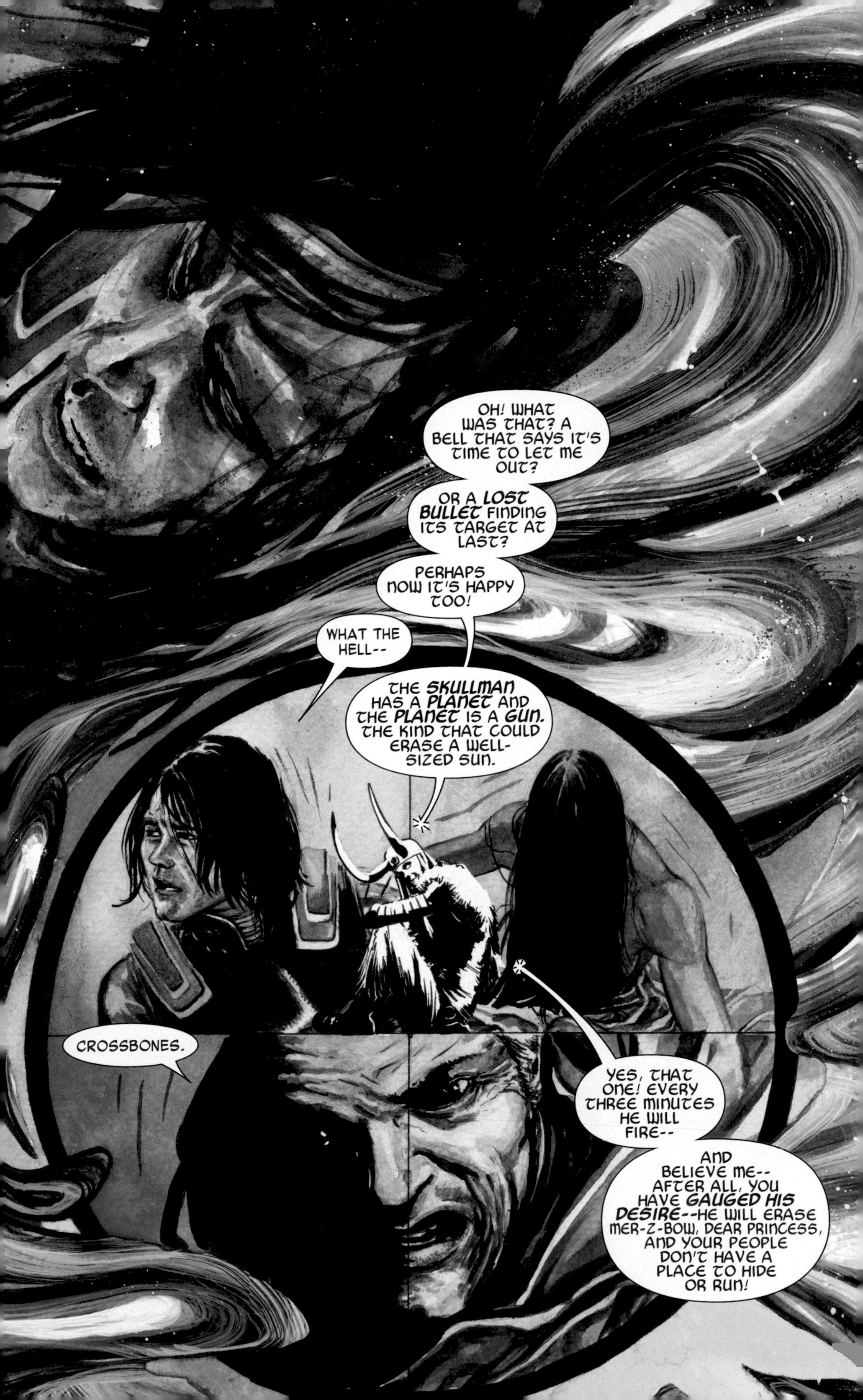
OH! WHAT WAS THAT? A BELL THAT SAYS IT'S TIME TO LET ME OUT?
OR A LOST BULLET FINDING ITS TARGET AT LAST?
PERHAPS NOW IT'S HAPPY TOO!
WHAT THE HELL--
THE SKULLMAN HAS A PLANET AND THE PLANET IS A GUN. THE KIND THAT COULD ERASE A WELL-SIZED SUN.
CROSSBONES.
YES, THAT ONE! EVERY THREE MINUTES HE WILL FIRE--
AND BELIEVE ME--AFTER ALL, YOU HAVE GAUGED HIS DESIRE--HE WILL ERASE MER-Z-BOW, DEAR PRINCESS, AND YOUR PEOPLE DON'T HAVE A PLACE TO HIDE OR RUN!

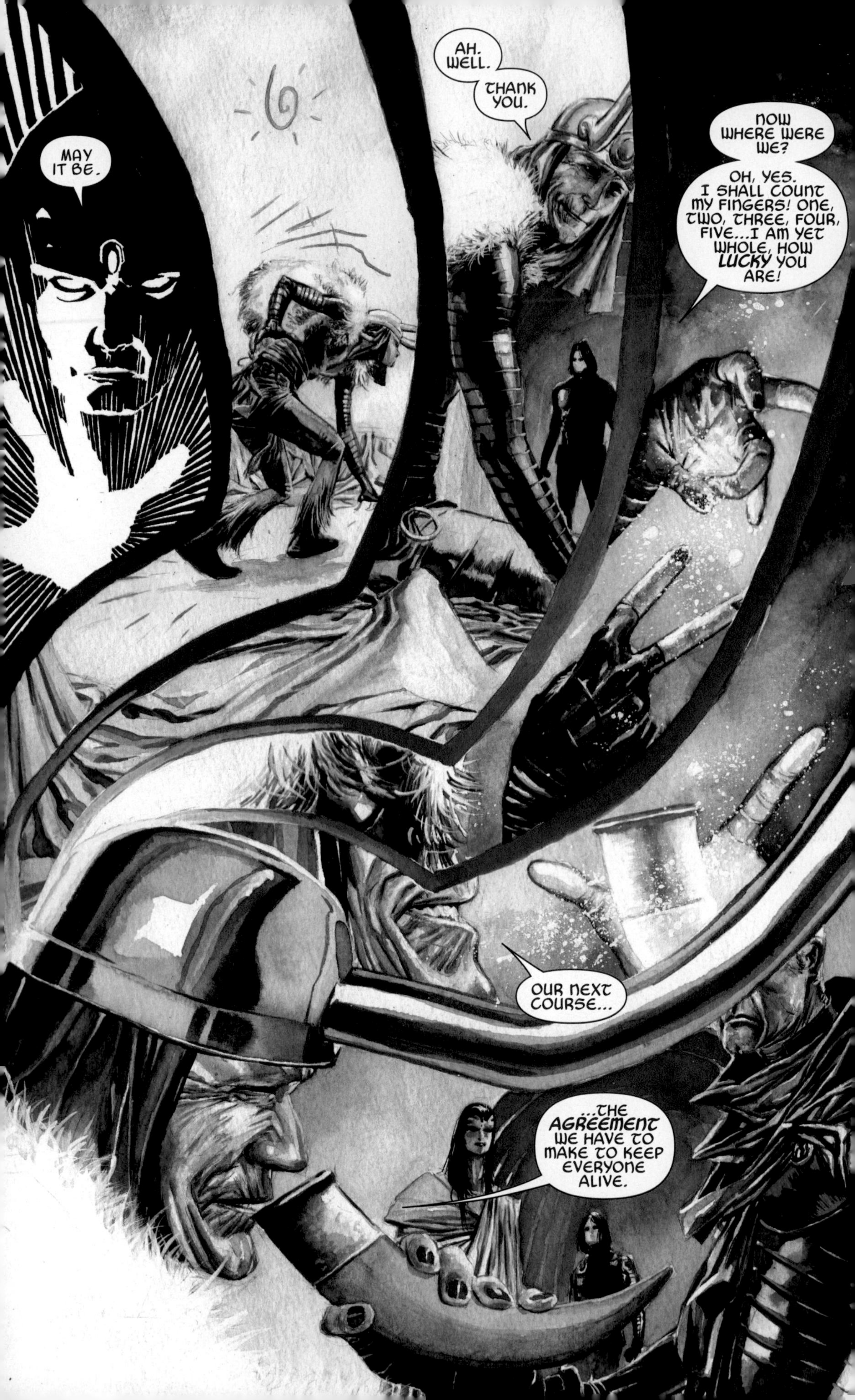
MAY IT BE.
AH. WELL.
THANK YOU.
NOW WHERE WERE WE?
OH, YES. I SHALL COUNT MY FINGERS! ONE, TWO, THREE, FOUR, FIVE...I AM YET WHOLE, HOW LUCKY YOU ARE!
OUR NEXT COURSE...
...THE AGREEMENT WE HAVE TO MAKE TO KEEP EVERYONE ALIVE.

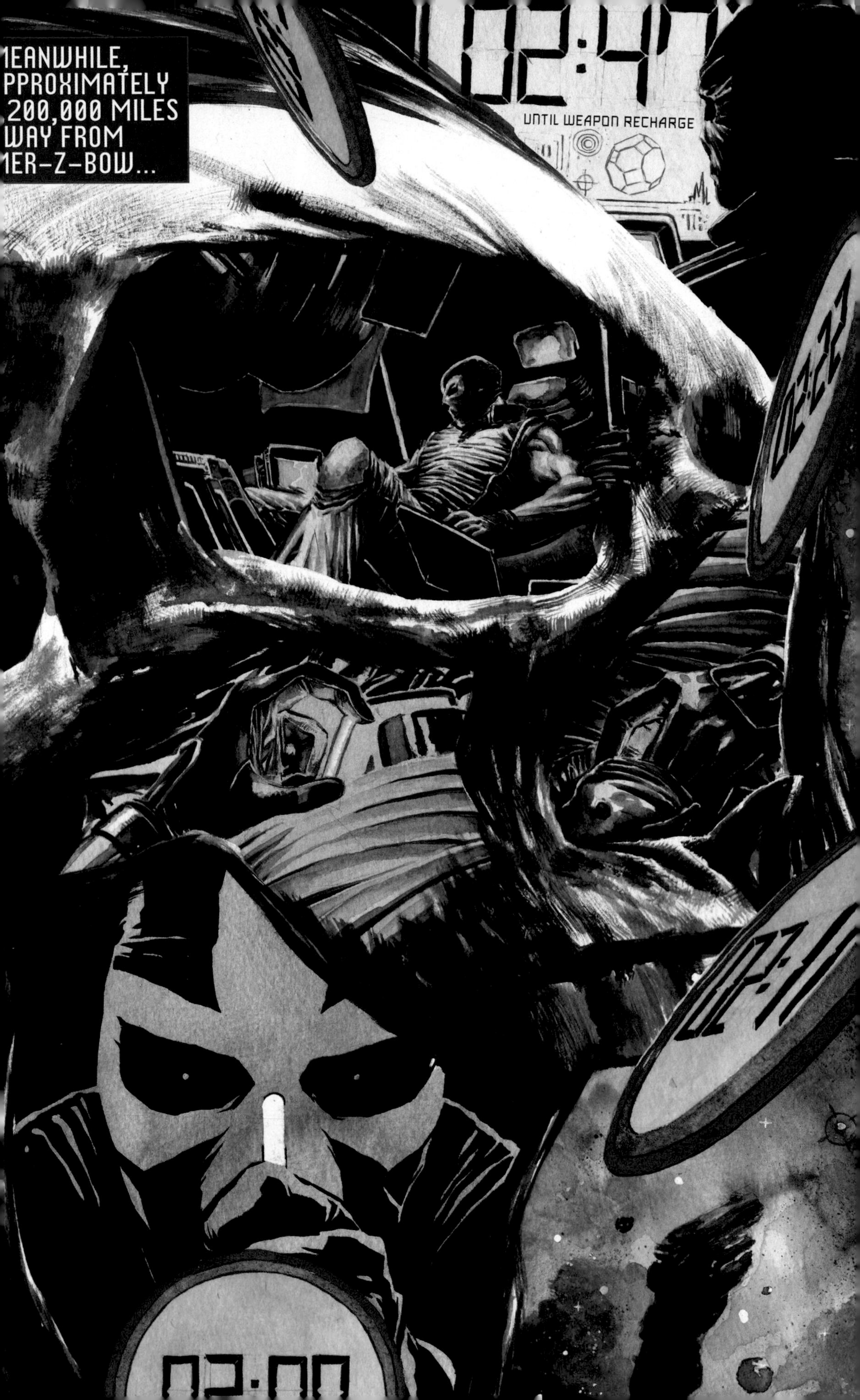

EANWHILE, PPROXIMATELY 200,000 MILES WAY FROM ER-Z-BOW...
UNTIL WEAPON RECHARGE

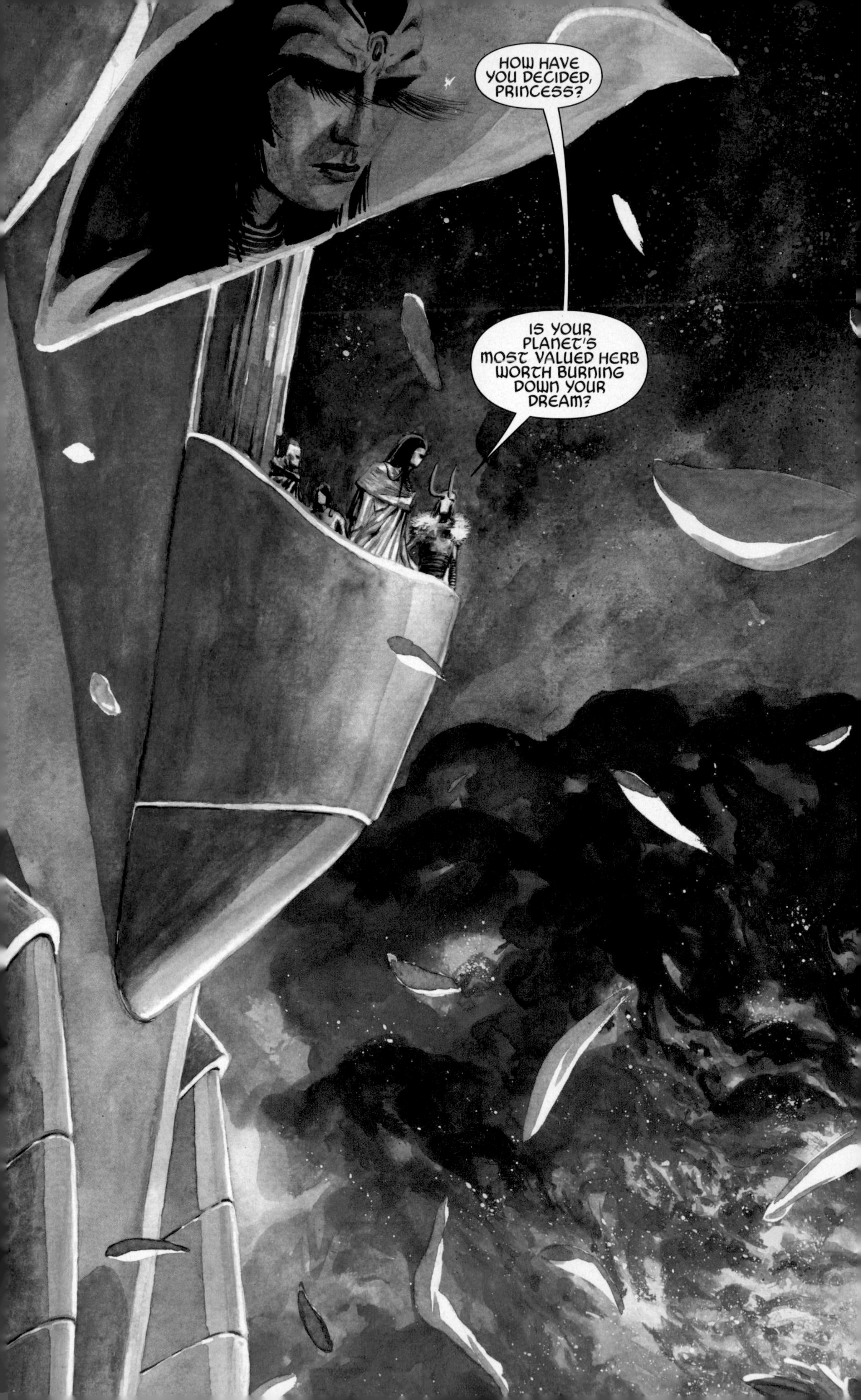
HOW HAVE YOU DECIDED, PRINCESS?
IS YOUR PLANET'S MOST VALUED HERB WORTH BURNING DOWN YOUR DREAM?

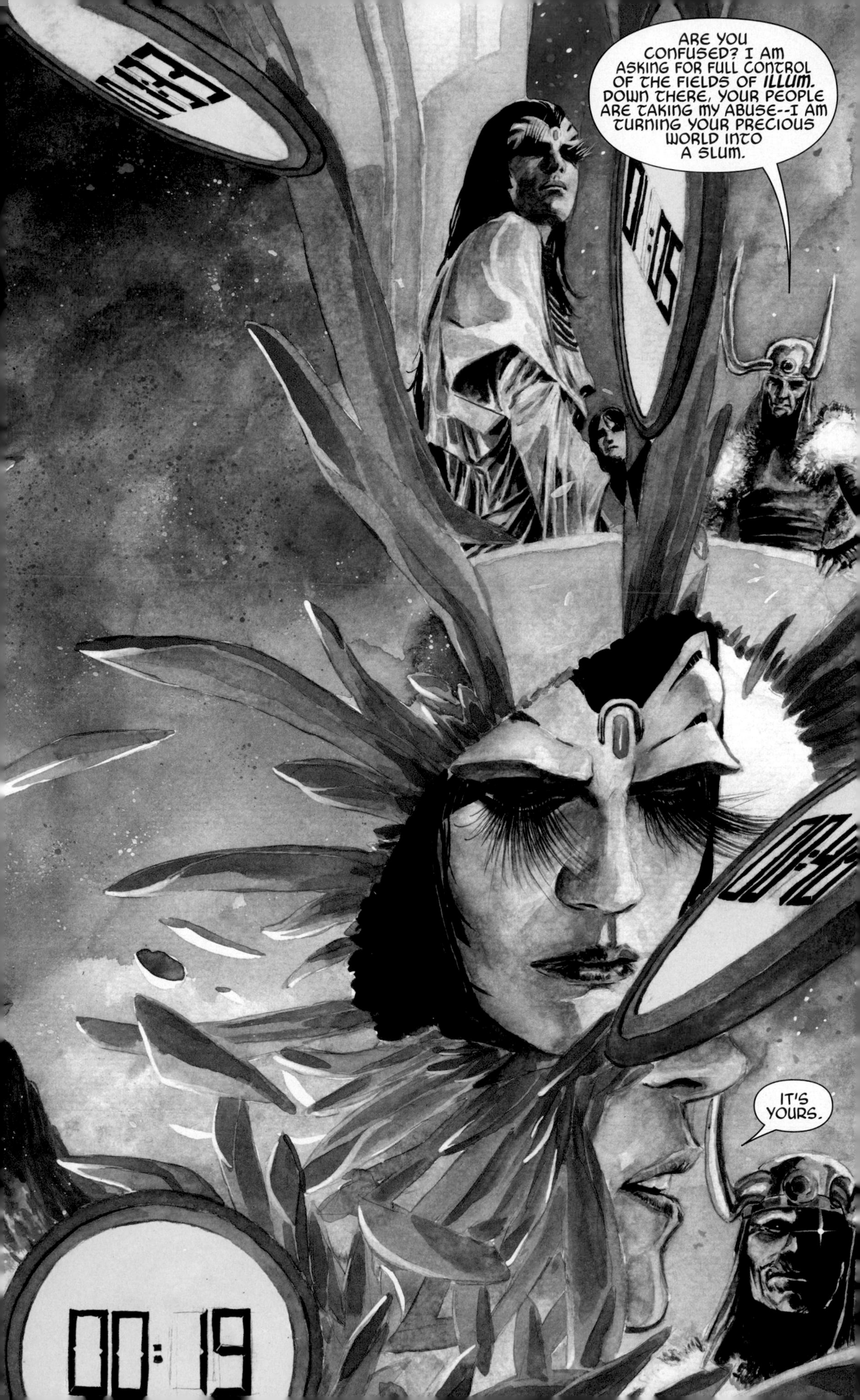
ARE YOU CONFUSED? I AM ASKING FOR FULL CONTROL OF THE FIELDS OF ILLUM. DOWN THERE, YOUR PEOPLE ARE TAKING MY ABUSE--I AM TURNING YOUR PRECIOUS WORLD INTO A SLUM.
01:05
IT'S YOURS.
00:19

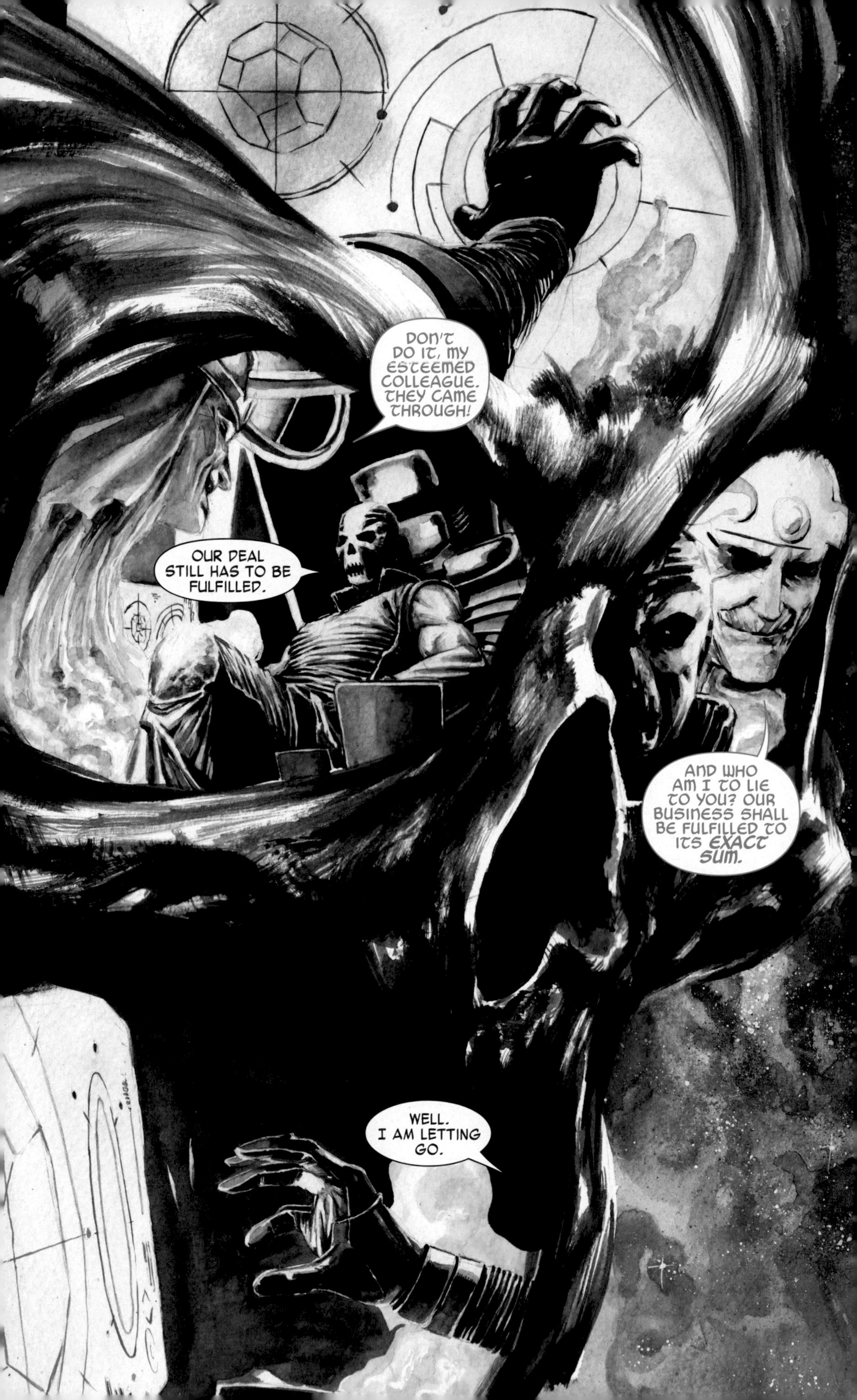
DON'T DO IT, MY ESTEEMED COLLEAGUE. THEY CAME THROUGH!
OUR DEAL STILL HAS TO BE FULFILLED.
AND WHO AM I TO LIE TO YOU? OUR BUSINESS SHALL BE FULFILLED TO ITS EXACT SUM.
WELL. I AM LETTING GO.

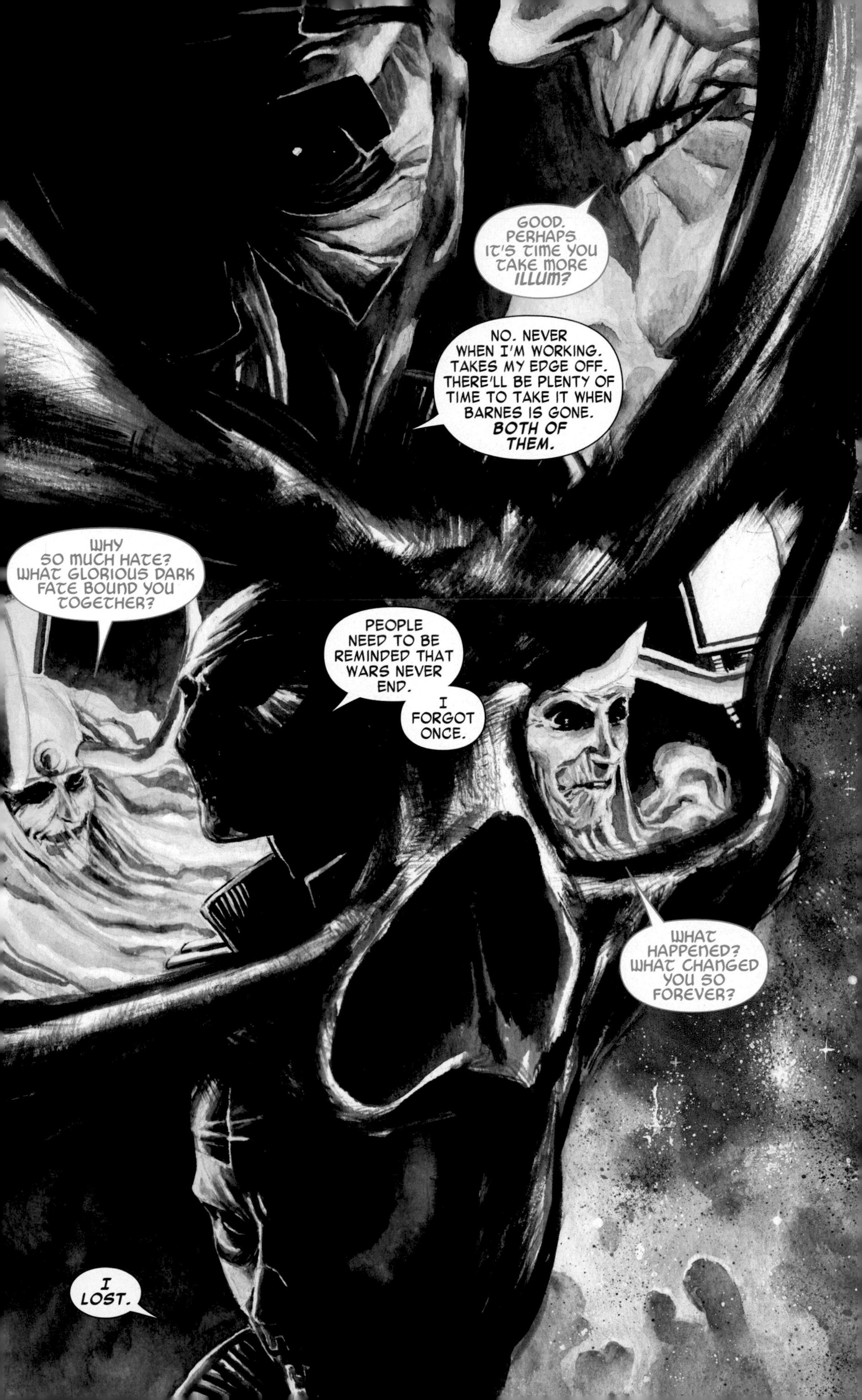
GOOD. PERHAPS IT'S TIME YOU TAKE MORE ILLUM?
NO. NEVER WHEN I'M WORKING. TAKES MY EDGE OFF. THERE'LL BE PLENTY OF TIME TO TAKE IT WHEN BARNES IS GONE. BOTH OF THEM.
WHY SO MUCH HATE? WHAT GLORIOUS DARK FATE BOUND YOU TOGETHER?
PEOPLE NEED TO BE REMINDED THAT WARS NEVER END.
I FORGOT ONCE.
WHAT HAPPENED? WHAT CHANGED YOU SO FOREVER?
I LOST.

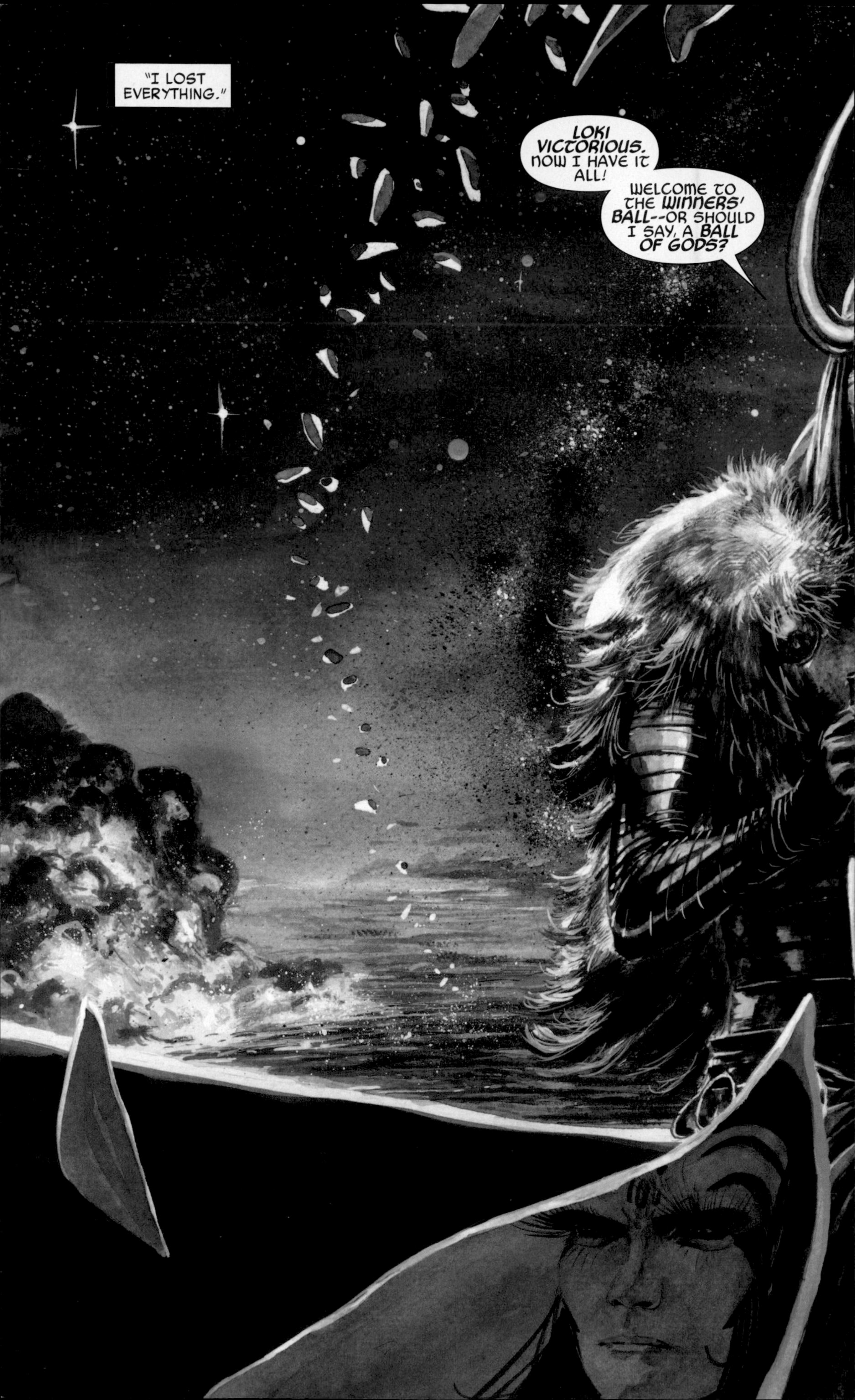
"I LOST EVERYTHING."
LOKI VICTORIOUS. NOW I HAVE IT ALL!
WELCOME TO THE WINNERS' BALL--OR SHOULD I SAY, A BALL OF GODS?

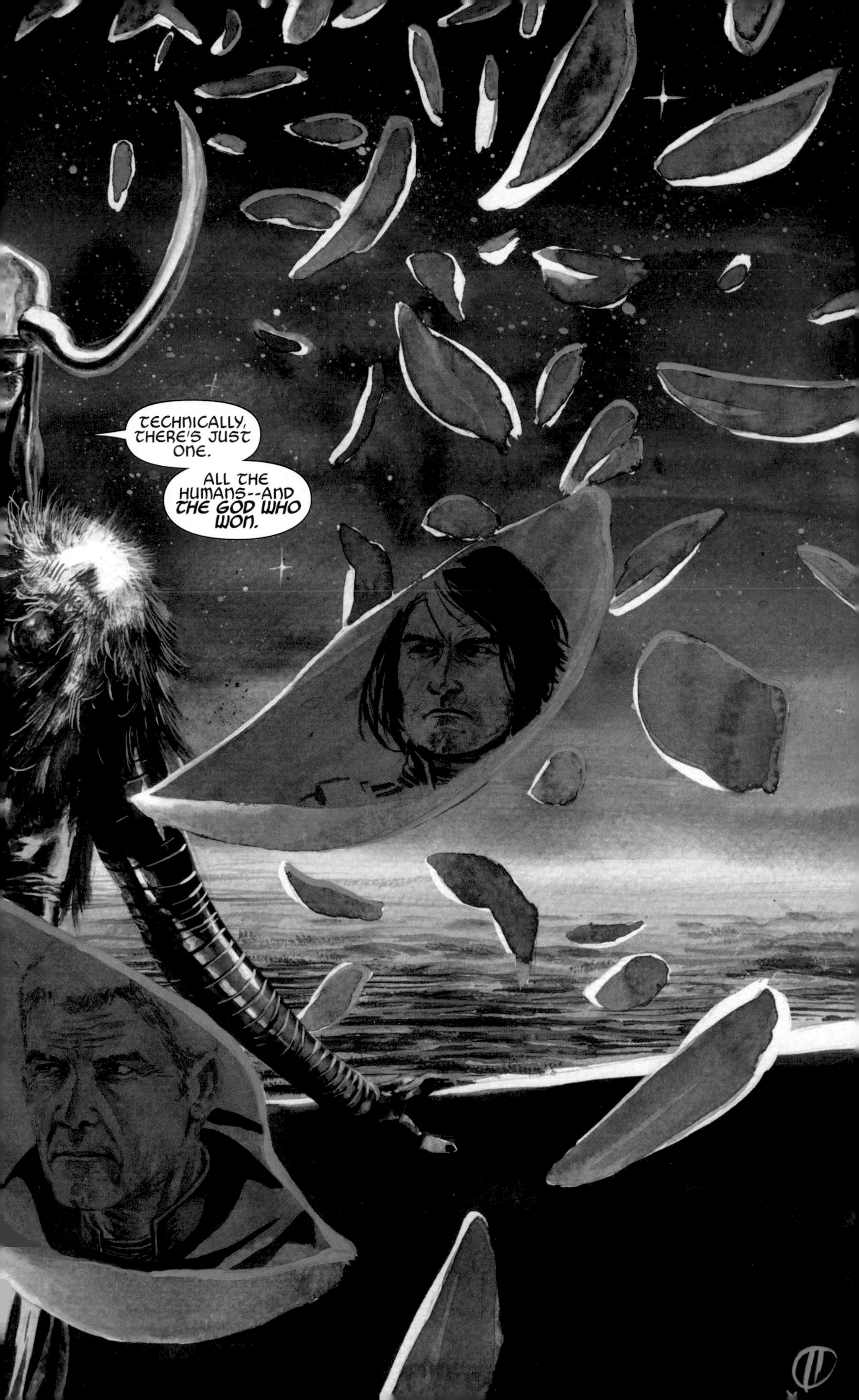
TECHNICALLY, THERE'S JUST ONE.
ALL THE HUMANS--AND *THE GOD WHO WON.*

YOU SIT ON THIS TREASURE, AND WHY? TO ENCOURAGE YOUR NATION'S GROWTH?
SURELY YOU MUST LOATHE YOUR PEOPLE'S CONSTANT DISPLEASURE!
THIS PLANET RESONATES WITH MUSIC, YET THEY DON'T UNDERSTAND WHAT THEY ARE USING!
ALL OF YOU COULD BE GODS OF SPACE AND TIME.
BUT INSTEAD OF TRANSCENDING YOUR OWN SLIME AND GRIME--
--YOU SIT ON IT AND LET THE UNIVERSE JUST FLOW.
IT'S NOT AMUSING! JUST VERY, VERY SAD, AND IT DRIVES UNCLE LOKI...IN SEARCH OF A BETTER RHYME.

VENTOLIN-- DON'T YOU UNDERSTAND? ILLUM WAS THE WAY TO ENSURE THE PROSPERITY OF YOUR LAND.
ALL YOU HAD TO DO WAS **SELL.**
NOW I GET IT FOR FREE.
AND WHAT DO I DO WITH IT?
I GIVE IT TO MY ADMIRERS SO THEY CAN WORSHIP-- ME!
SEE, IT'S ALL ABOUT **BELIEF.**
IF A THIEF SAYS HE'S A GOD, AND ENOUGH PEOPLE SO WILL, ILLUM OPENS THEM UP, AND THE POWERS OF THEIR MINDS GO STILL WITH THE FLOW OF HIS VOICE AS IT CHANTS WITH THE POWER OF HONEY-LIKE RELIEF...
**...LOKI IS GOD.**
MORE POWERFUL BY THE MINUTE.
THE **MORE ILLUM**--THE MORE POWERFUL **MY SPIRIT.**

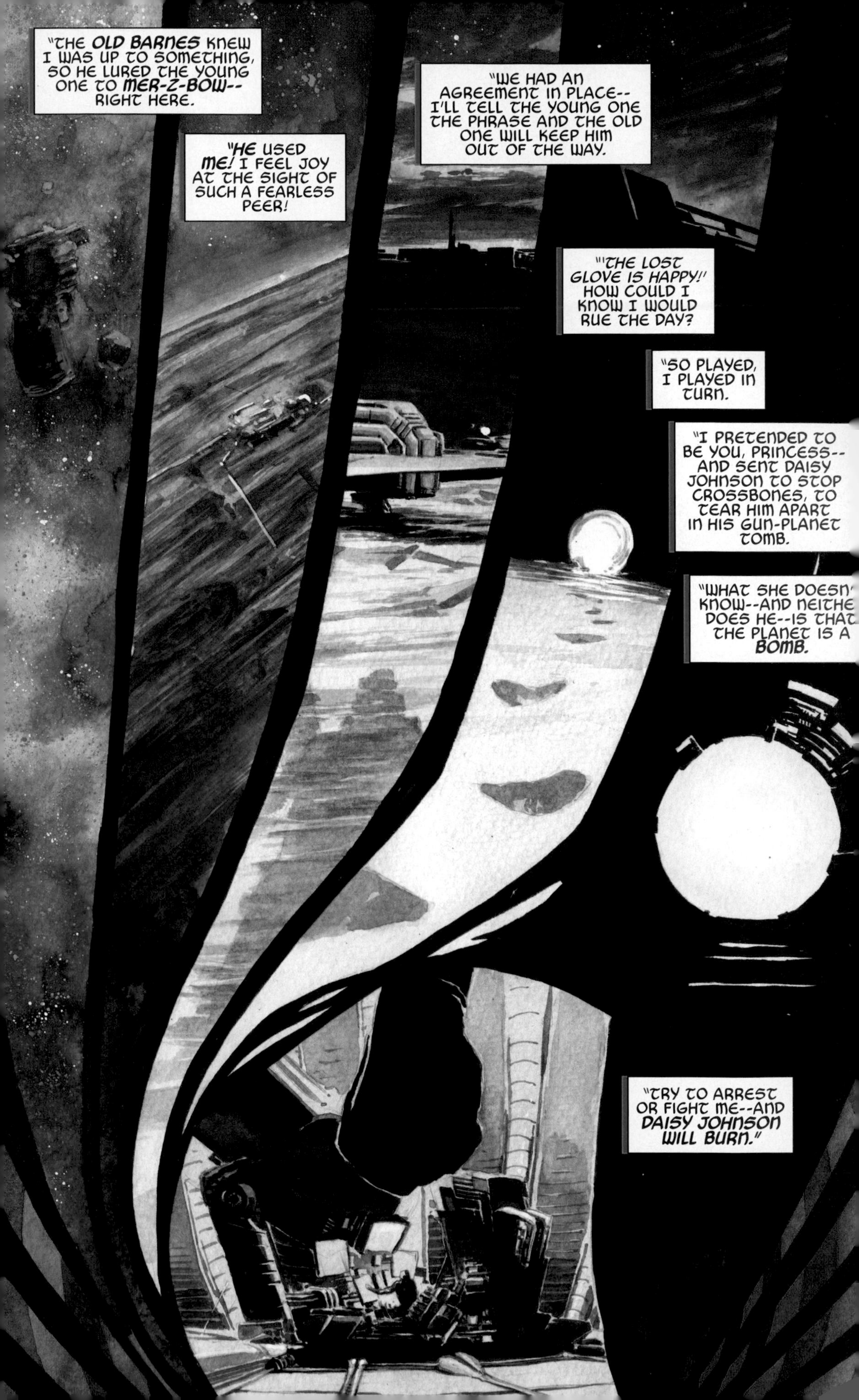
"THE OLD BARNES KNEW I WAS UP TO SOMETHING, SO HE LURED THE YOUNG ONE TO MER-Z-BOW-- RIGHT HERE.
"HE USED ME! I FEEL JOY AT THE SIGHT OF SUCH A FEARLESS PEER!
"WE HAD AN AGREEMENT IN PLACE-- I'LL TELL THE YOUNG ONE THE PHRASE AND THE OLD ONE WILL KEEP HIM OUT OF THE WAY.
"'THE LOST GLOVE IS HAPPY!' HOW COULD I KNOW I WOULD RUE THE DAY?
"SO PLAYED, I PLAYED IN TURN.
"I PRETENDED TO BE YOU, PRINCESS-- AND SENT DAISY JOHNSON TO STOP CROSSBONES, TO TEAR HIM APART IN HIS GUN-PLANET TOMB.
"WHAT SHE DOESN' KNOW--AND NEITHE DOES HE--IS THAT THE PLANET IS A BOMB.
"TRY TO ARREST OR FIGHT ME--AND DAISY JOHNSON WILL BURN."

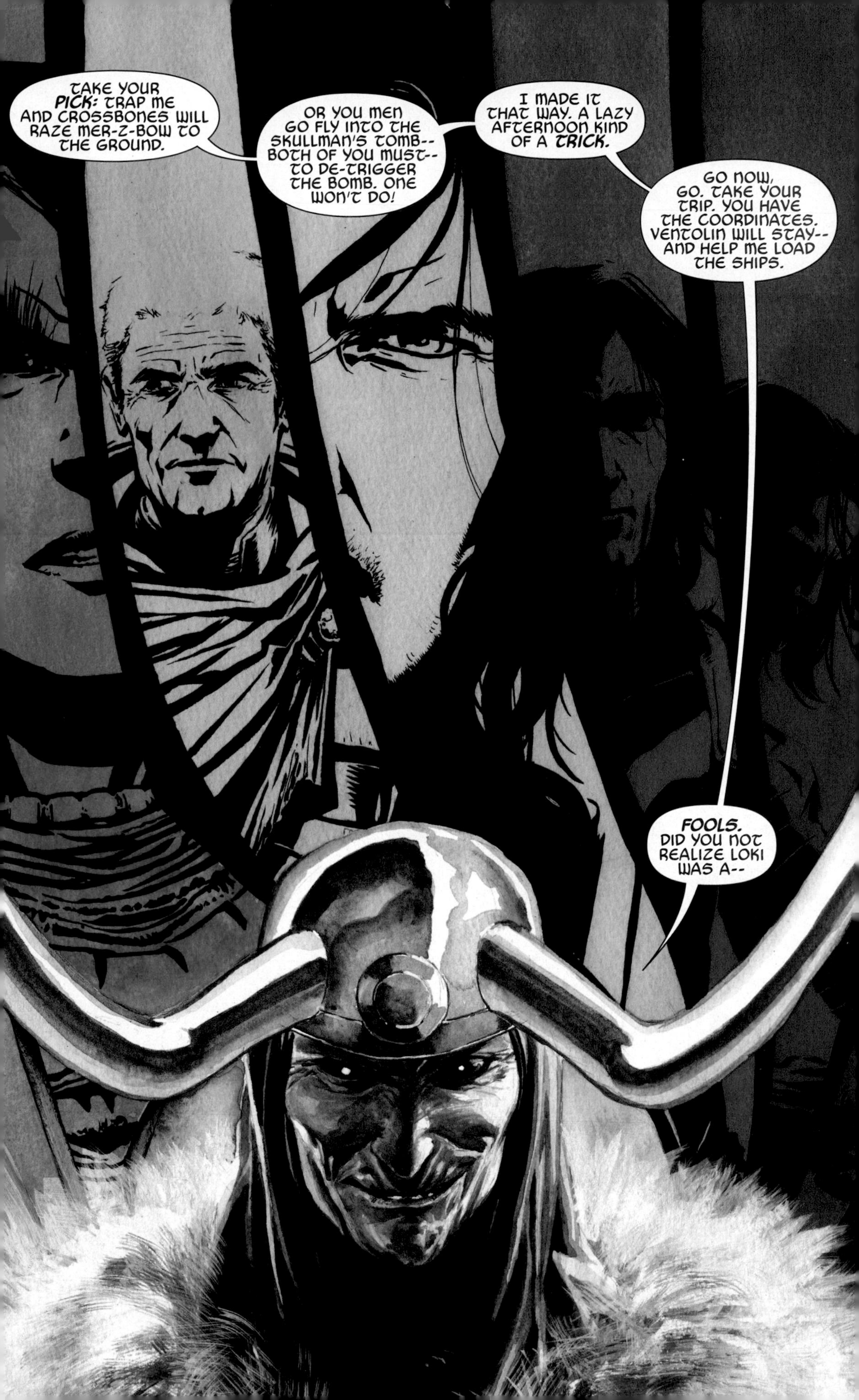
TAKE YOUR PICK: TRAP ME AND CROSSBONES WILL RAZE MER-Z-BOW TO THE GROUND.
OR YOU MEN GO FLY INTO THE SKULLMAN'S TOMB-- BOTH OF YOU MUST-- TO DE-TRIGGER THE BOMB. ONE WON'T DO!
I MADE IT THAT WAY. A LAZY AFTERNOON KIND OF A TRICK.
GO NOW, GO. TAKE YOUR TRIP. YOU HAVE THE COORDINATES. VENTOLIN WILL STAY-- AND HELP ME LOAD THE SHIPS.
FOOLS. DID YOU NOT REALIZE LOKI WAS A--

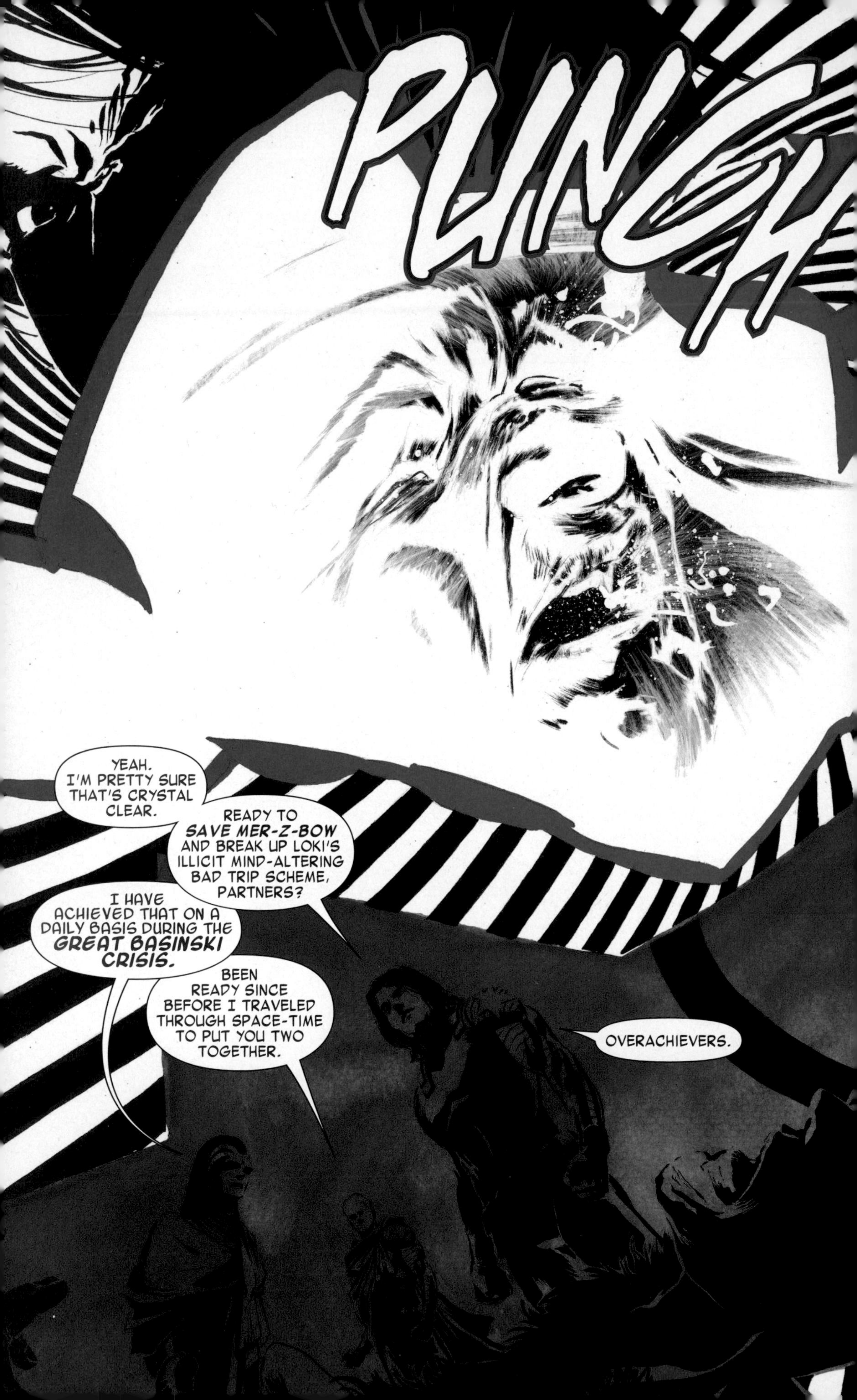
PUNCH
YEAH. I'M PRETTY SURE THAT'S CRYSTAL CLEAR.
READY TO SAVE MER-Z-BOW AND BREAK UP LOKI'S ILLICIT MIND-ALTERING BAD TRIP SCHEME, PARTNERS?
I HAVE ACHIEVED THAT ON A DAILY BASIS DURING THE GREAT BASINSKI CRISIS.
BEEN READY SINCE BEFORE I TRAVELED THROUGH SPACE-TIME TO PUT YOU TWO TOGETHER.
OVERACHIEVERS.

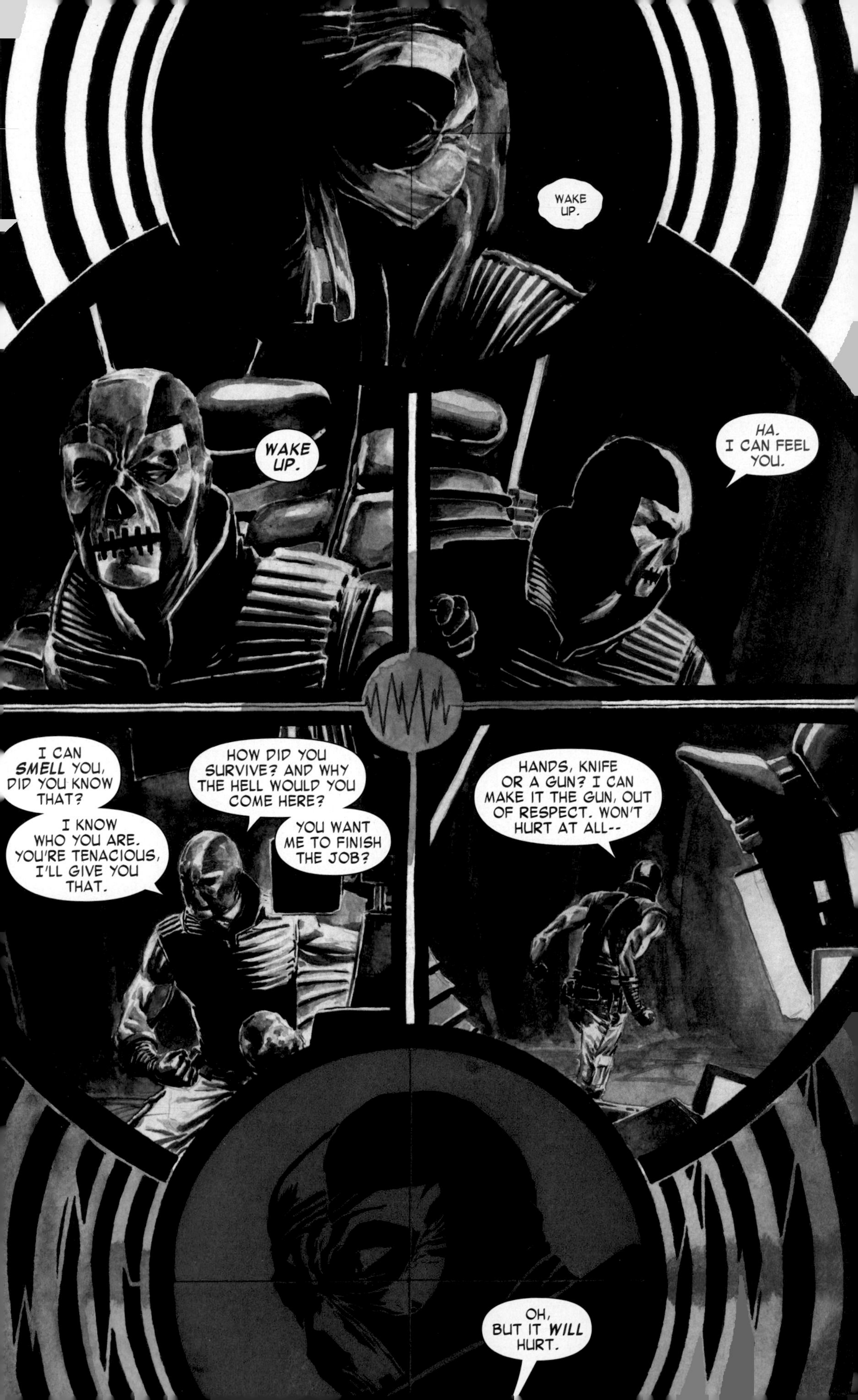

WAKE UP.
WAKE UP.
HA. I CAN FEEL YOU.
I CAN SMELL YOU, DID YOU KNOW THAT?
I KNOW WHO YOU ARE. YOU'RE TENACIOUS, I'LL GIVE YOU THAT.
HOW DID YOU SURVIVE? AND WHY THE HELL WOULD YOU COME HERE?
YOU WANT ME TO FINISH THE JOB?
HANDS, KNIFE OR A GUN? I CAN MAKE IT THE GUN, OUT OF RESPECT. WON'T HURT AT ALL--
OH, BUT IT WILL HURT.

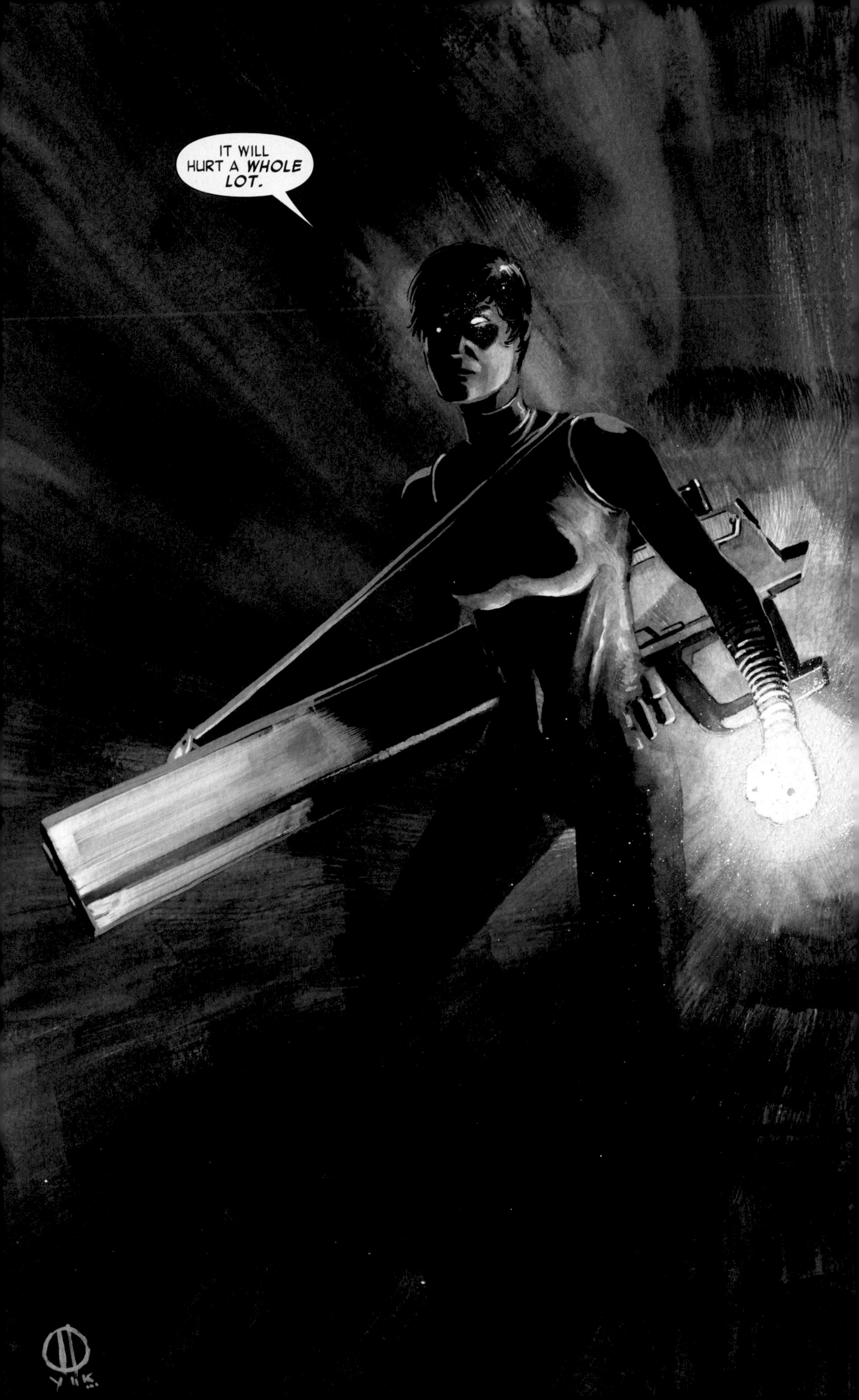
IT WILL HURT A WHOLE LOT.

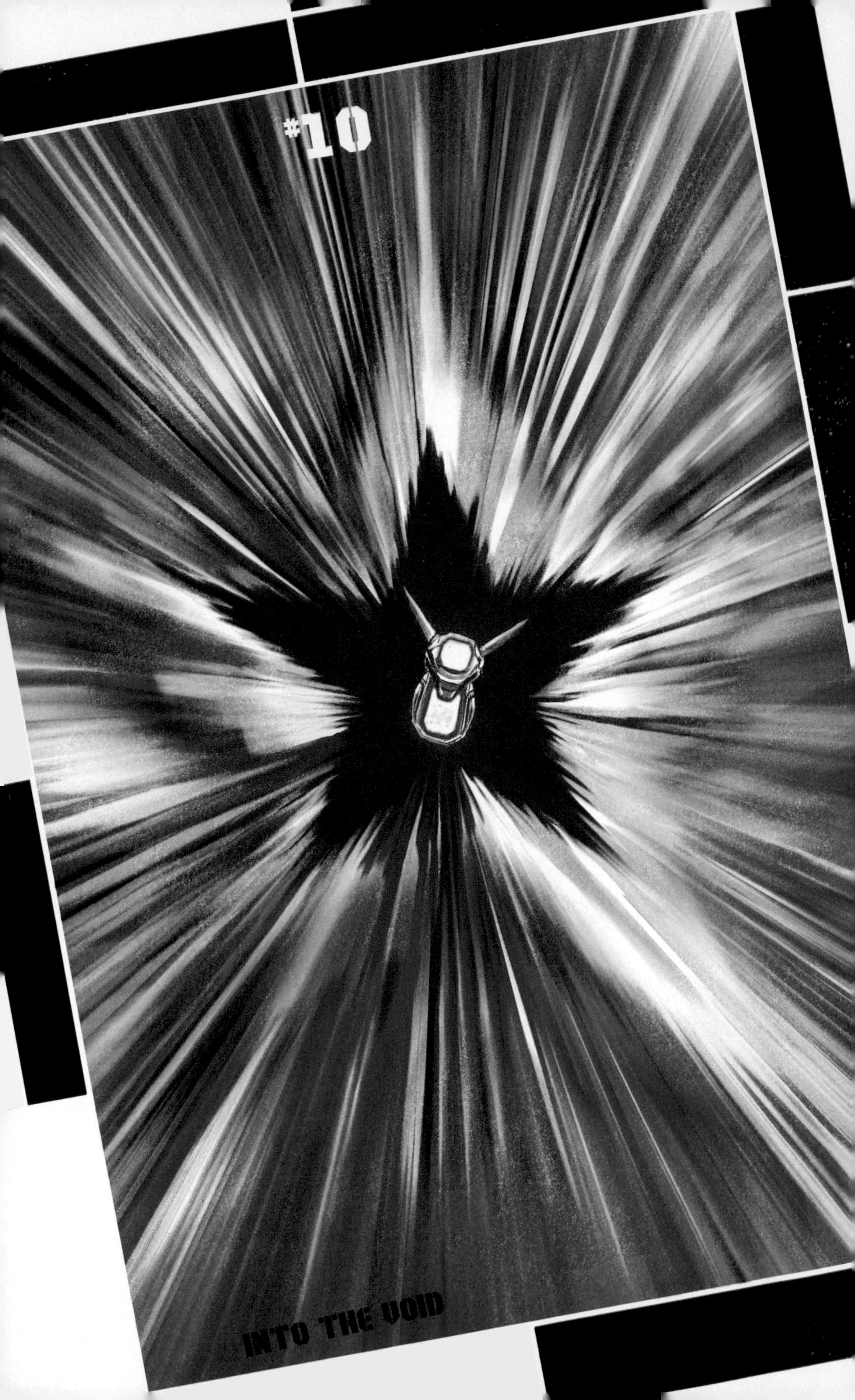
#10
INTO THE VOID

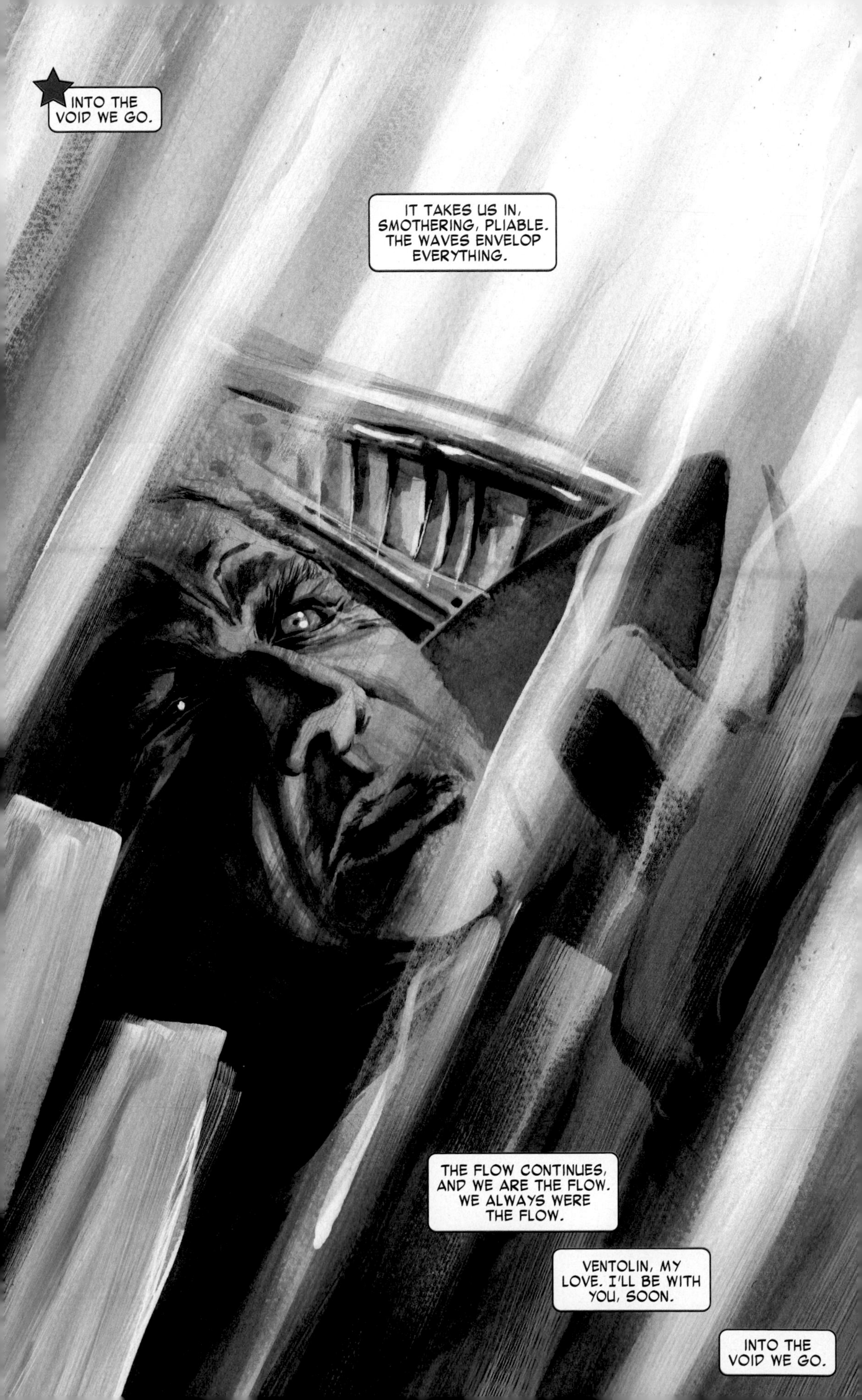
INTO THE VOID WE GO.
IT TAKES US IN, SMOTHERING, PLIABLE. THE WAVES ENVELOP EVERYTHING.
THE FLOW CONTINUES, AND WE ARE THE FLOW. WE ALWAYS WERE THE FLOW.
VENTOLIN, MY LOVE. I'LL BE WITH YOU, SOON.
INTO THE VOID WE GO.

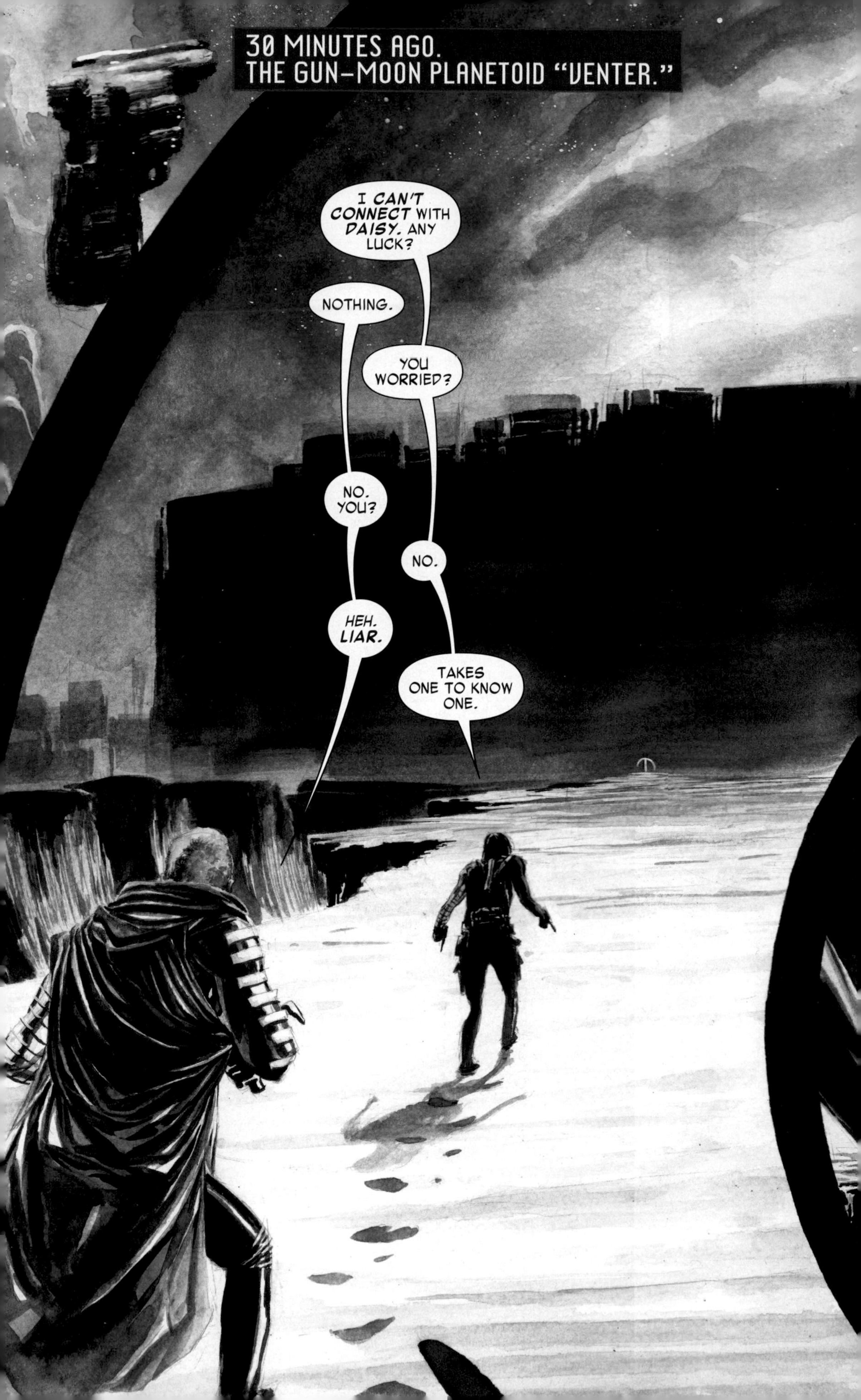
30 MINUTES AGO.
THE GUN-MOON PLANETOID "VENTER."
I CAN'T CONNECT WITH DAISY. ANY LUCK?
NOTHING.
YOU WORRIED?
NO. YOU?
NO.
HEH. LIAR.
TAKES ONE TO KNOW ONE.

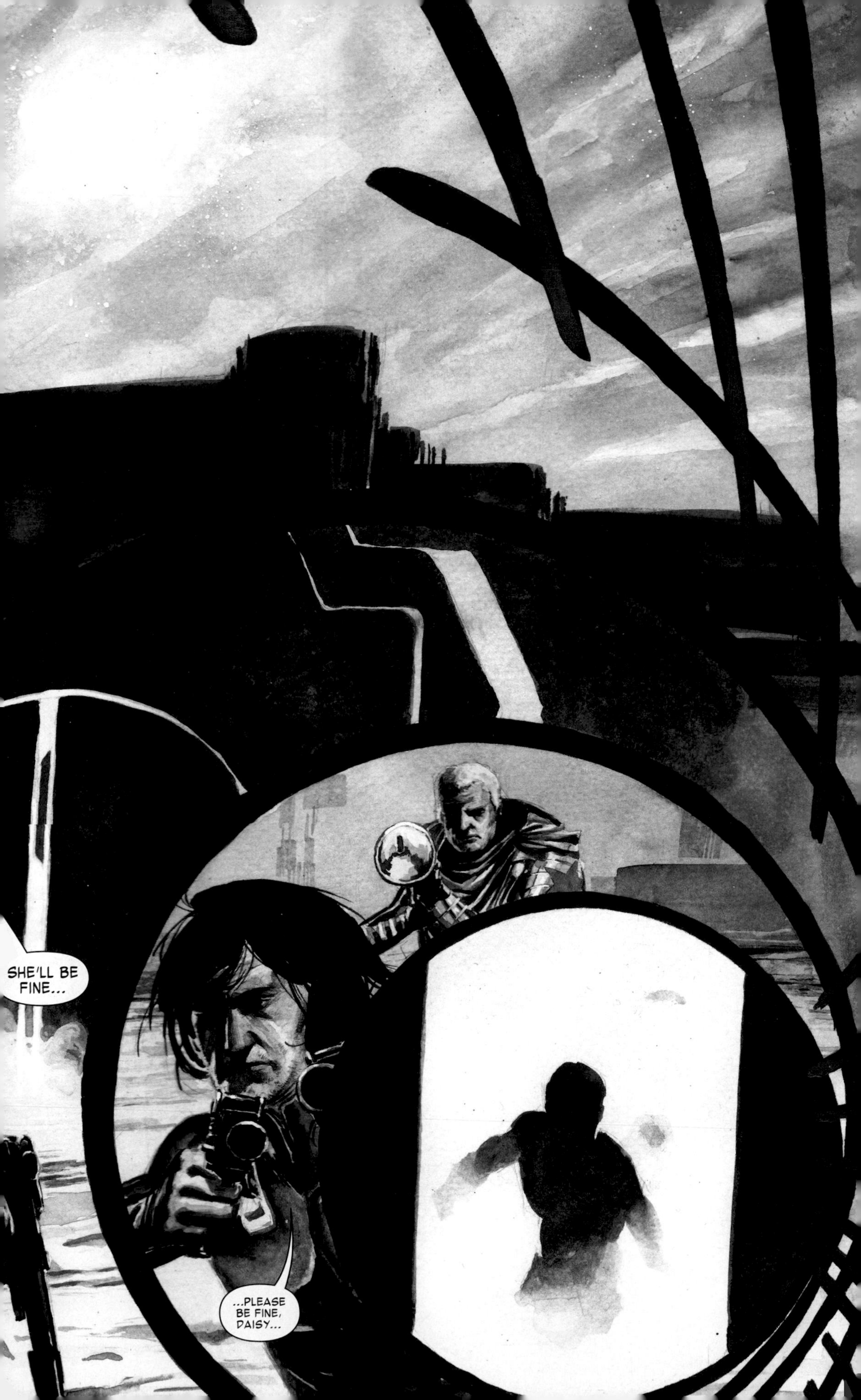
SHE'LL BE FINE...
...PLEASE BE FINE, DAISY...

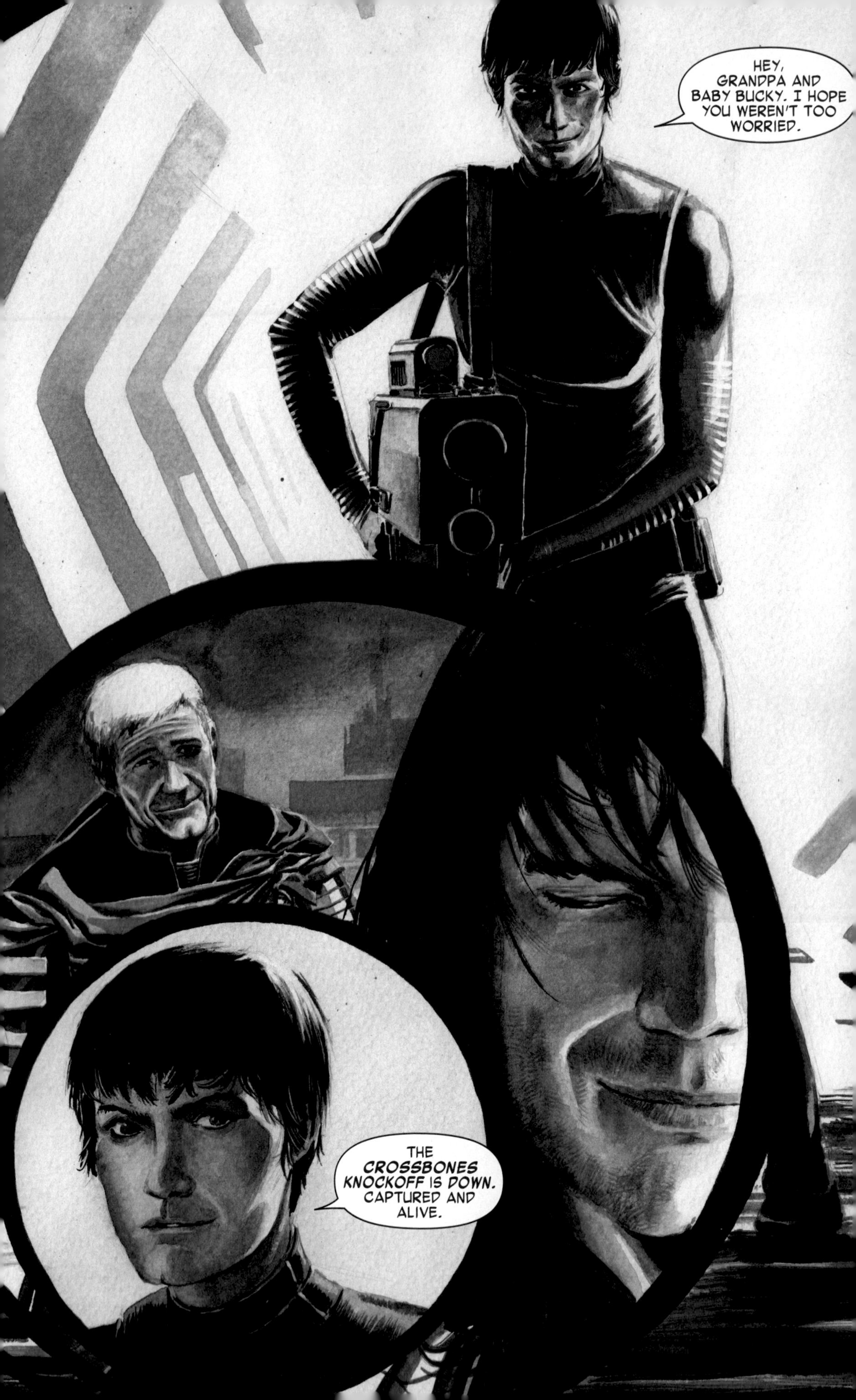
HEY, GRANDPA AND BABY BUCKY. I HOPE YOU WEREN'T TOO WORRIED.
THE *CROSSBONES KNOCKOFF* IS DOWN. CAPTURED AND ALIVE.

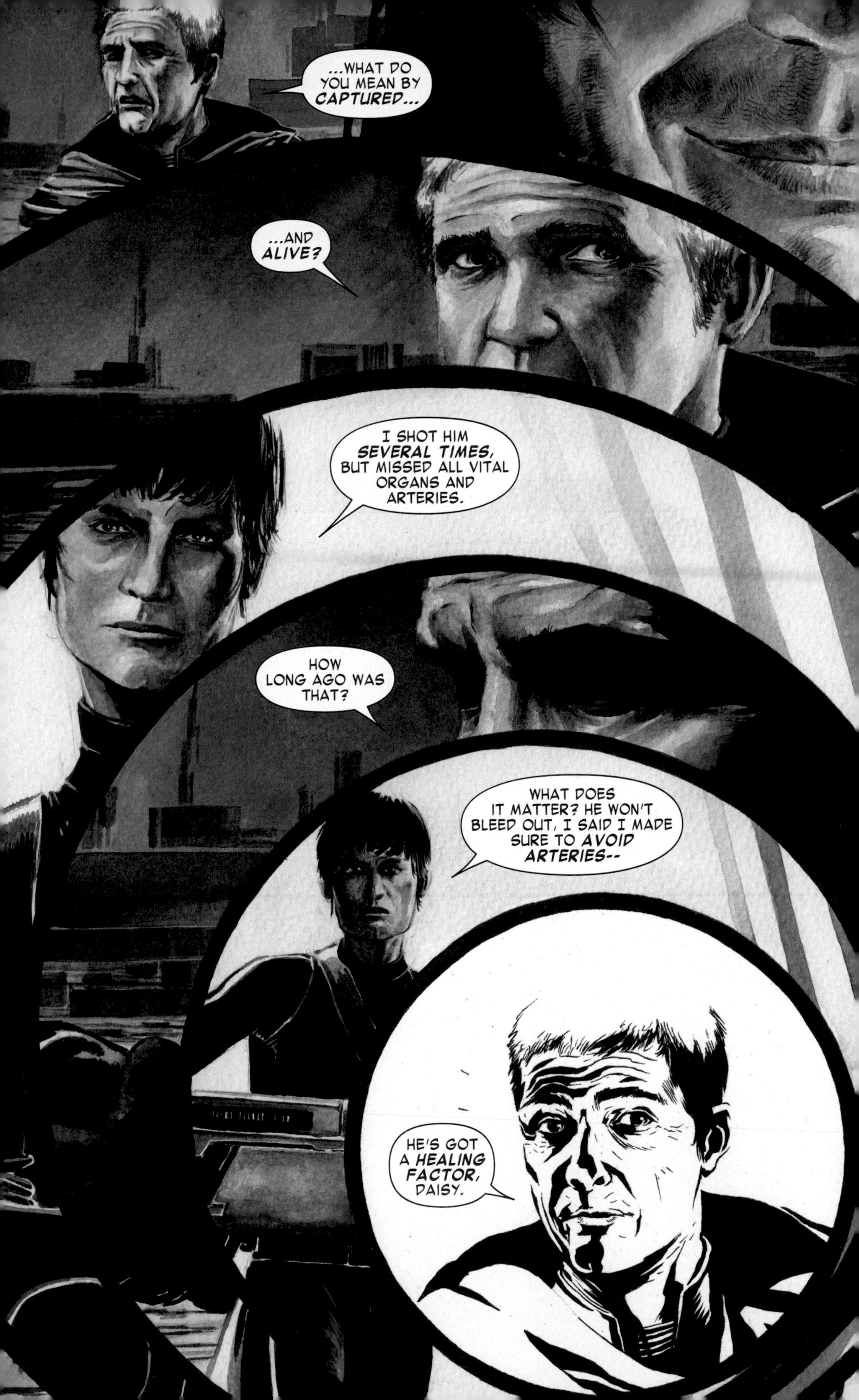
...WHAT DO YOU MEAN BY CAPTURED...
...AND ALIVE?
I SHOT HIM SEVERAL TIMES, BUT MISSED ALL VITAL ORGANS AND ARTERIES.
HOW LONG AGO WAS THAT?
WHAT DOES IT MATTER? HE WON'T BLEED OUT, I SAID I MADE SURE TO AVOID ARTERIES--
HE'S GOT A HEALING FACTOR, DAISY.

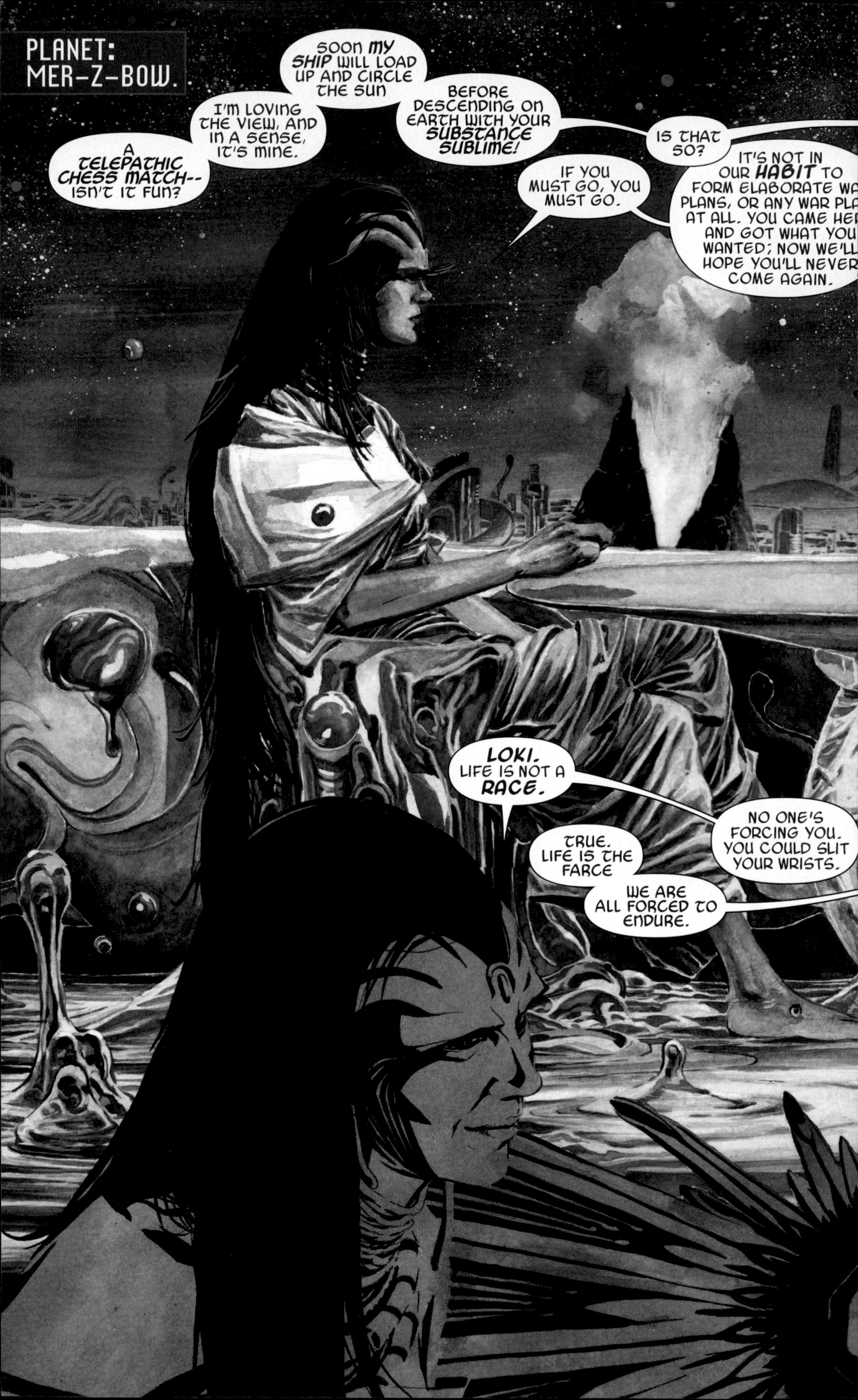
PLANET: MER-Z-BOW.
A TELEPATHIC CHESS MATCH-- ISN'T IT FUN?
I'M LOVING THE VIEW, AND IN A SENSE, IT'S MINE.
SOON MY SHIP WILL LOAD UP AND CIRCLE THE SUN
BEFORE DESCENDING ON EARTH WITH YOUR SUBSTANCE SUBLIME!
IS THAT SO?
IF YOU MUST GO, YOU MUST GO.
LOKI. LIFE IS NOT A RACE.
TRUE. LIFE IS THE FARCE
WE ARE ALL FORCED TO ENDURE.
NO ONE'S FORCING YOU. YOU COULD SLIT YOUR WRISTS.

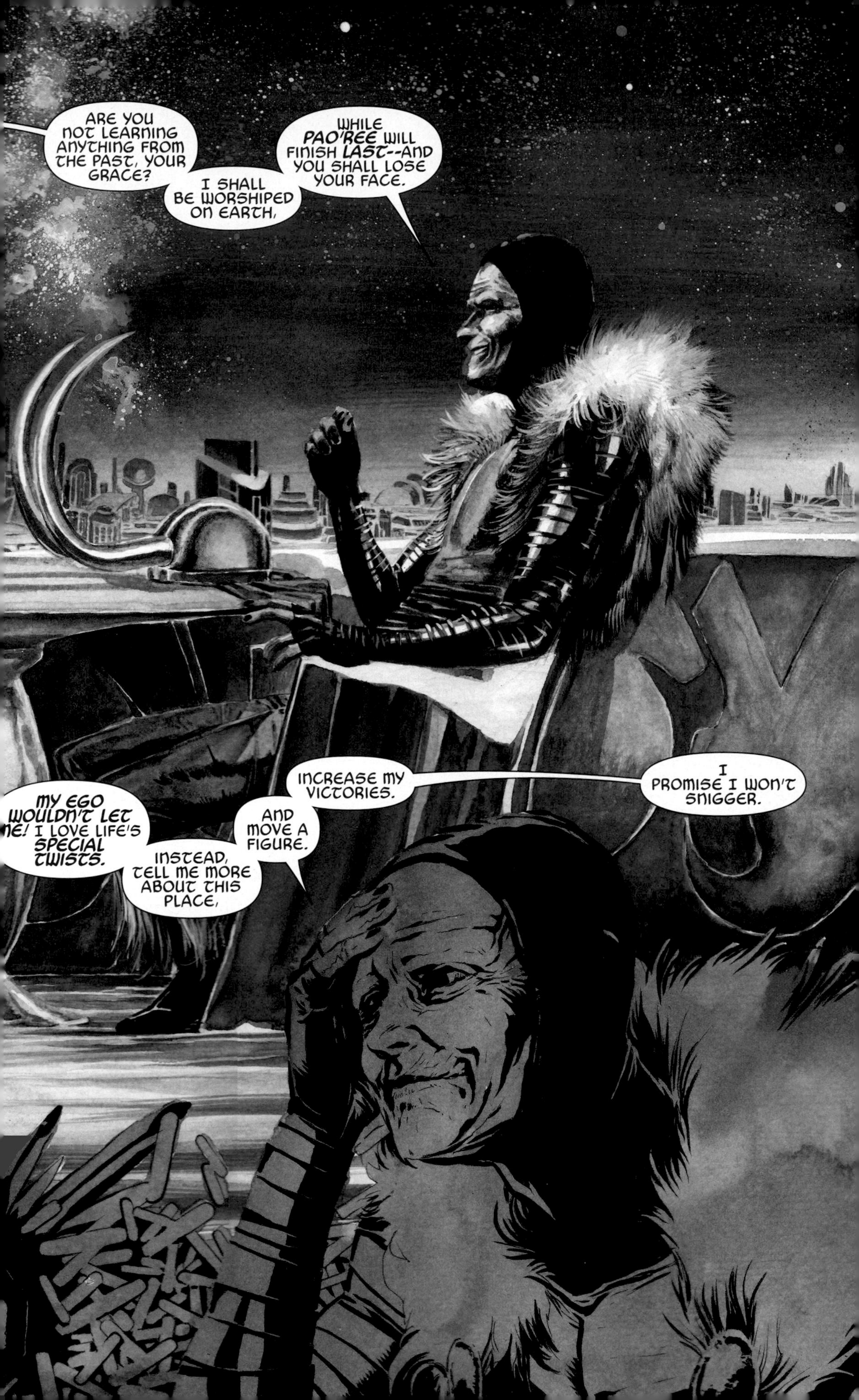
ARE YOU NOT LEARNING ANYTHING FROM THE PAST, YOUR GRACE?
I SHALL BE WORSHIPED ON EARTH,
WHILE PAO'REE WILL FINISH LAST--AND YOU SHALL LOSE YOUR FACE.
I PROMISE I WON'T SNIGGER.
INCREASE MY VICTORIES.
AND MOVE A FIGURE.
INSTEAD, TELL ME MORE ABOUT THIS PLACE,
MY EGO WOULDN'T LET ME! I LOVE LIFE'S SPECIAL TWISTS.

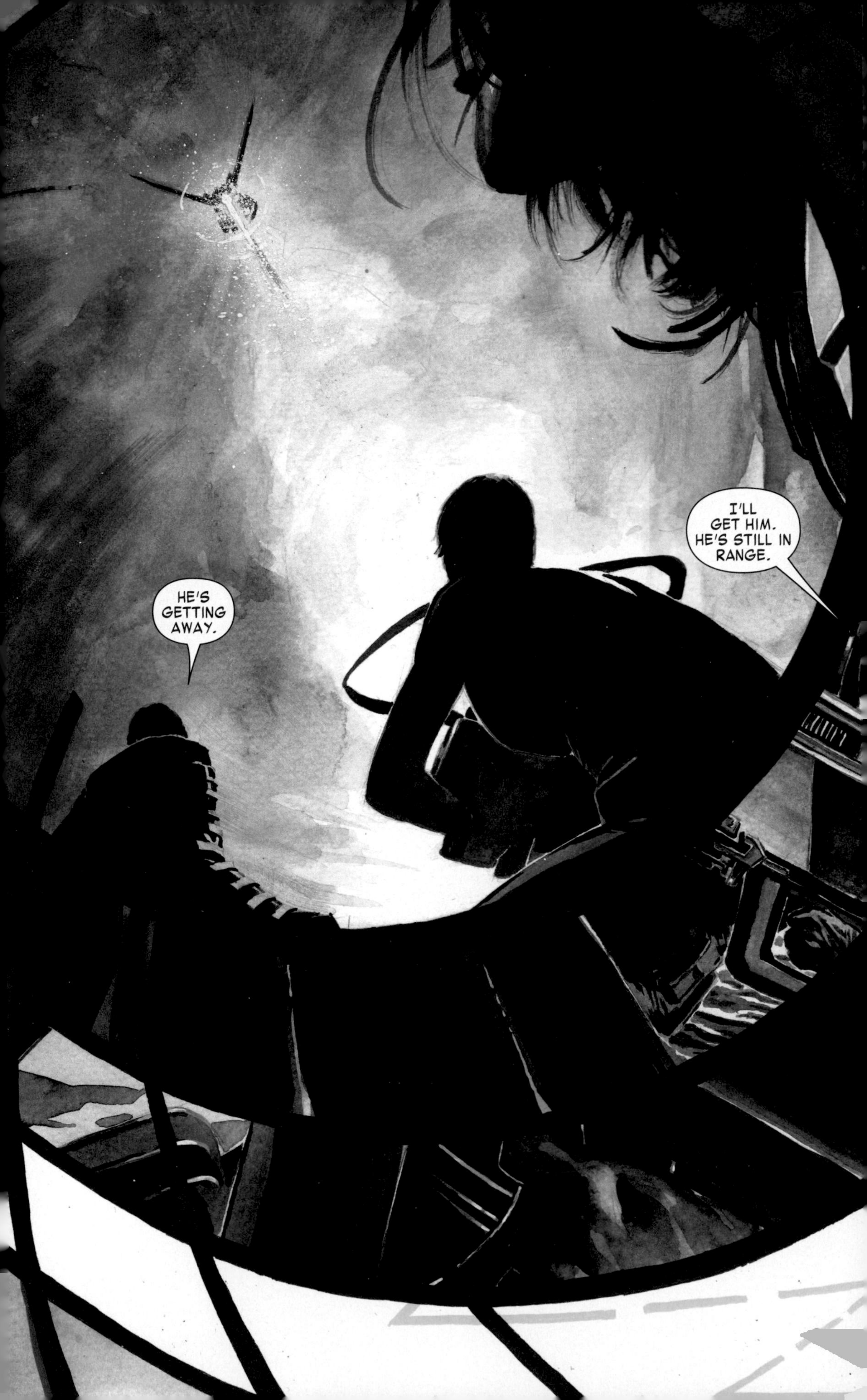
HE'S GETTING AWAY.
I'LL GET HIM. HE'S STILL IN RANGE.

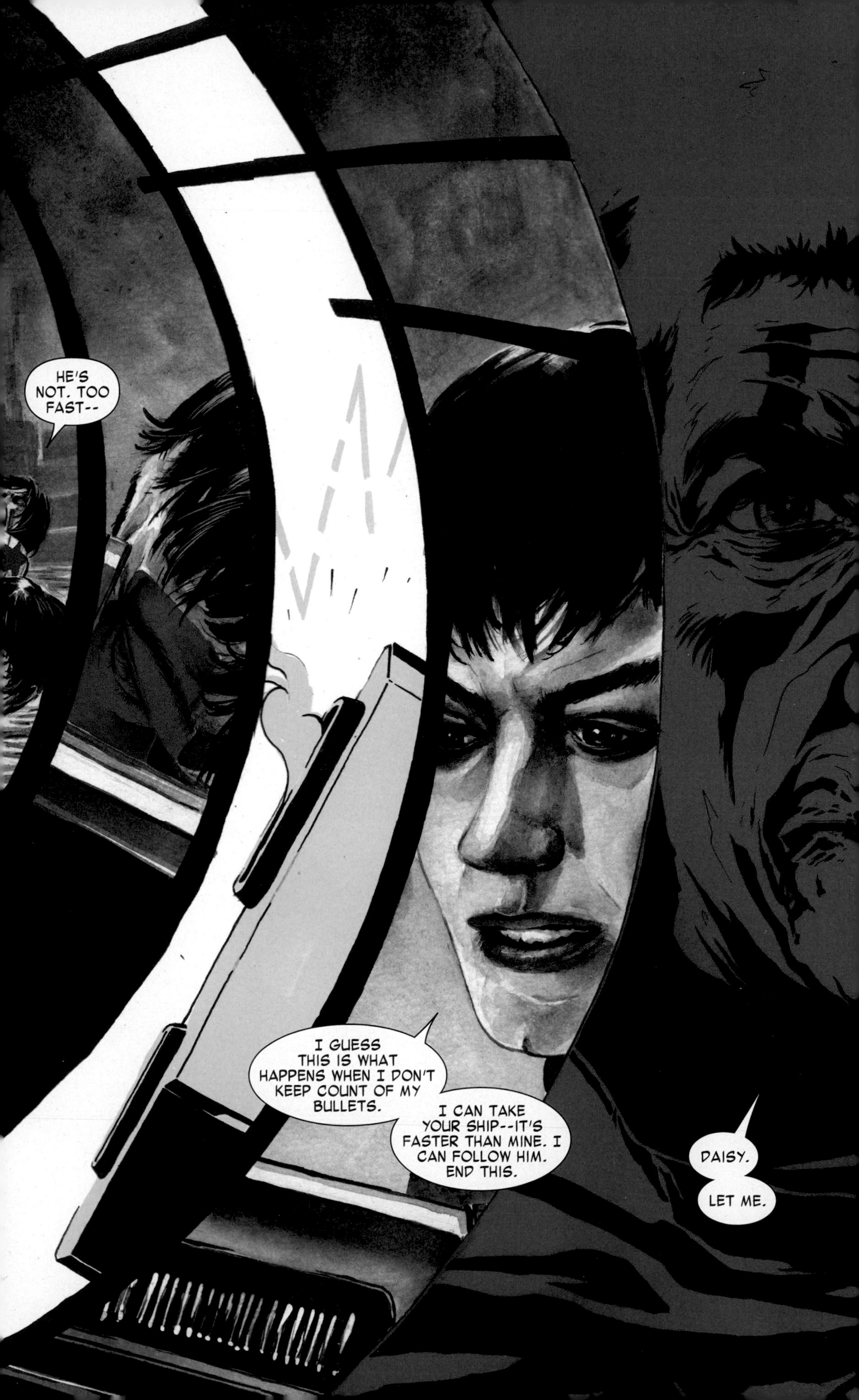
HE'S NOT. TOO FAST--
I GUESS THIS IS WHAT HAPPENS WHEN I DON'T KEEP COUNT OF MY BULLETS.
I CAN TAKE YOUR SHIP--IT'S FASTER THAN MINE. I CAN FOLLOW HIM. END THIS.
DAISY.
LET ME.

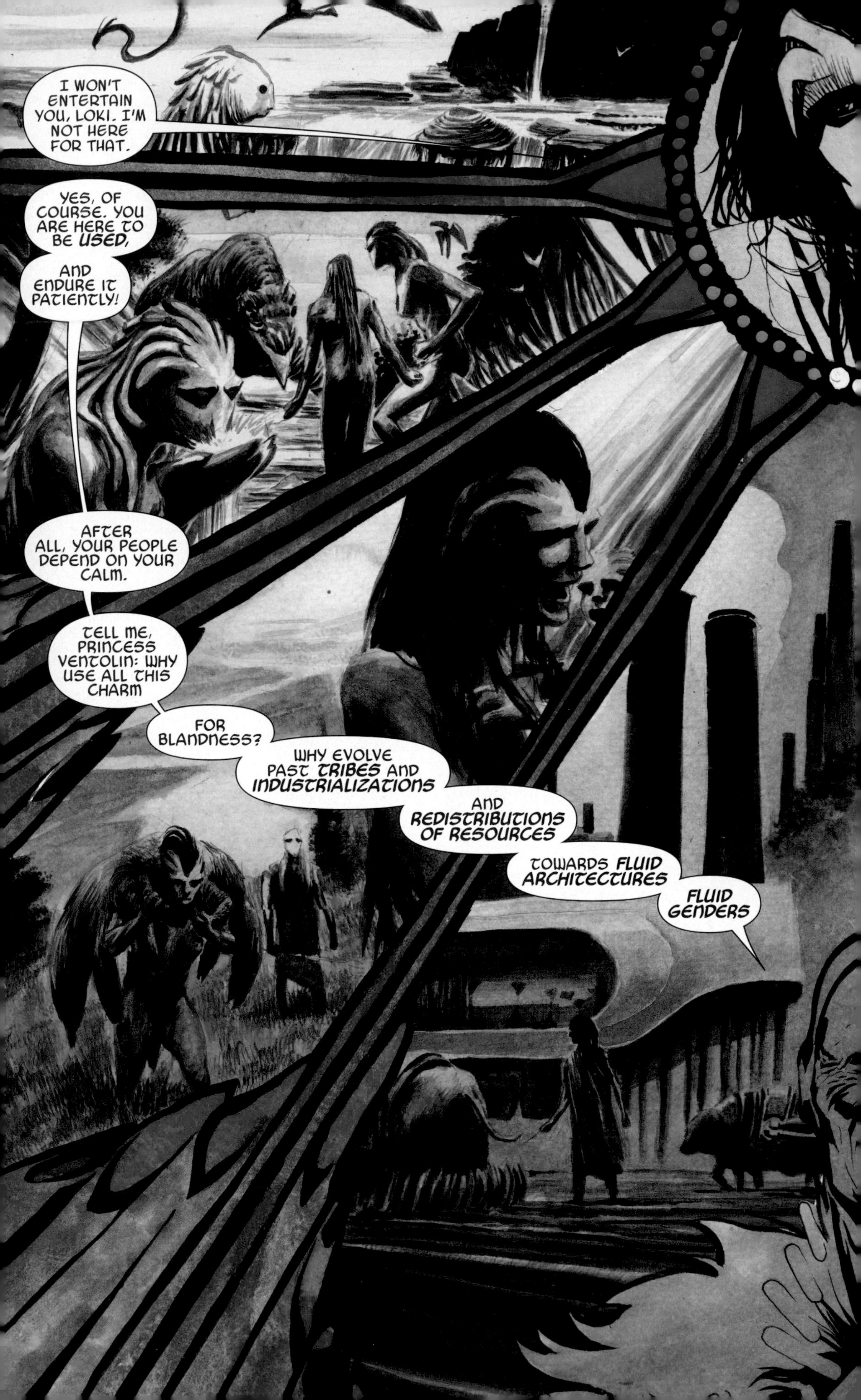
I WON'T ENTERTAIN YOU, LOKI. I'M NOT HERE FOR THAT.
YES, OF COURSE. YOU ARE HERE TO BE USED,
AND ENDURE IT PATIENTLY!
AFTER ALL, YOUR PEOPLE DEPEND ON YOUR CALM.
TELL ME, PRINCESS VENTOLIN: WHY USE ALL THIS CHARM
FOR BLANDNESS?
WHY EVOLVE PAST TRIBES AND INDUSTRIALIZATIONS
AND REDISTRIBUTIONS OF RESOURCES
TOWARDS FLUID ARCHITECTURES
FLUID GENDERS

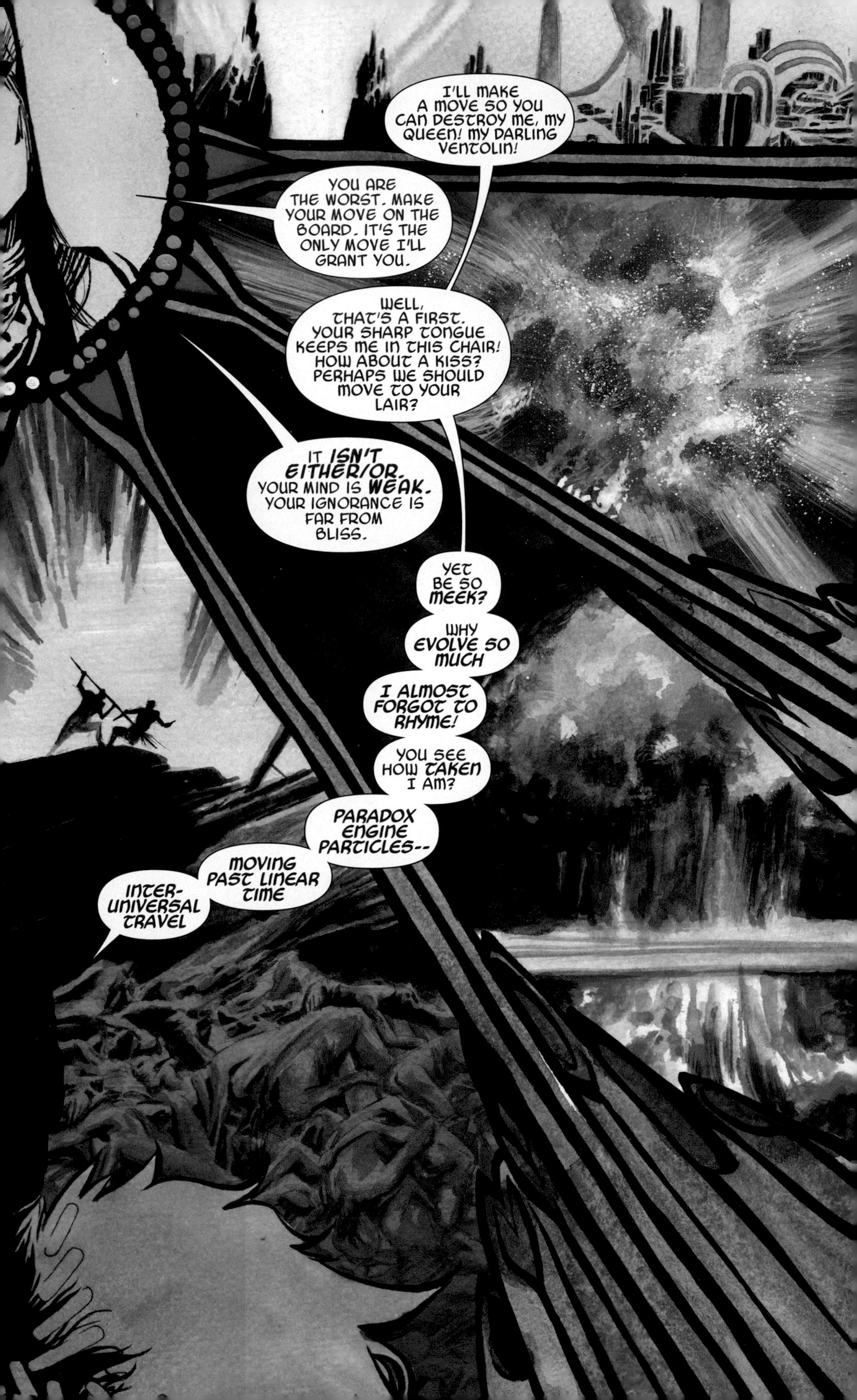
I'LL MAKE A MOVE SO YOU CAN DESTROY ME, MY QUEEN! MY DARLING VENTOLIN!
YOU ARE THE WORST. MAKE YOUR MOVE ON THE BOARD. IT'S THE ONLY MOVE I'LL GRANT YOU.
WELL, THAT'S A FIRST. YOUR SHARP TONGUE KEEPS ME IN THIS CHAIR! HOW ABOUT A KISS? PERHAPS WE SHOULD MOVE TO YOUR LAIR?
IT ISN'T EITHER/OR. YOUR MIND IS WEAK. YOUR IGNORANCE IS FAR FROM BLISS.
YET BE SO MEEK?
WHY EVOLVE SO MUCH
I ALMOST FORGOT TO RHYME!
YOU SEE HOW TAKEN I AM?
PARADOX ENGINE PARTICLES--
MOVING PAST LINEAR TIME
INTER-UNIVERSAL TRAVEL

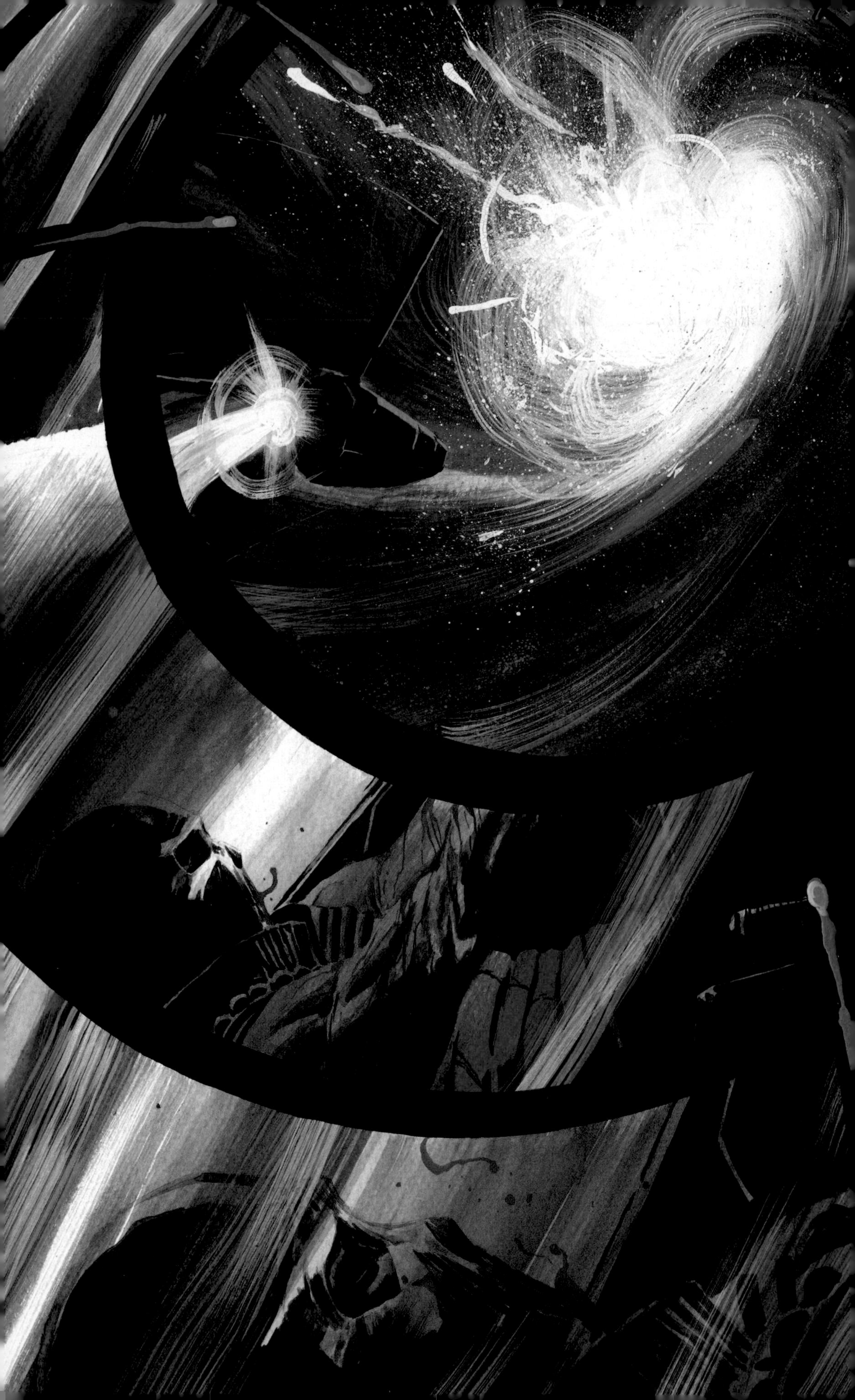

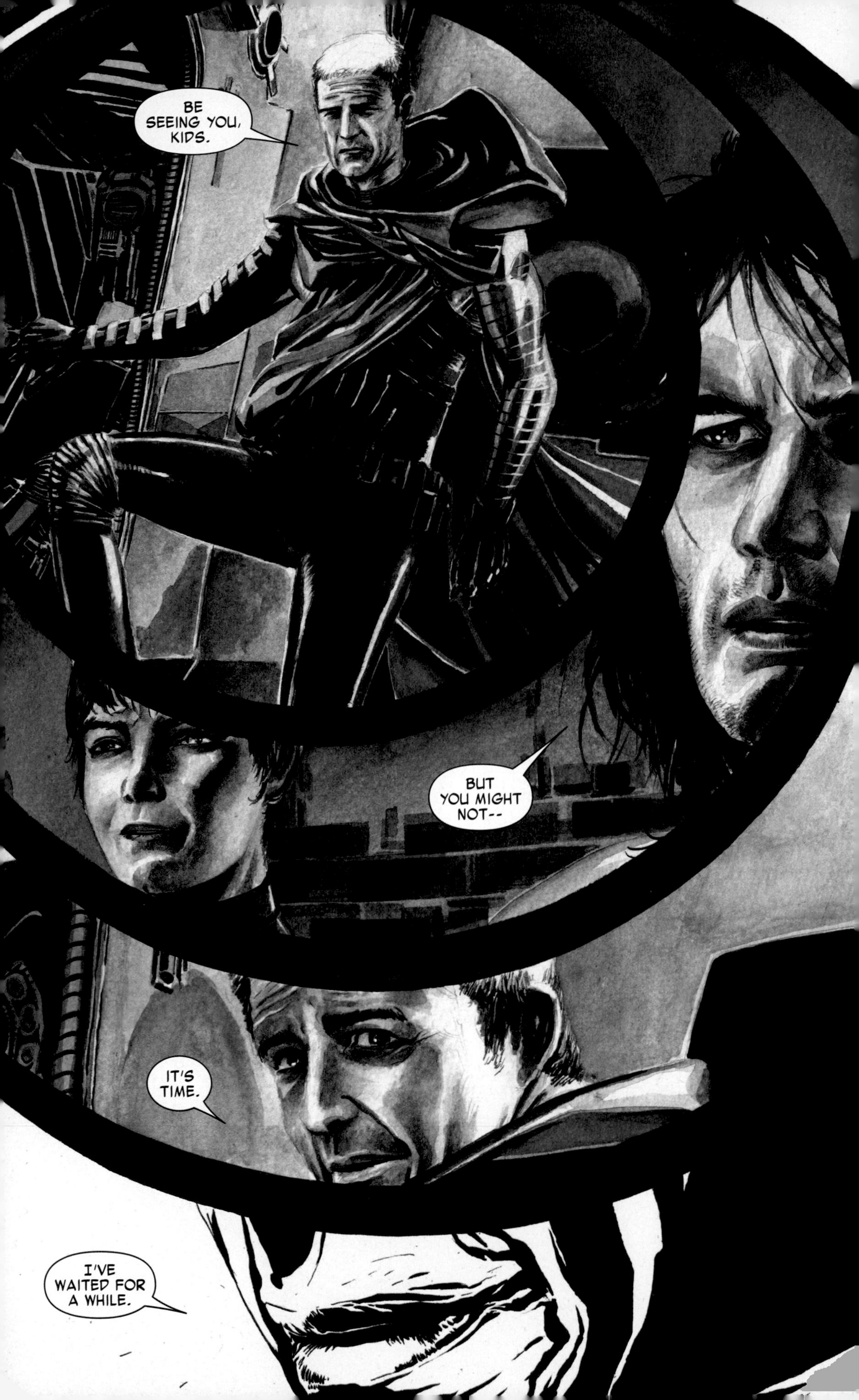
BE SEEING YOU, KIDS.
BUT YOU MIGHT NOT--
IT'S TIME.
I'VE WAITED FOR A WHILE.

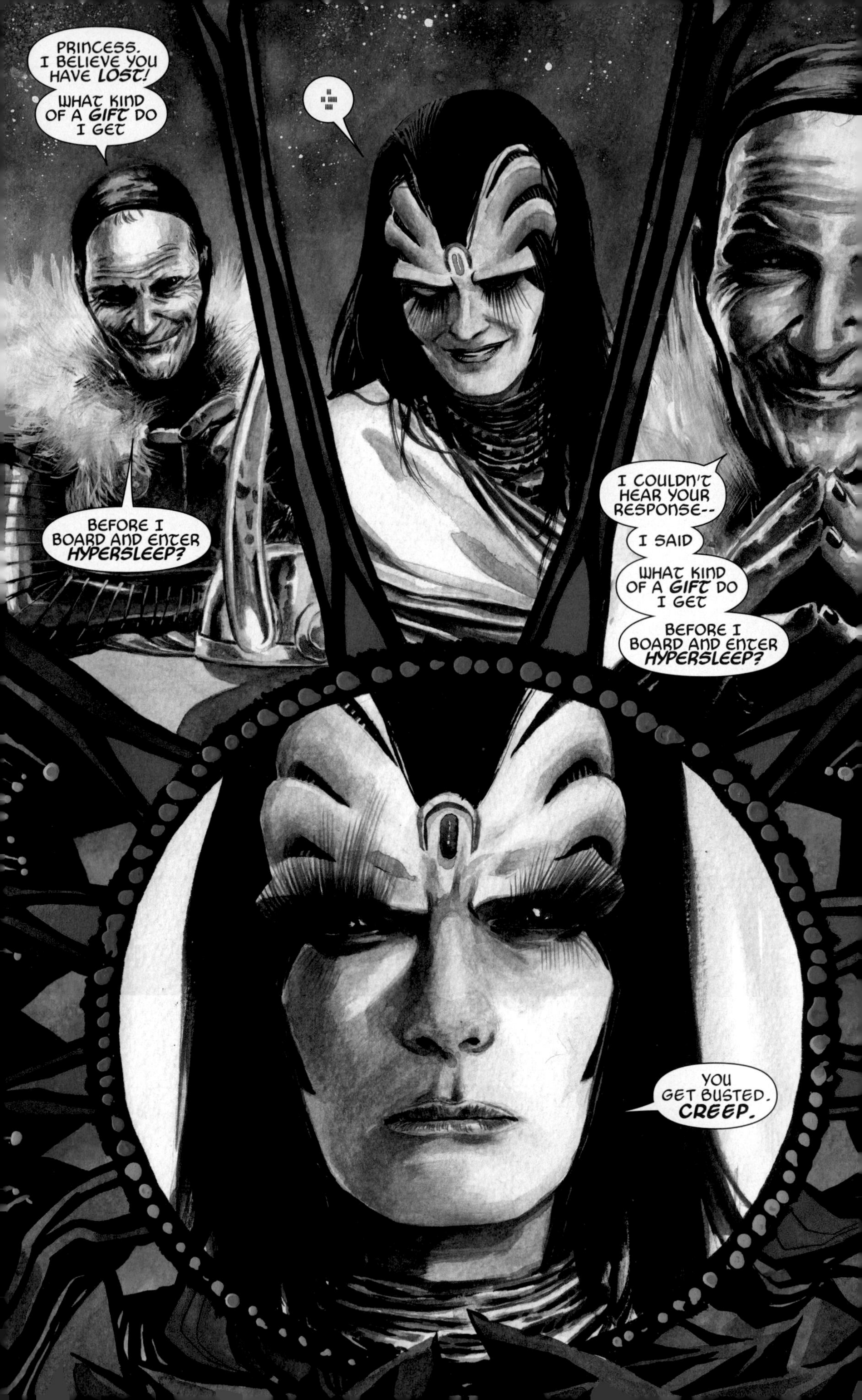

PRINCESS. I BELIEVE YOU HAVE LOST!
WHAT KIND OF A GIFT DO I GET
...
BEFORE I BOARD AND ENTER HYPERSLEEP?
I COULDN'T HEAR YOUR RESPONSE--
I SAID
WHAT KIND OF A GIFT DO I GET
BEFORE I BOARD AND ENTER HYPERSLEEP?
YOU GET BUSTED. CREEP.

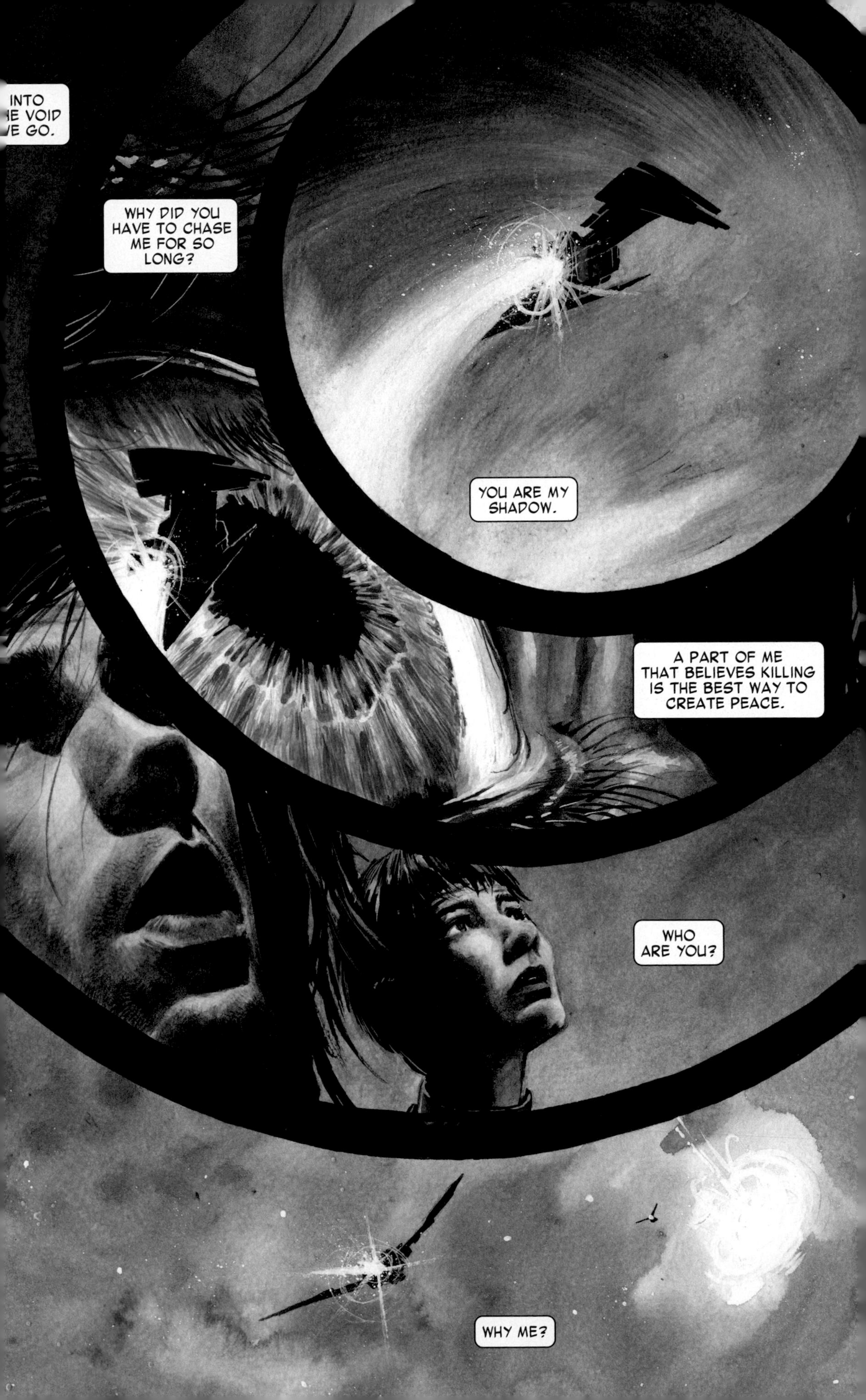
INTO
IE VOID
/E GO.
WHY DID YOU HAVE TO CHASE ME FOR SO LONG?
YOU ARE MY SHADOW.
A PART OF ME THAT BELIEVES KILLING IS THE BEST WAY TO CREATE PEACE.
WHO ARE YOU?
WHY ME?

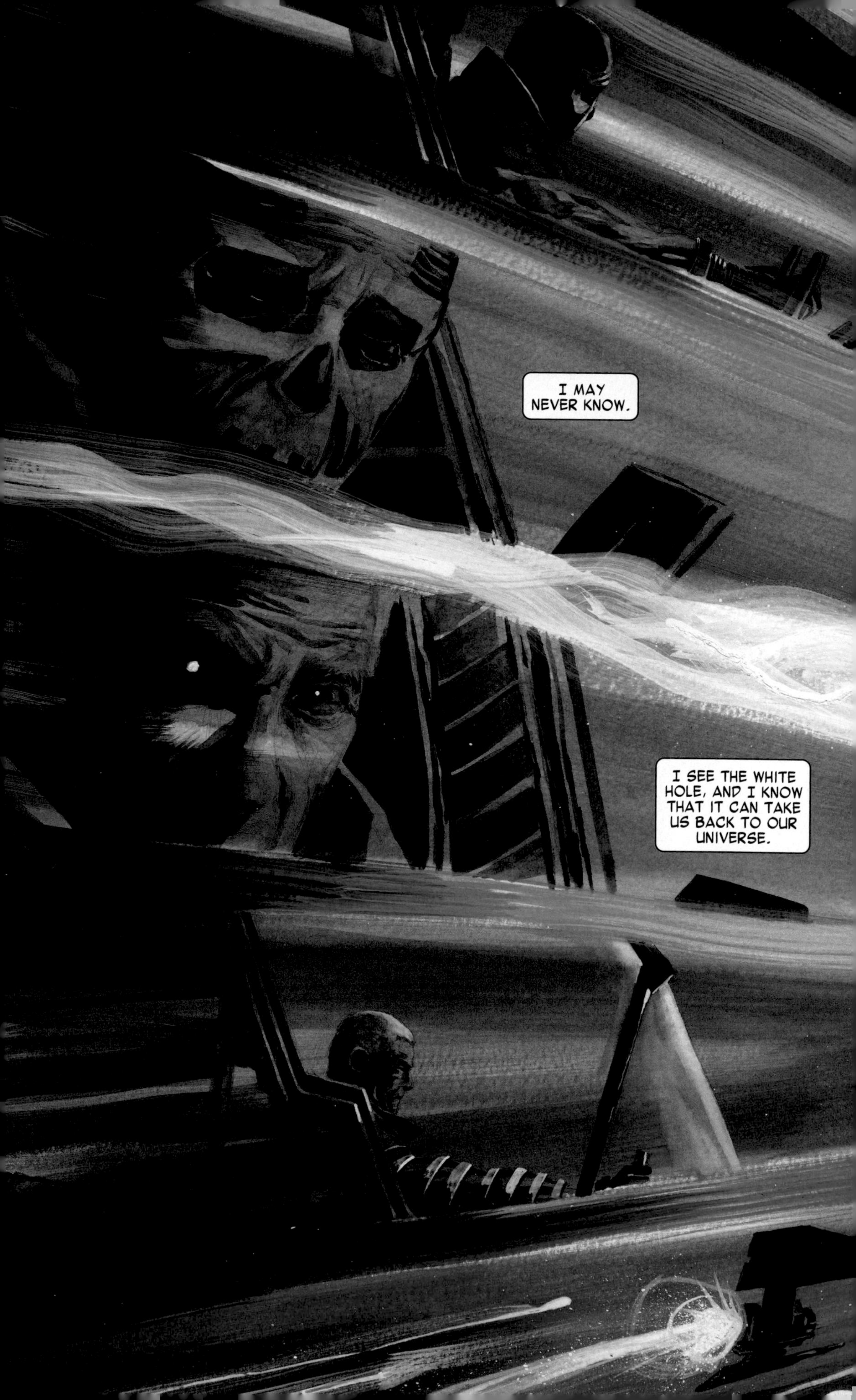
I MAY NEVER KNOW.
I SEE THE WHITE HOLE, AND I KNOW THAT IT CAN TAKE US BACK TO OUR UNIVERSE.

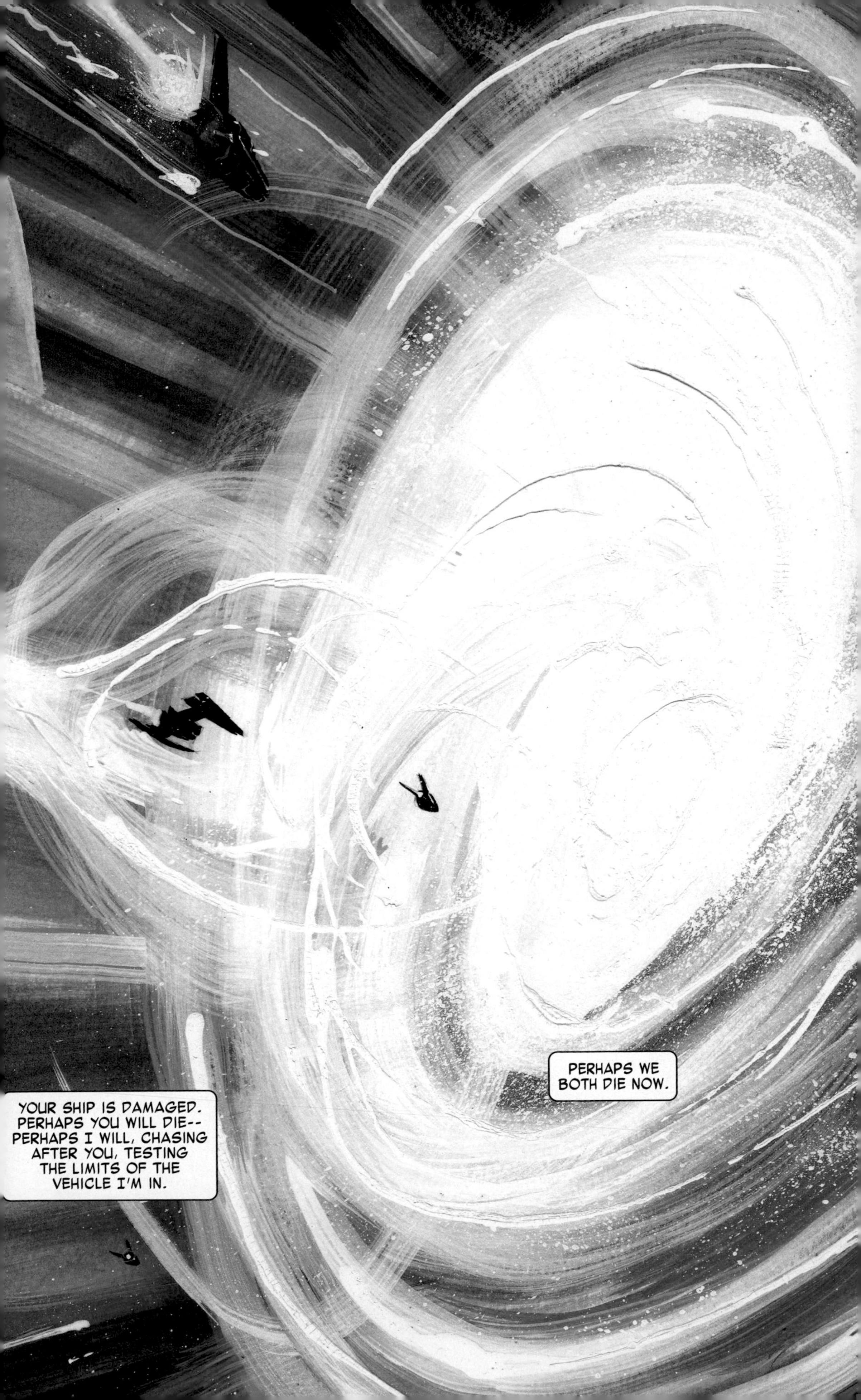
YOUR SHIP IS DAMAGED. PERHAPS YOU WILL DIE-- PERHAPS I WILL, CHASING AFTER YOU, TESTING THE LIMITS OF THE VEHICLE I'M IN.
PERHAPS WE BOTH DIE NOW.

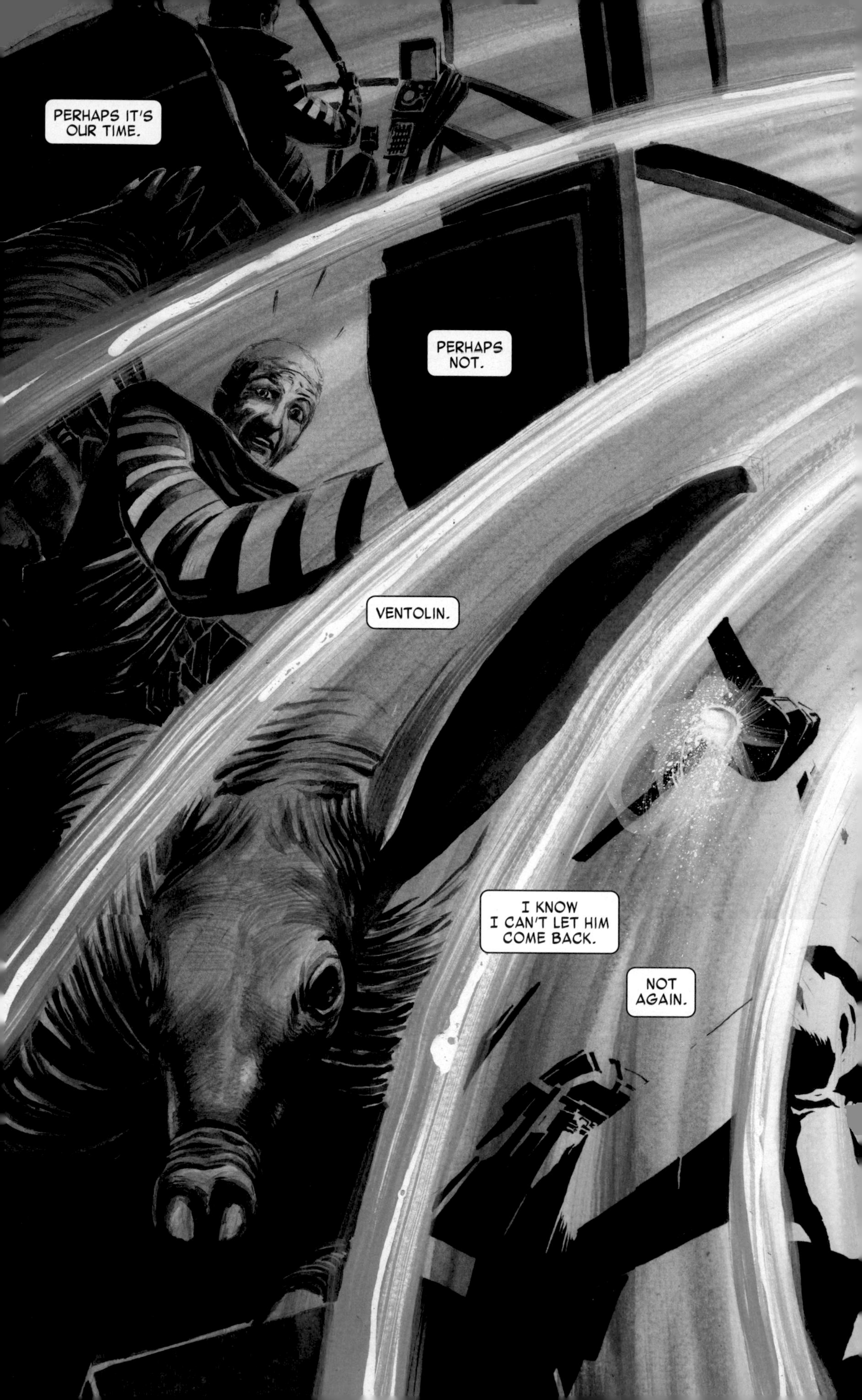
PERHAPS IT'S OUR TIME.
PERHAPS NOT.
VENTOLIN.
I KNOW I CAN'T LET HIM COME BACK.
NOT AGAIN.

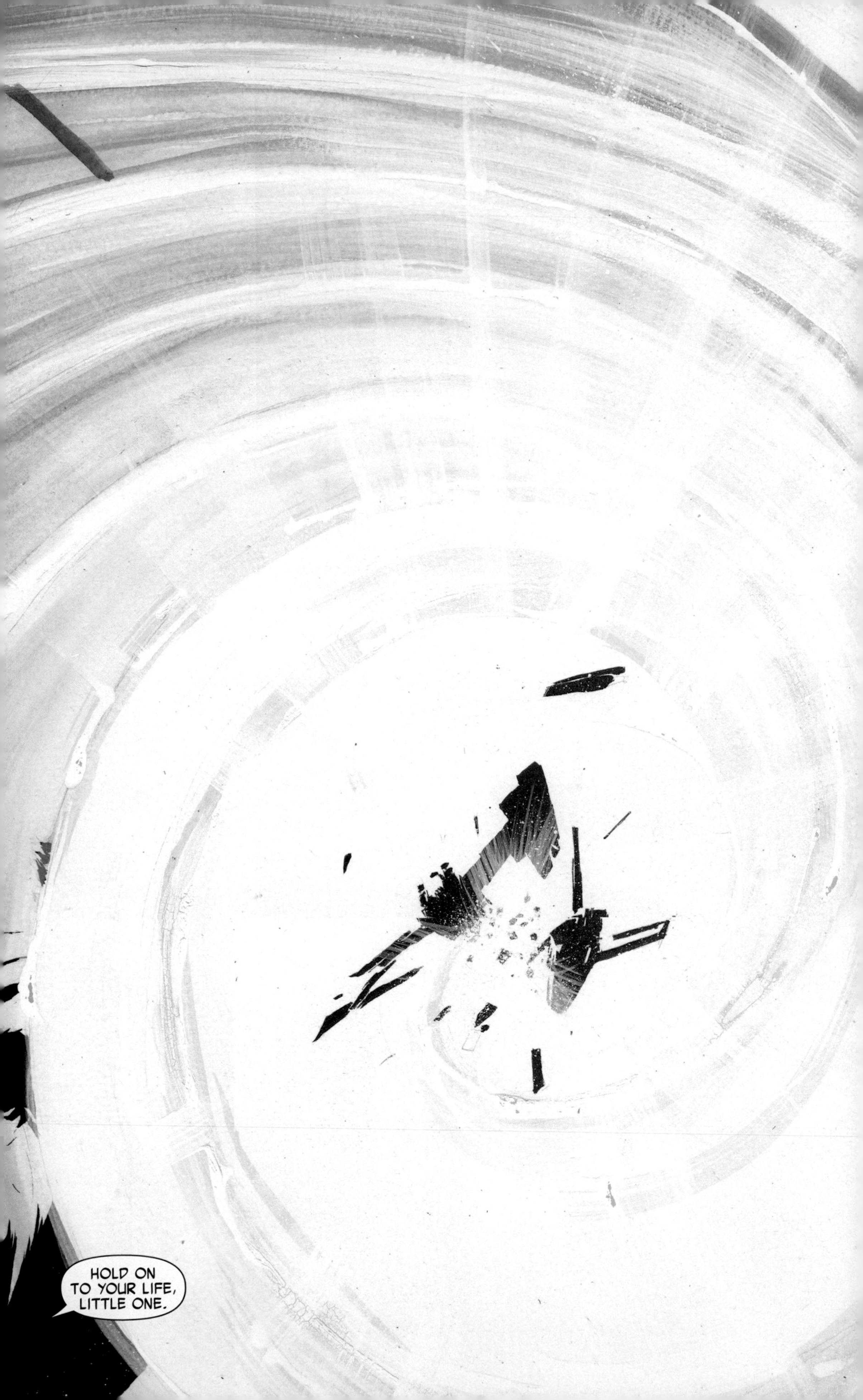
HOLD ON TO YOUR LIFE, LITTLE ONE.

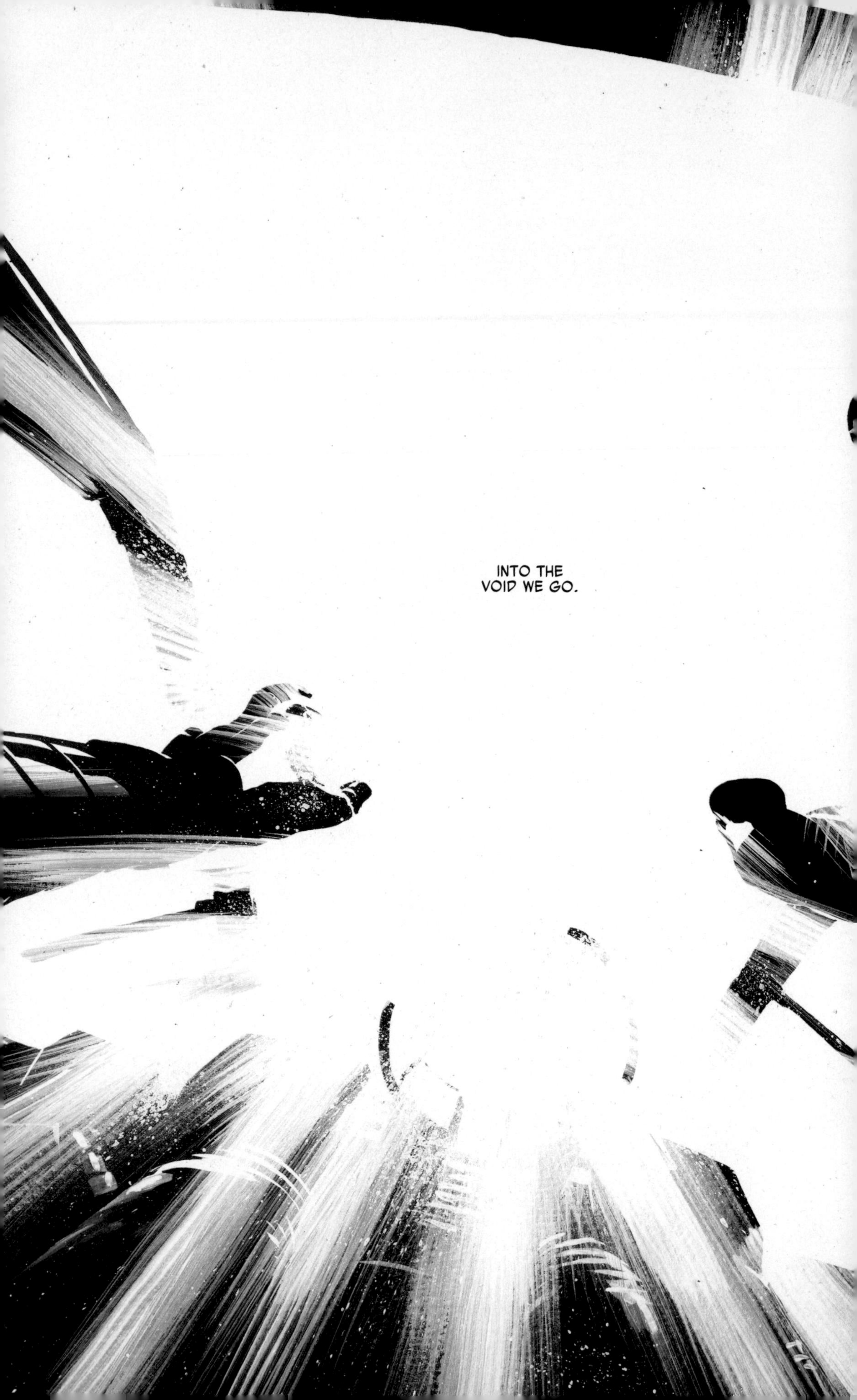
INTO THE VOID WE GO.

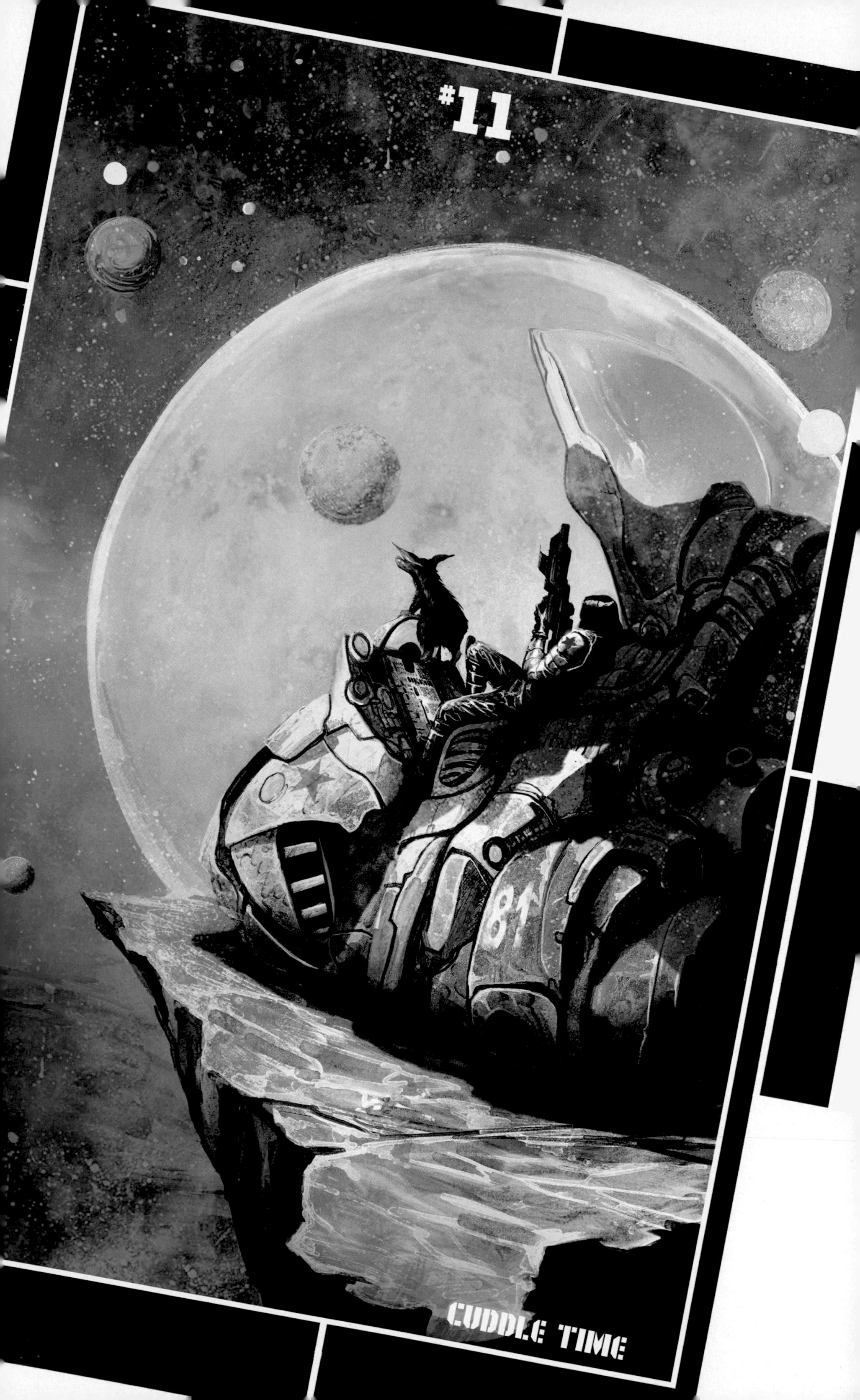
#11
CUDDLE TIME

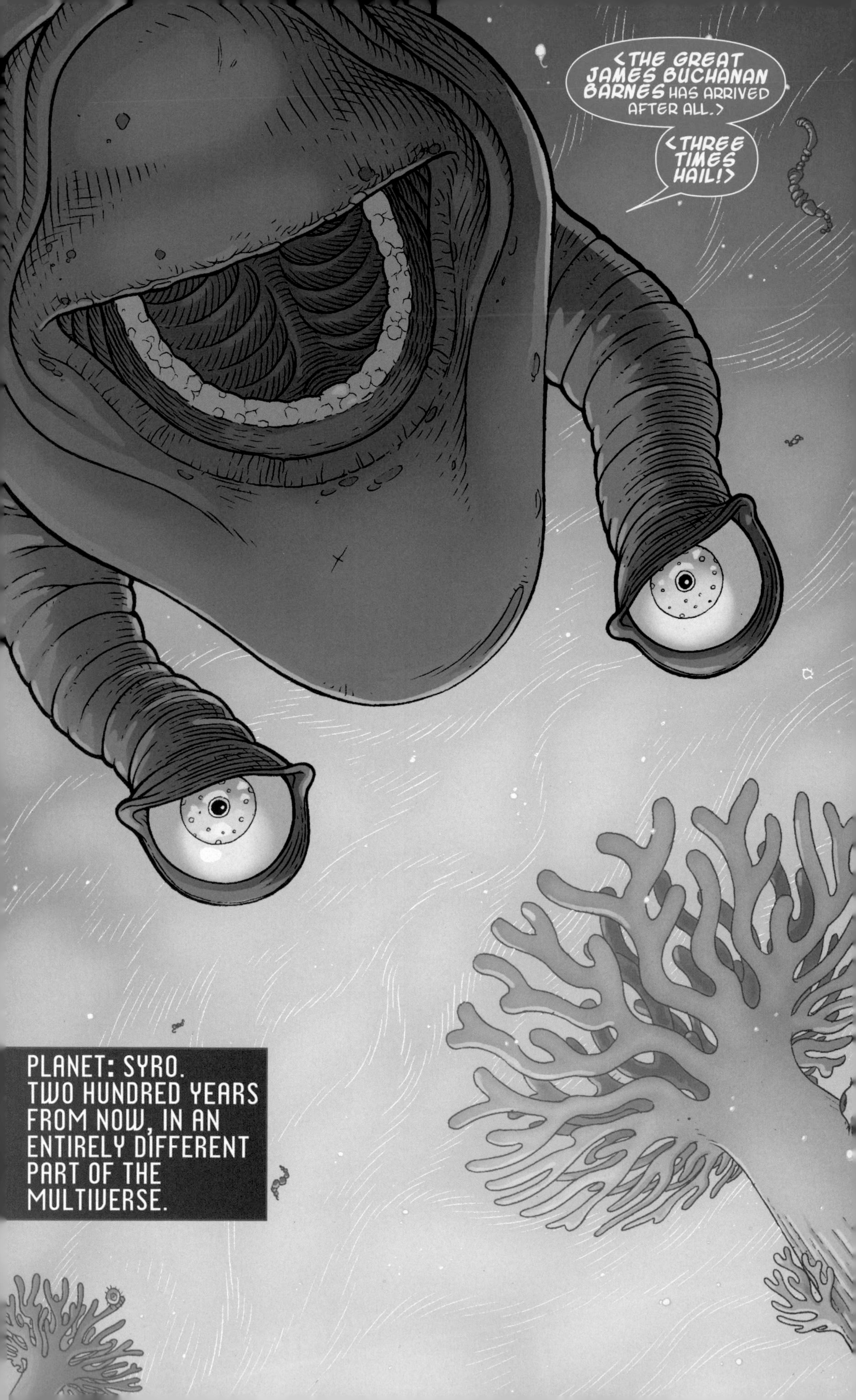
<THE GREAT JAMES BUCHANAN BARNES HAS ARRIVED AFTER ALL.>
<THREE TIMES HAIL!>
PLANET: SYRO. TWO HUNDRED YEARS FROM NOW, IN AN ENTIRELY DIFFERENT PART OF THE MULTIVERSE.

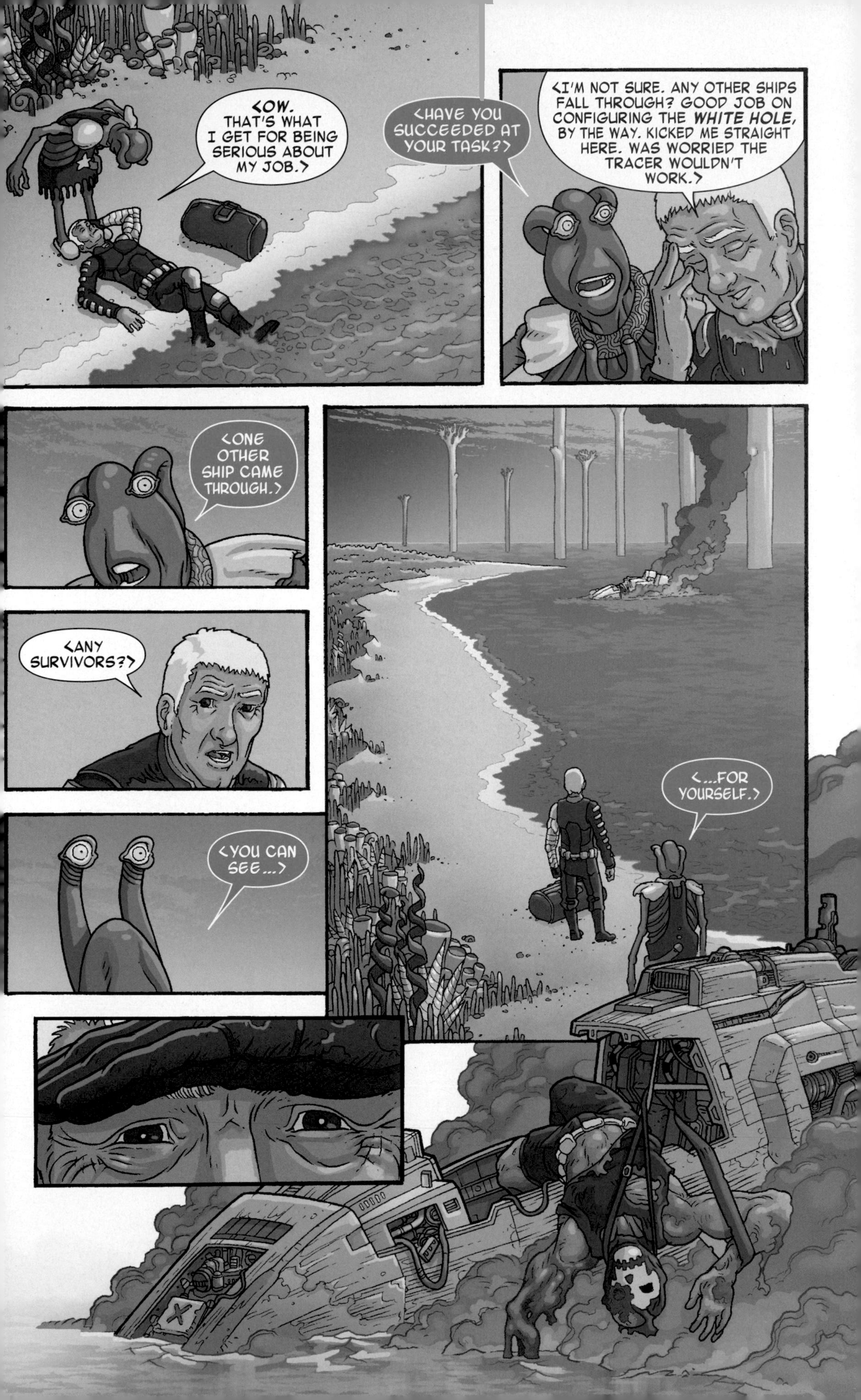
<OW. THAT'S WHAT I GET FOR BEING SERIOUS ABOUT MY JOB.>
<HAVE YOU SUCCEEDED AT YOUR TASK?>
<I'M NOT SURE. ANY OTHER SHIPS FALL THROUGH? GOOD JOB ON CONFIGURING THE *WHITE HOLE*, BY THE WAY. KICKED ME STRAIGHT HERE. WAS WORRIED THE TRACER WOULDN'T WORK.>
<ONE OTHER SHIP CAME THROUGH.>
<ANY SURVIVORS?>
<YOU CAN SEE...>
<...FOR YOURSELF.>

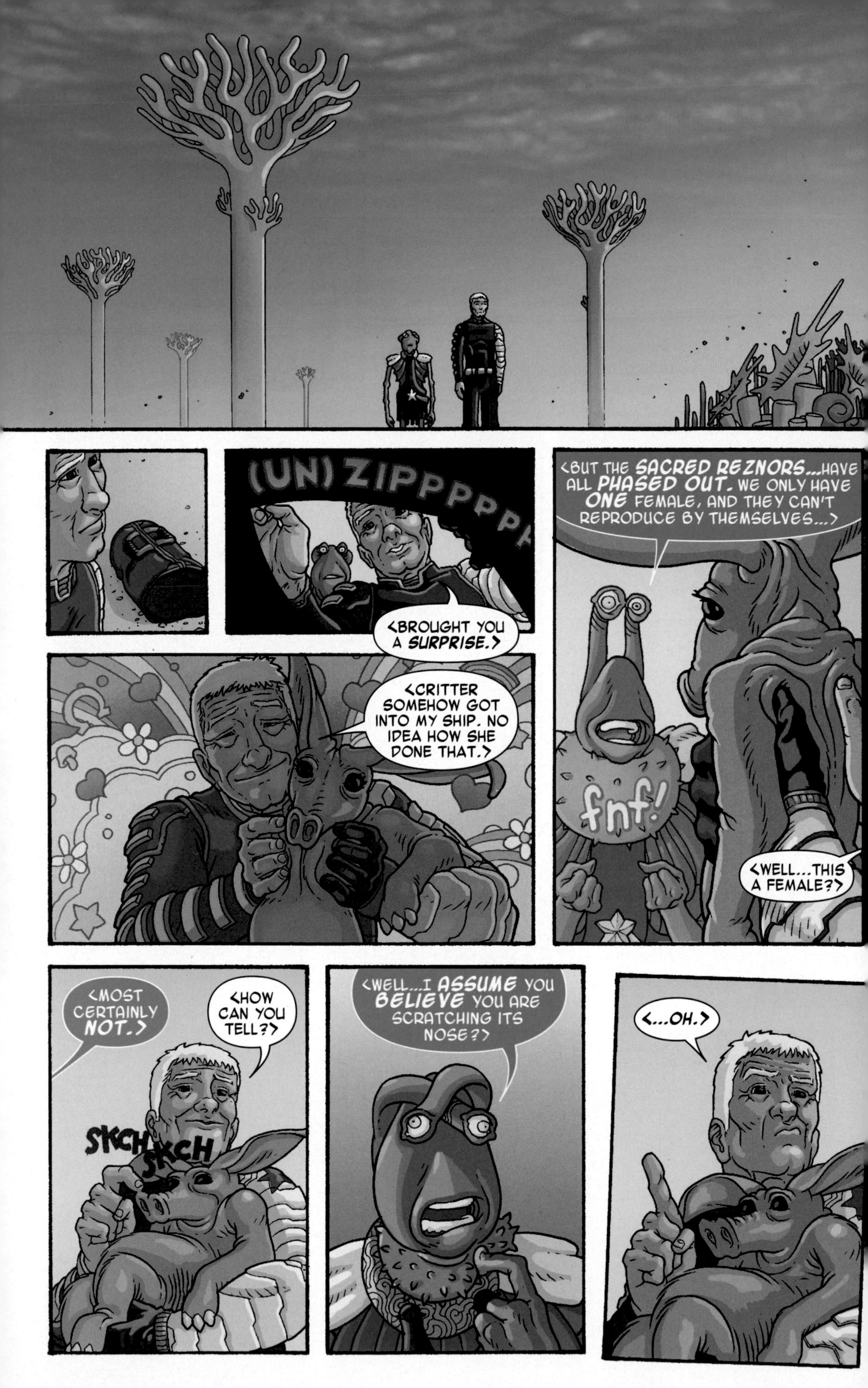
(UN) ZIPPPPPP
<BROUGHT YOU A SURPRISE.>
<BUT THE SACRED REZNORS...HAVE ALL PHASED OUT. WE ONLY HAVE ONE FEMALE, AND THEY CAN'T REPRODUCE BY THEMSELVES...>
<CRITTER SOMEHOW GOT INTO MY SHIP. NO IDEA HOW SHE DONE THAT.>
fnf!
<WELL...THIS A FEMALE?>
<MOST CERTAINLY NOT.>
<HOW CAN YOU TELL?>
SKCH SKCH
<WELL...I ASSUME YOU BELIEVE YOU ARE SCRATCHING ITS NOSE?>
<...OH.>

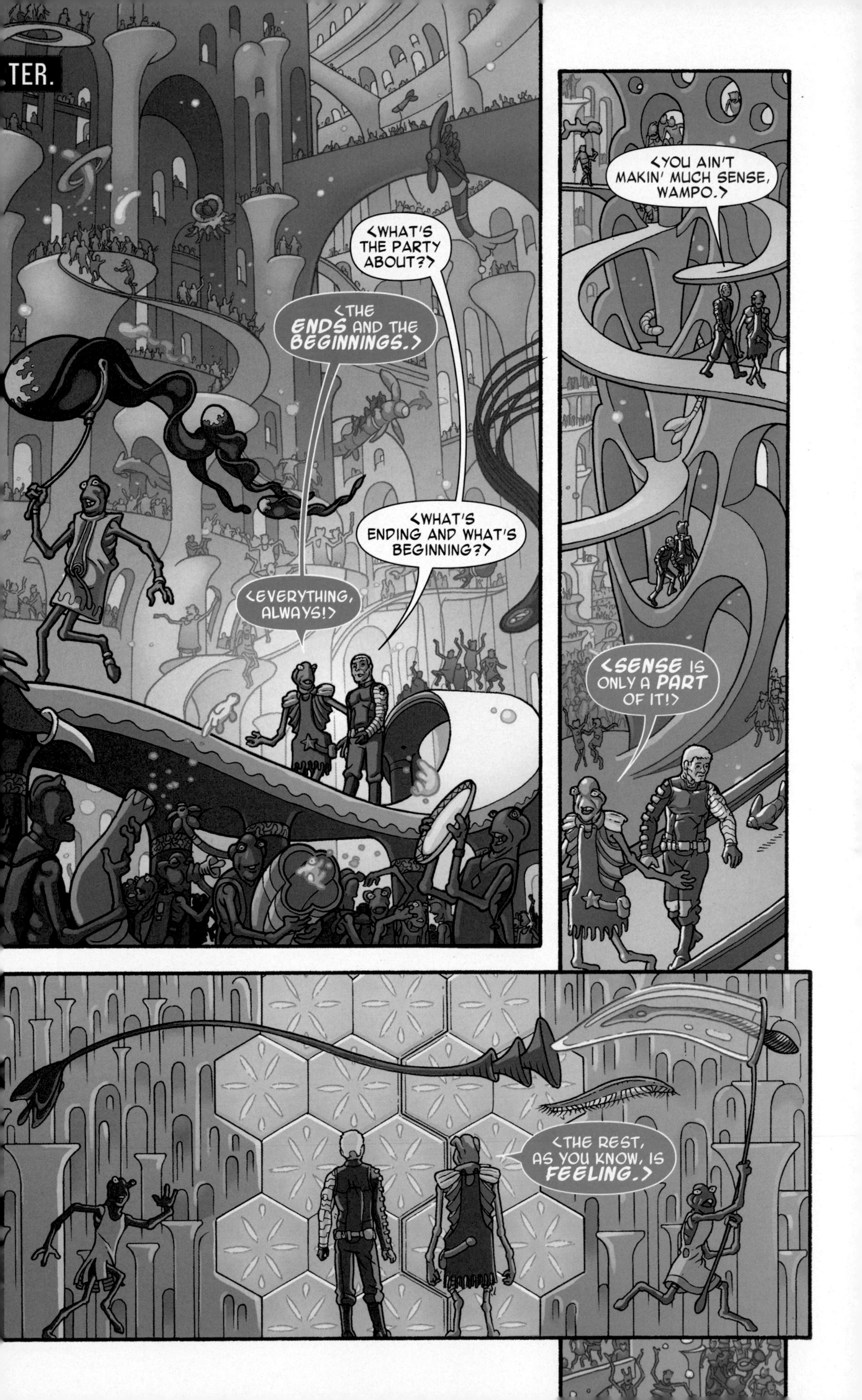
TER.
<WHAT'S THE PARTY ABOUT?>
<THE ENDS AND THE BEGINNINGS.>
<WHAT'S ENDING AND WHAT'S BEGINNING?>
<EVERYTHING, ALWAYS!>
<YOU AIN'T MAKIN' MUCH SENSE, WAMPO.>
<SENSE IS ONLY A PART OF IT!>
<THE REST, AS YOU KNOW, IS FEELING.>

<AFTER ALL, ISN'T THAT WHY YOU CHOSE NOT TO ASSASSINATE OUR THEN-RULER, ENOCHIAN CUP-QUARK, WHEN YOU FIRST CAME HERE ALL THOSE YEARS AGO?>
<BECAUSE YOU FELT IT WASN'T RIGHT?>
<I REMEMBER YOU SAYING "I DON'T THINK I SHOULD BE AN INSTRUMENT OF WAR.">
<ARE YOU NERVOUS?>
<OF COURSE I'M NERVOUS. WE HAVEN'T SEEN EACH OTHER IN NEARLY A DECADE. THIS PLACE FEELS SO *DIFFERENT.*>
<WE HAD SOME GREAT HELP WITH REBUILDING. AND ABOUT THE OTHER THING...>
<REAL LOVE FINDS ITS WAY. EVERYTHING WE LOVE, WE MUST RESPECT ITS COMPLETE FREEDOM, ALWAYS.>
<...IT'S NICE HAVING YOU BACK, BY THE WAY.>

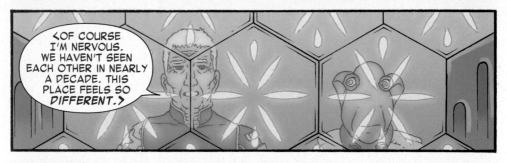

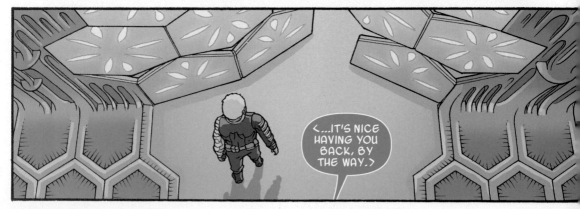

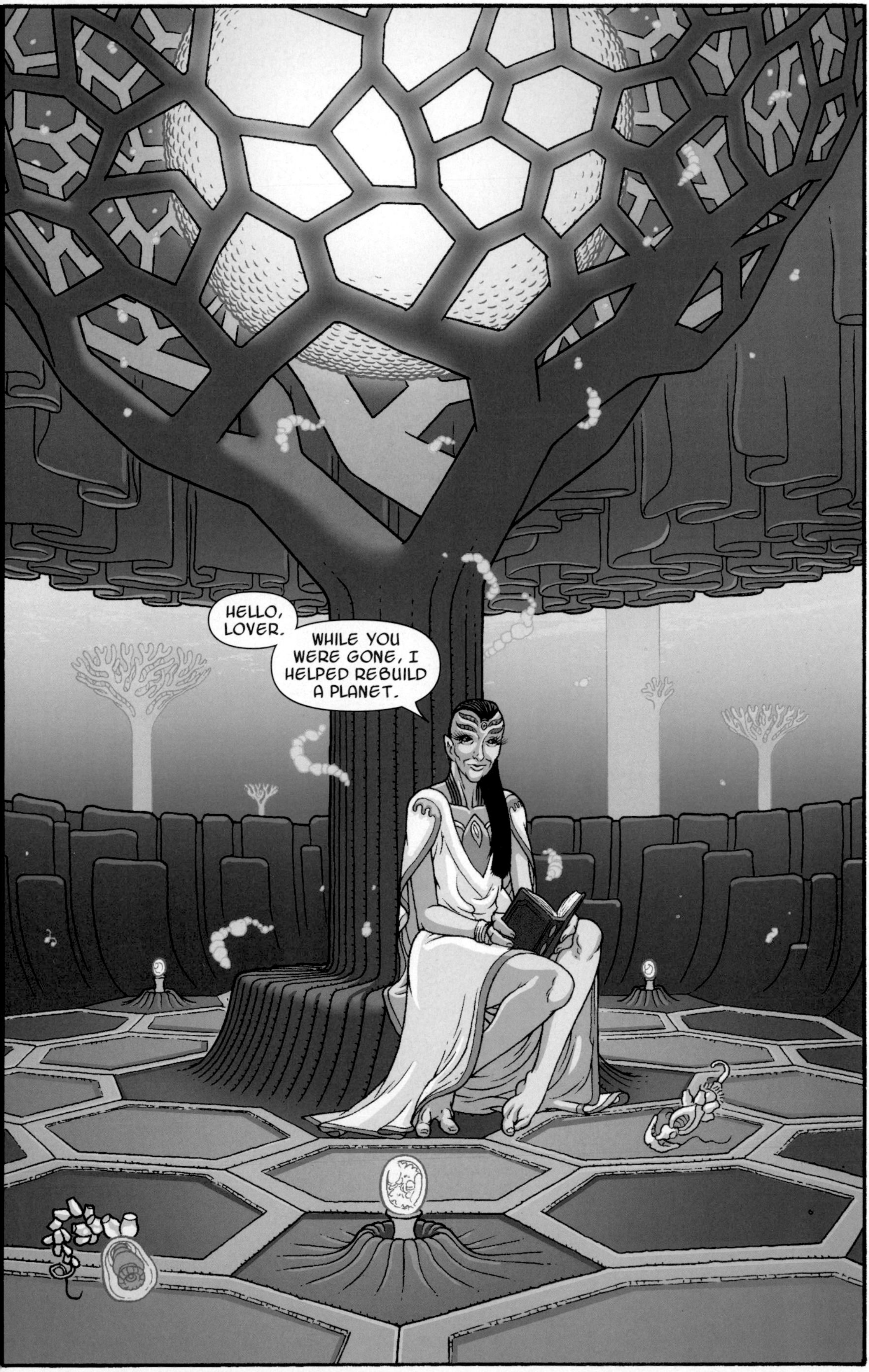
HELLO, LOVER.
WHILE YOU WERE GONE, I HELPED REBUILD A PLANET.

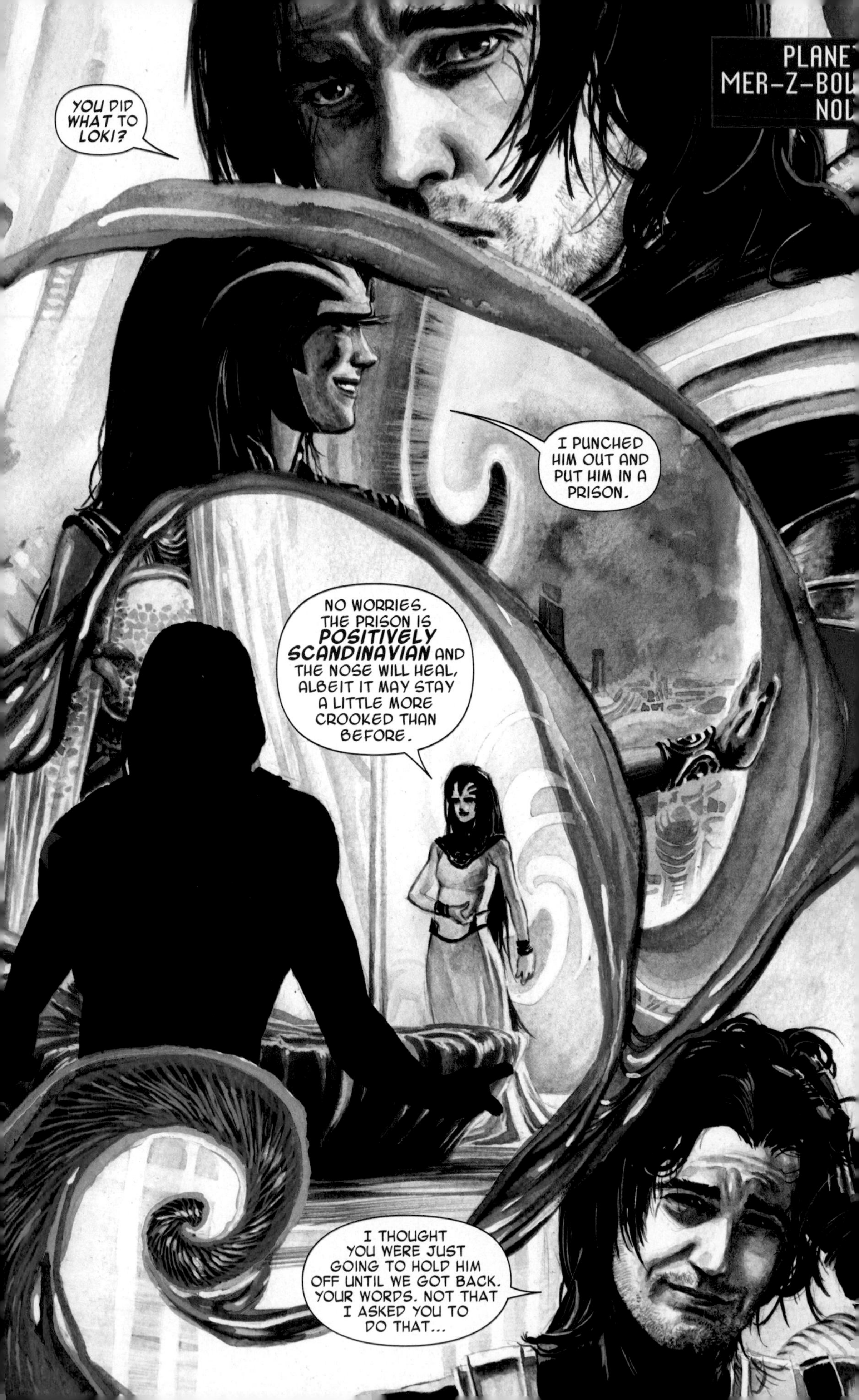
PLANET
MER-Z-BOL
NOL
YOU DID WHAT TO LOKI?
I PUNCHED HIM OUT AND PUT HIM IN A PRISON.
NO WORRIES. THE PRISON IS POSITIVELY SCANDINAVIAN AND THE NOSE WILL HEAL, ALBEIT IT MAY STAY A LITTLE MORE CROOKED THAN BEFORE.
I THOUGHT YOU WERE JUST GOING TO HOLD HIM OFF UNTIL WE GOT BACK. YOUR WORDS. NOT THAT I ASKED YOU TO DO THAT...

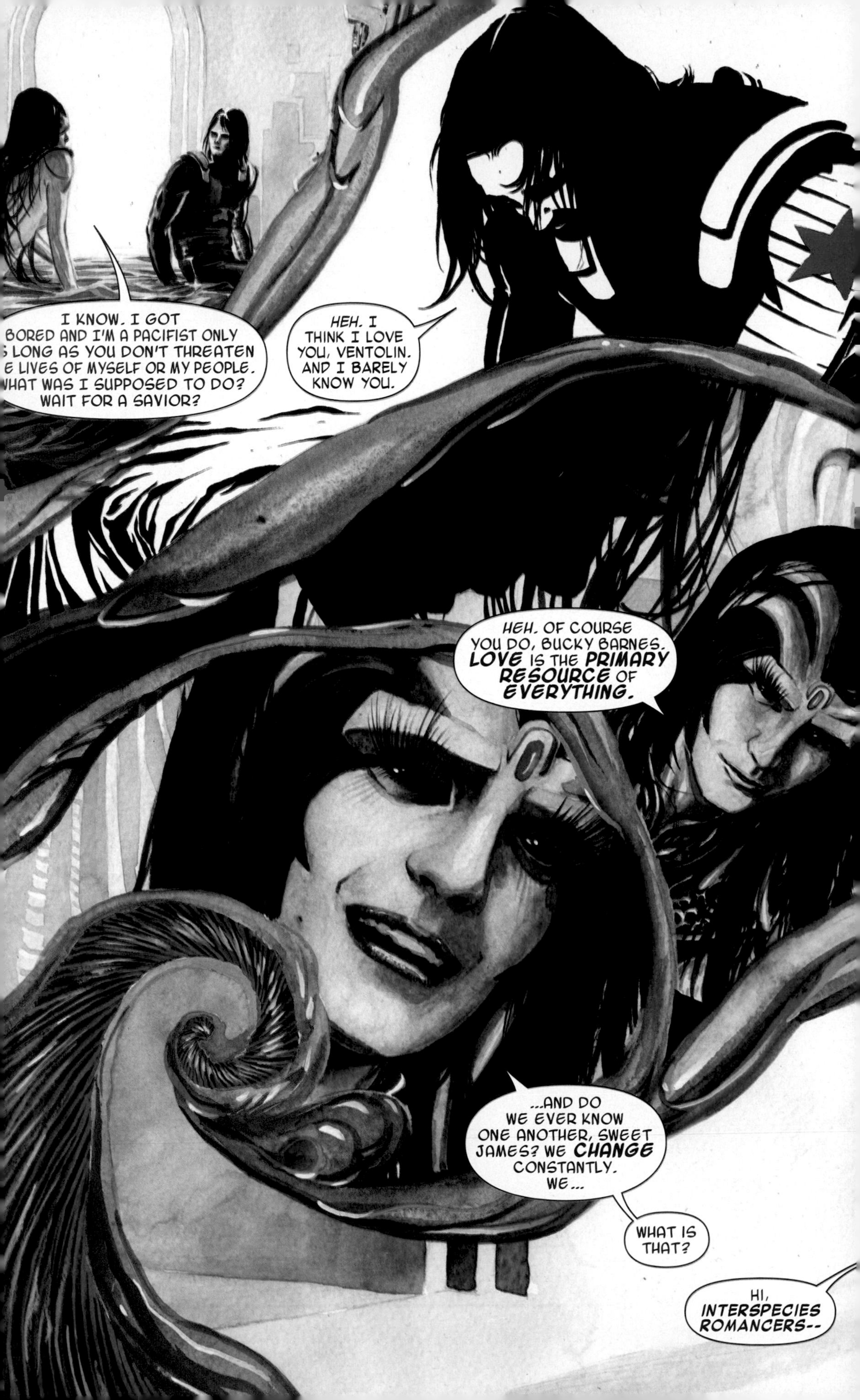
I KNOW. I GOT BORED AND I'M A PACIFIST ONLY S LONG AS YOU DON'T THREATEN E LIVES OF MYSELF OR MY PEOPLE. WHAT WAS I SUPPOSED TO DO? WAIT FOR A SAVIOR?
HEH. I THINK I LOVE YOU, VENTOLIN. AND I BARELY KNOW YOU.
HEH. OF COURSE YOU DO, BUCKY BARNES. LOVE IS THE PRIMARY RESOURCE OF EVERYTHING.
...AND DO WE EVER KNOW ONE ANOTHER, SWEET JAMES? WE CHANGE CONSTANTLY. WE...
WHAT IS THAT?
HI, INTERSPECIES ROMANCERS--

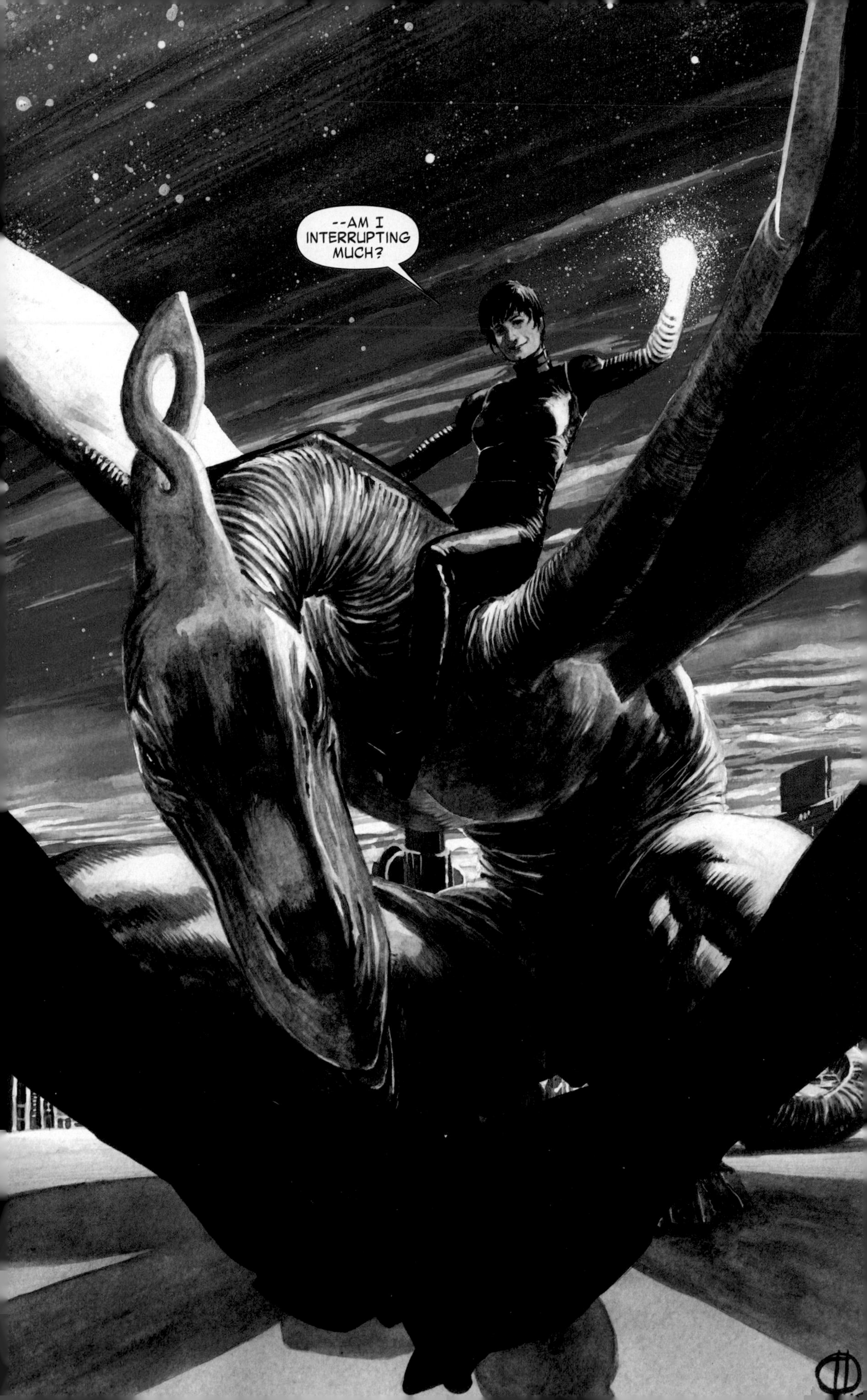
--AM I INTERRUPTING MUCH?

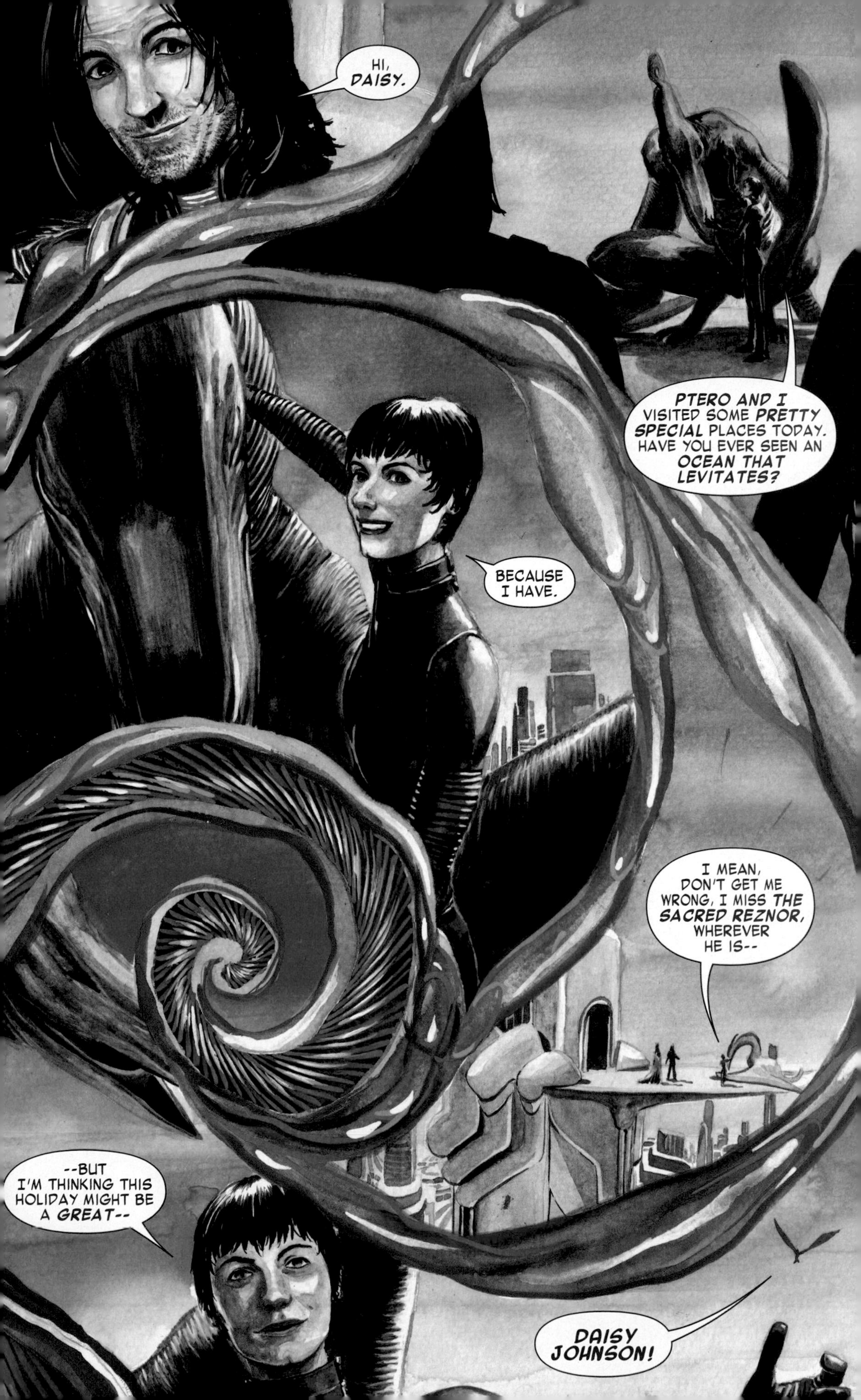
HI, DAISY.
PTERO AND I VISITED SOME PRETTY SPECIAL PLACES TODAY. HAVE YOU EVER SEEN AN OCEAN THAT LEVITATES?
BECAUSE I HAVE.
I MEAN, DON'T GET ME WRONG, I MISS THE SACRED REZNOR, WHEREVER HE IS--
--BUT I'M THINKING THIS HOLIDAY MIGHT BE A GREAT--
DAISY JOHNSON!

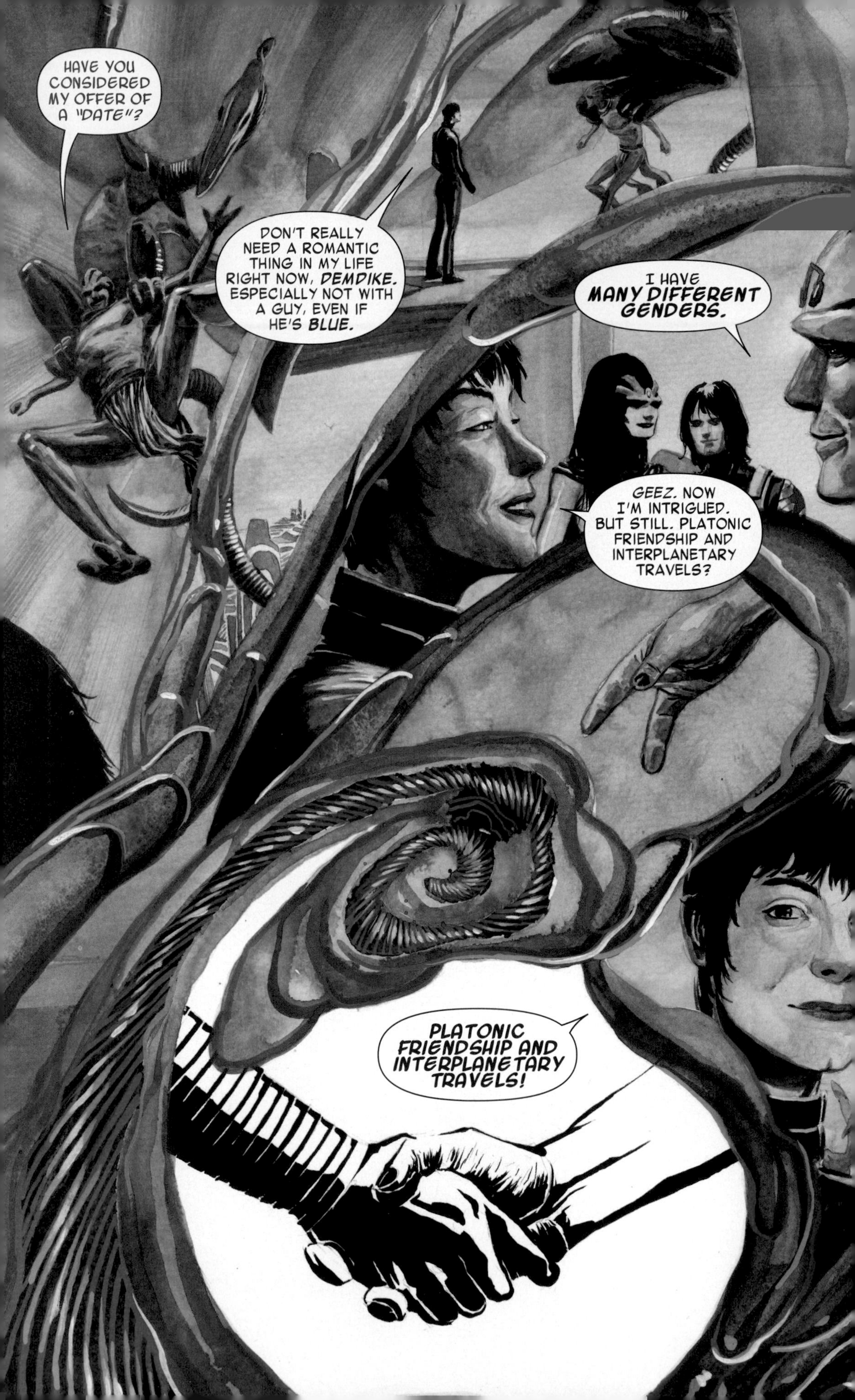
HAVE YOU CONSIDERED MY OFFER OF A "DATE"?
DON'T REALLY NEED A ROMANTIC THING IN MY LIFE RIGHT NOW, DEMDIKE. ESPECIALLY NOT WITH A GUY, EVEN IF HE'S BLUE.
I HAVE MANY DIFFERENT GENDERS.
GEEZ. NOW I'M INTRIGUED. BUT STILL. PLATONIC FRIENDSHIP AND INTERPLANETARY TRAVELS?
PLATONIC FRIENDSHIP AND INTERPLANETARY TRAVELS!

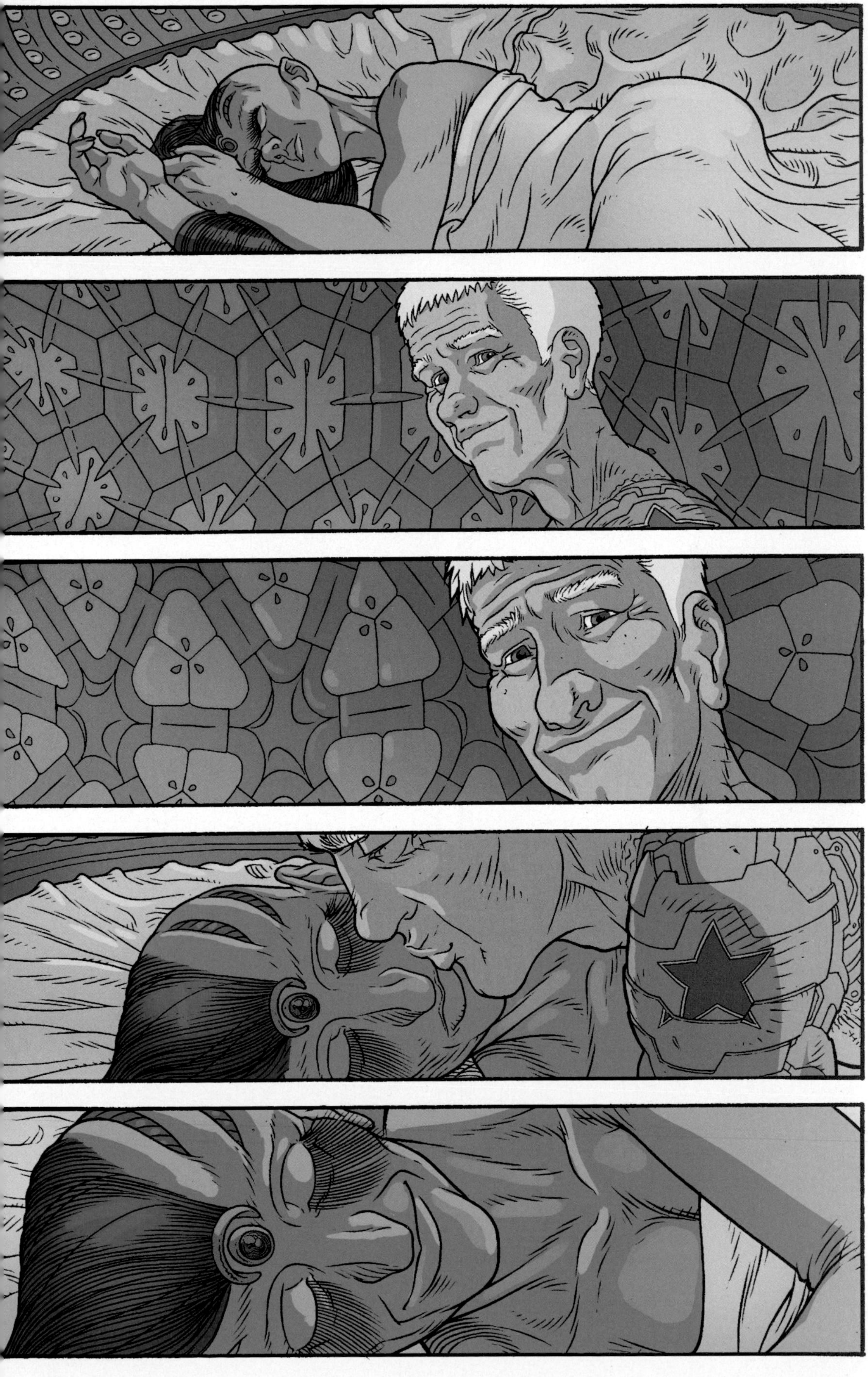

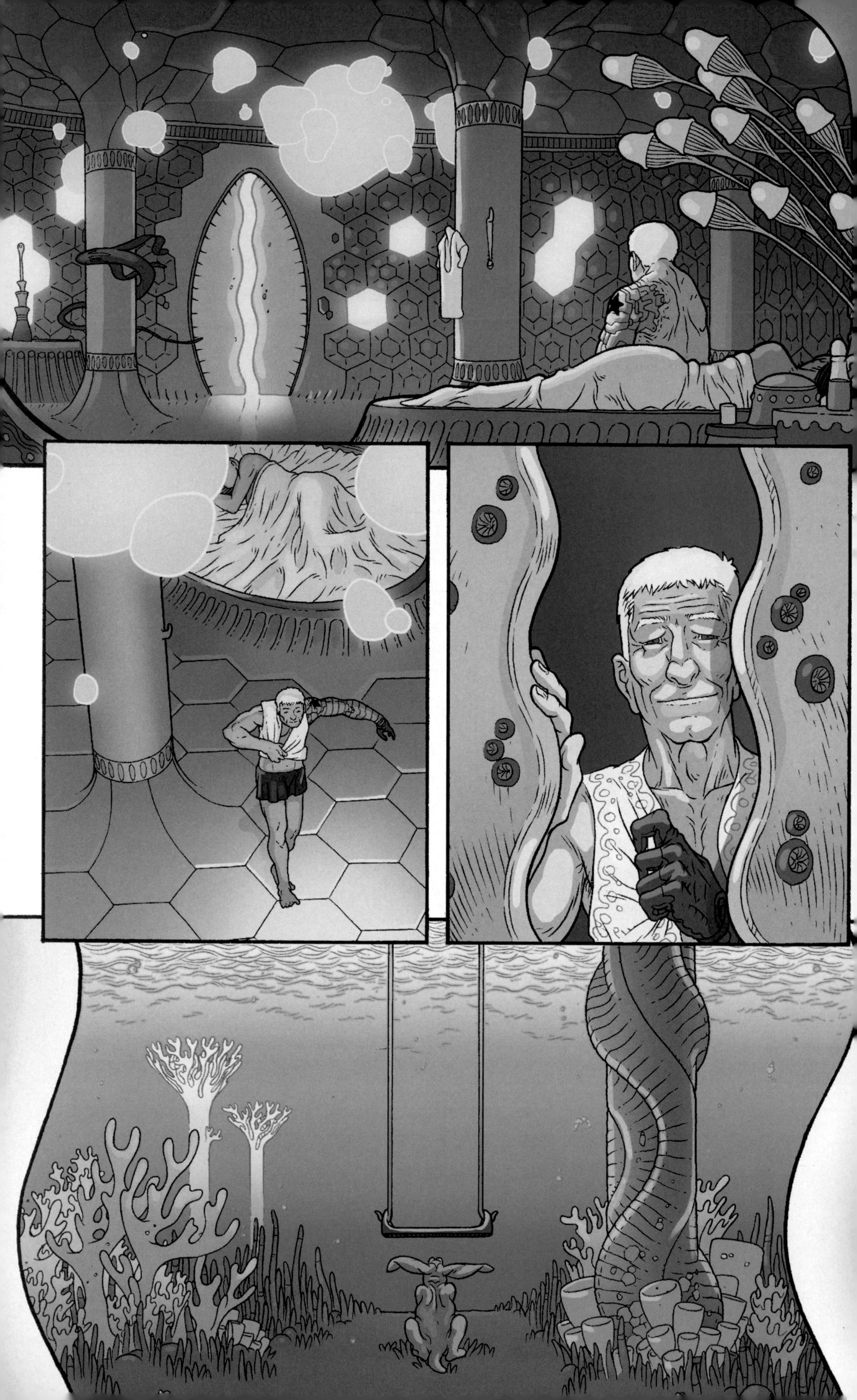

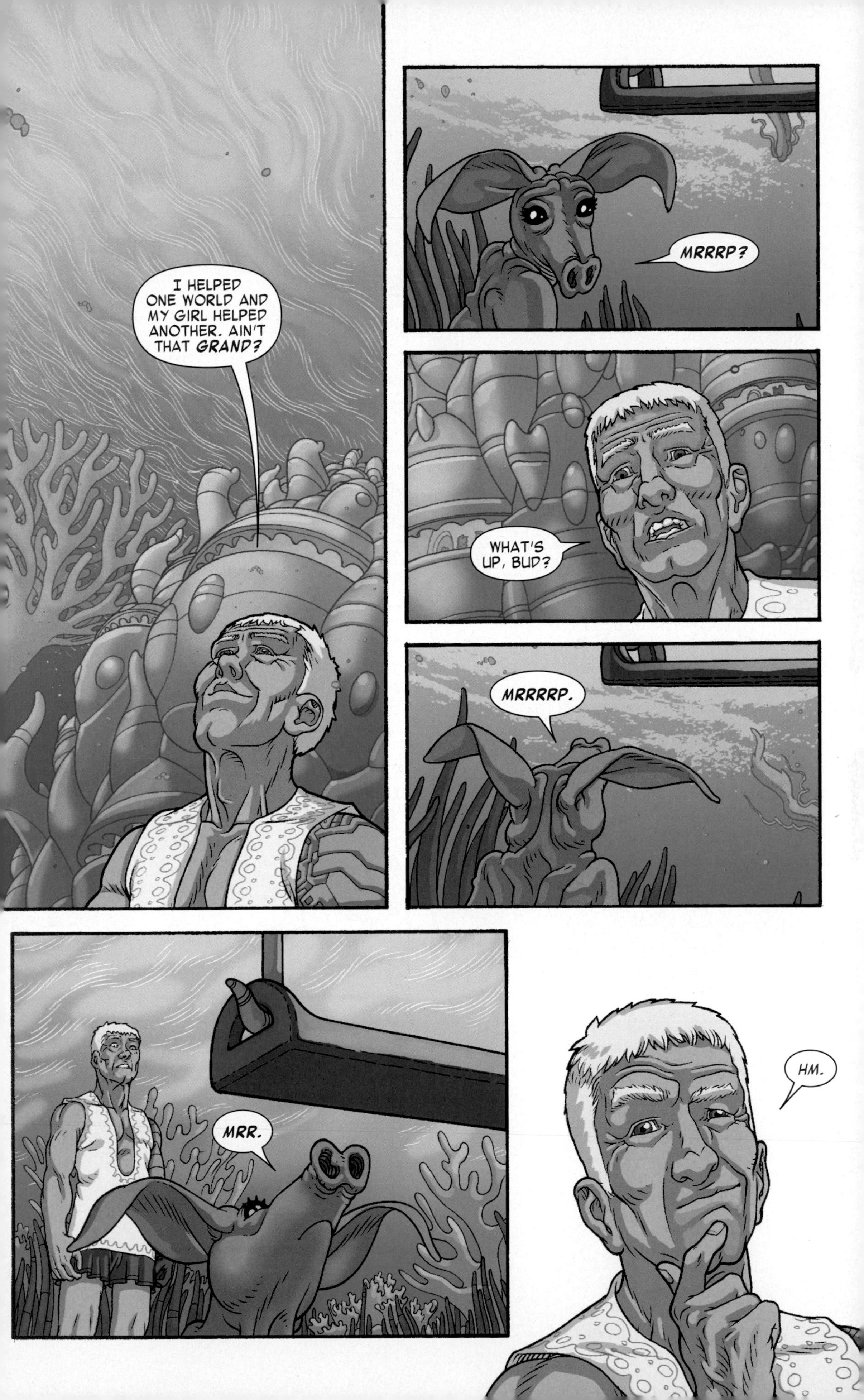
I HELPED ONE WORLD AND MY GIRL HELPED ANOTHER. AIN'T THAT GRAND?
MRRRP?
WHAT'S UP, BUD?
MRRRRP.
MRR.
HM.

YOU WANNA GET ON THAT?

ALL RIGHT, LITTLE ADVENTURER.

WE ALL GET WHAT WE WANT TODAY.

WE ALL GET WHAT WE WANT TODAY.

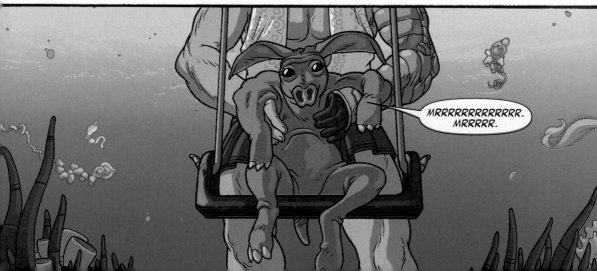

MRRRRRRRRRRRRR. MRRRRR.

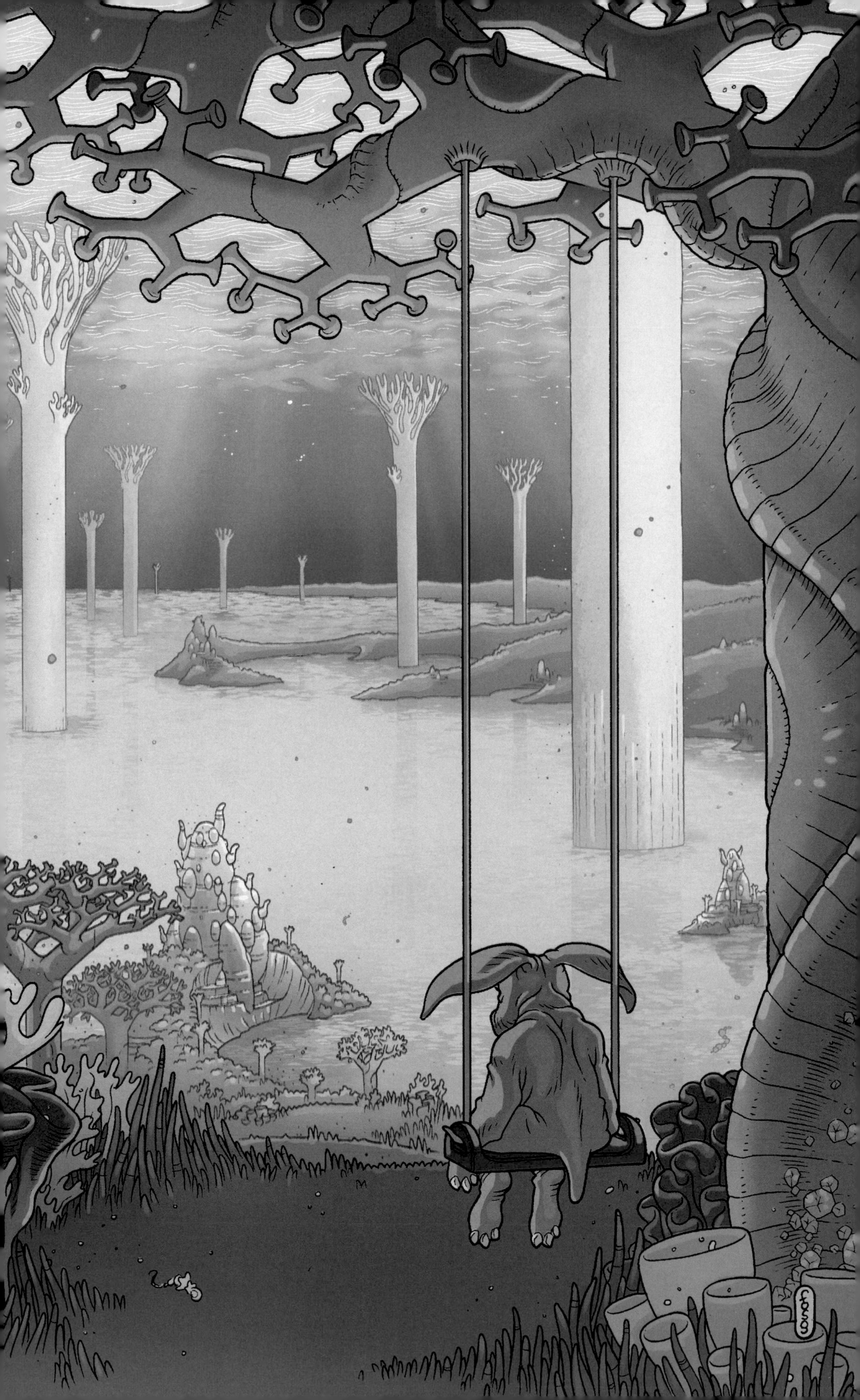

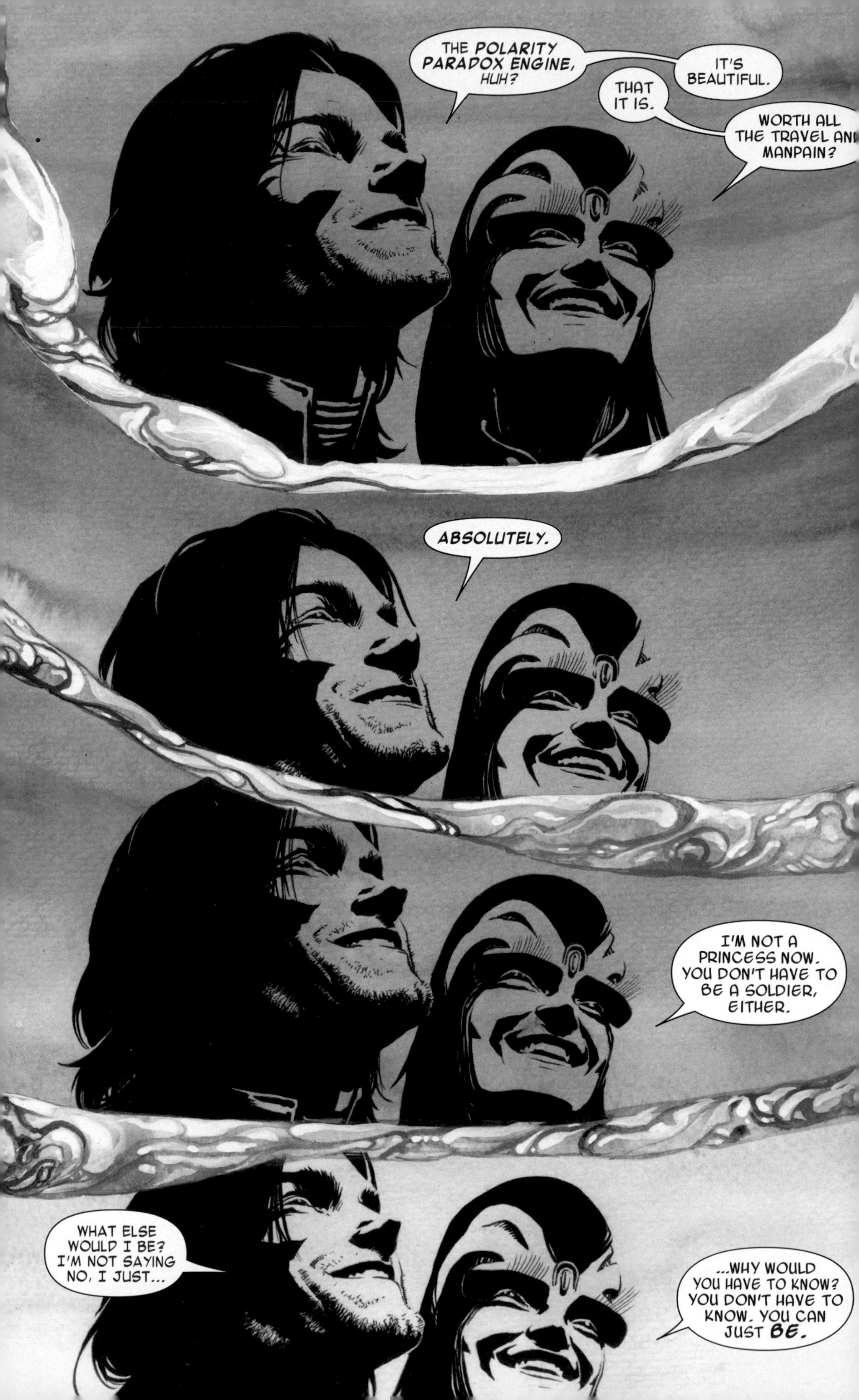
THE POLARITY PARADOX ENGINE, HUH?
IT'S BEAUTIFUL.
THAT IT IS.
WORTH ALL THE TRAVEL AND MANPAIN?
ABSOLUTELY.
I'M NOT A PRINCESS NOW. YOU DON'T HAVE TO BE A SOLDIER, EITHER.
WHAT ELSE WOULD I BE? I'M NOT SAYING NO, I JUST...
...WHY WOULD YOU HAVE TO KNOW? YOU DON'T HAVE TO KNOW. YOU CAN JUST BE.

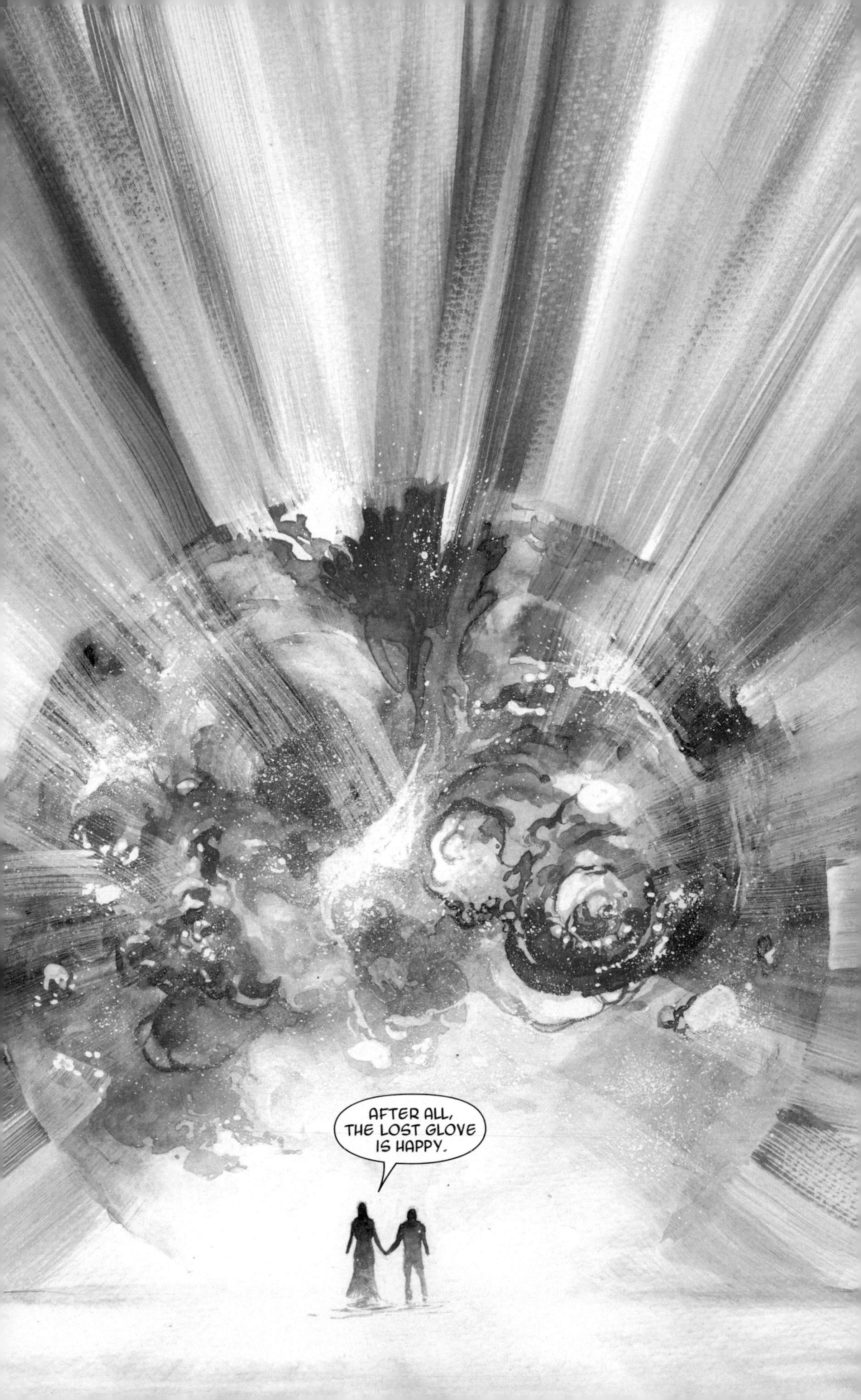
AFTER ALL, THE LOST GLOVE IS HAPPY.

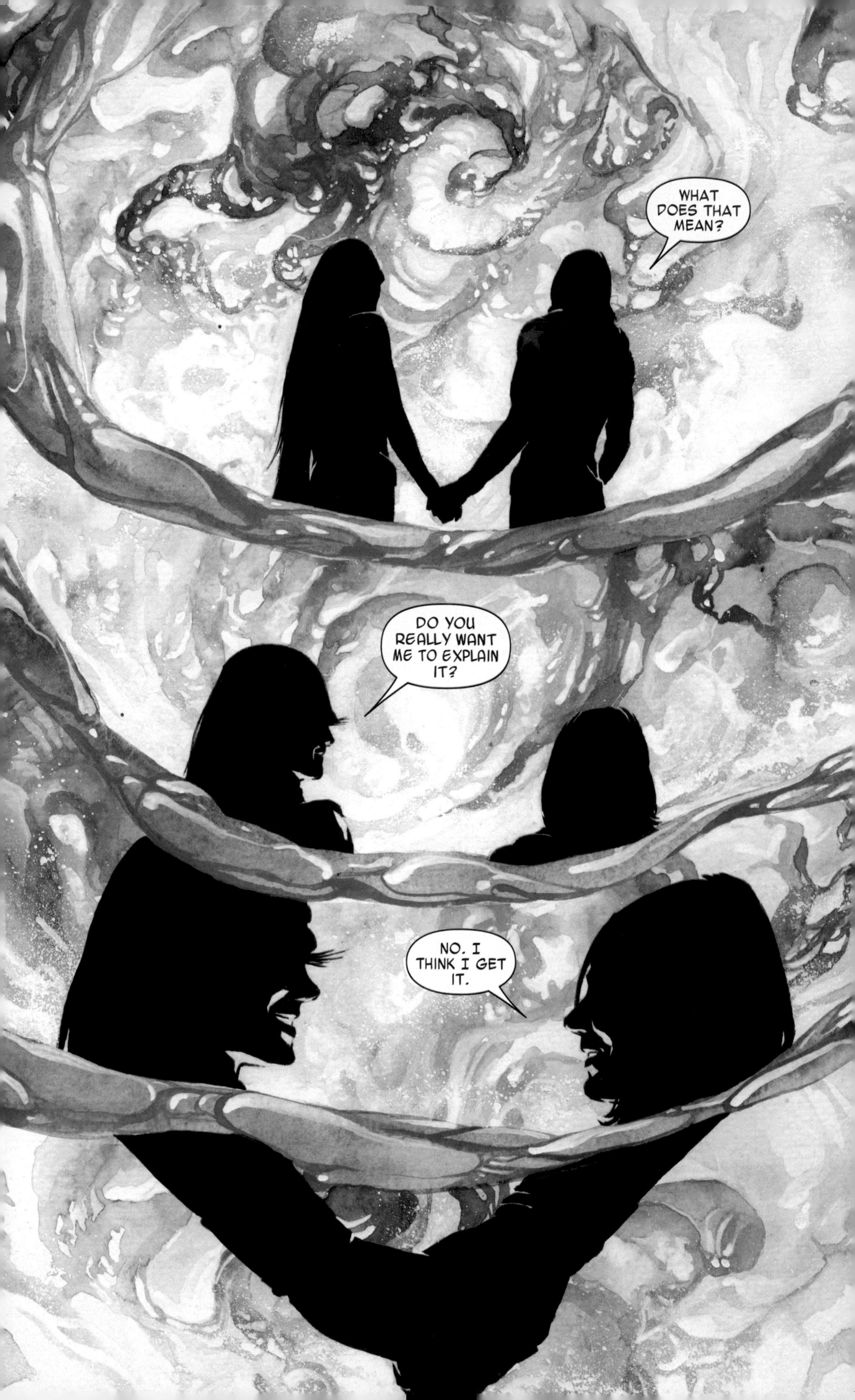
WHAT DOES THAT MEAN?
DO YOU REALLY WANT ME TO EXPLAIN IT?
NO. I THINK I GET IT.

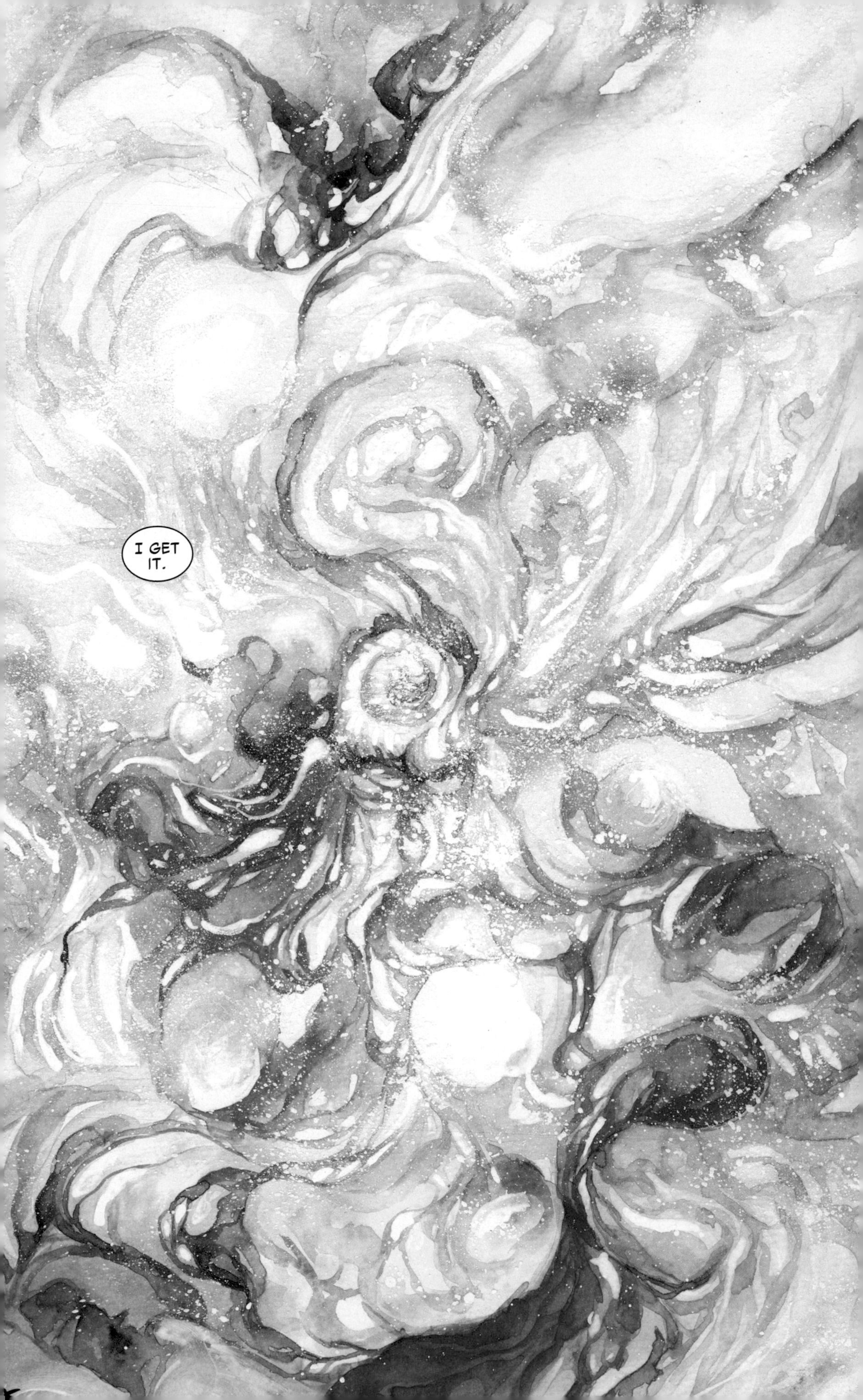
I GET IT.

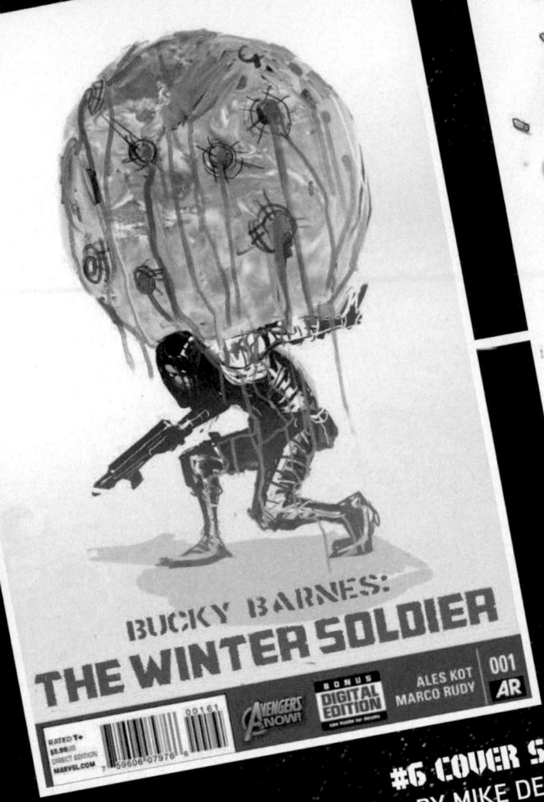
BUCKY BARNES:
THE WINTER SOLDIER
ALES KOT
MARCO RUDY
001
AR
BONUS
DIGITAL EDITION
AVENGERS NOW!
RATED T+

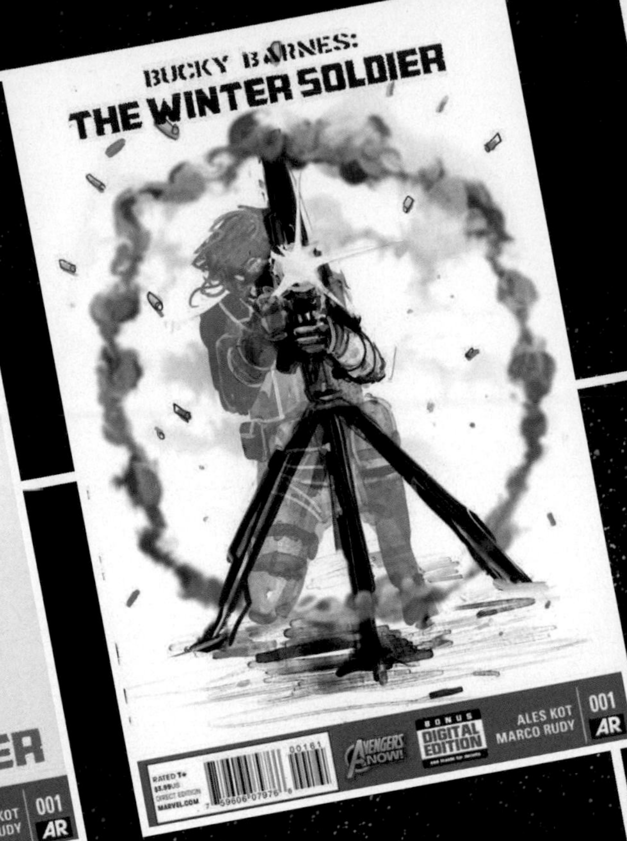
BUCKY BARNES:
THE WINTER SOLDIER
ALES KOT
MARCO RUDY
001
AR
BONUS
DIGITAL EDITION
AVENGERS NOW!
RATED T+

**#6 COVER SKETCHES**
BY MIKE DEL MUNDO

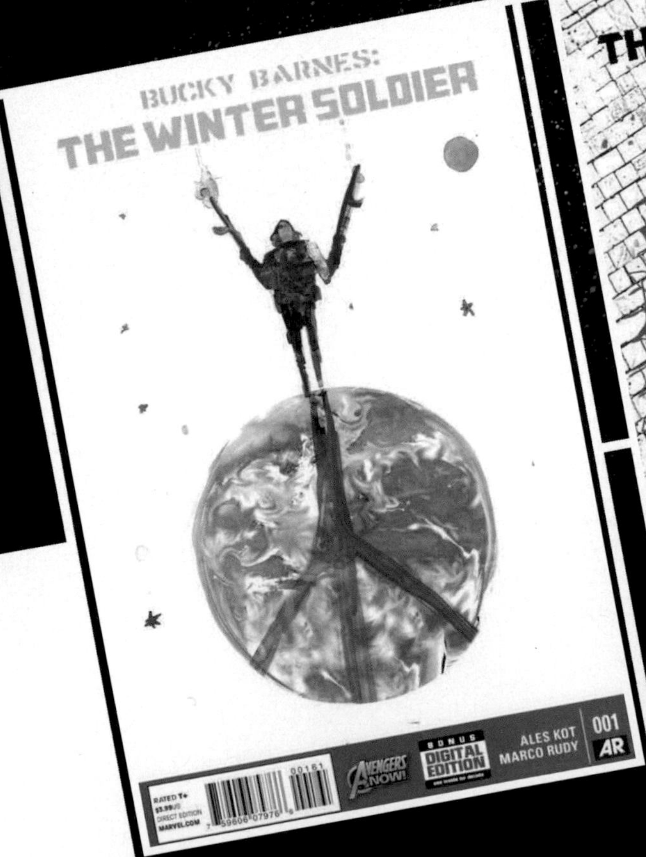
BUCKY BARNES:
THE WINTER SOLDIER
ALES KOT
MARCO RUDY
001
AR
BONUS
DIGITAL EDITION
AVENGERS NOW!
RATED T+

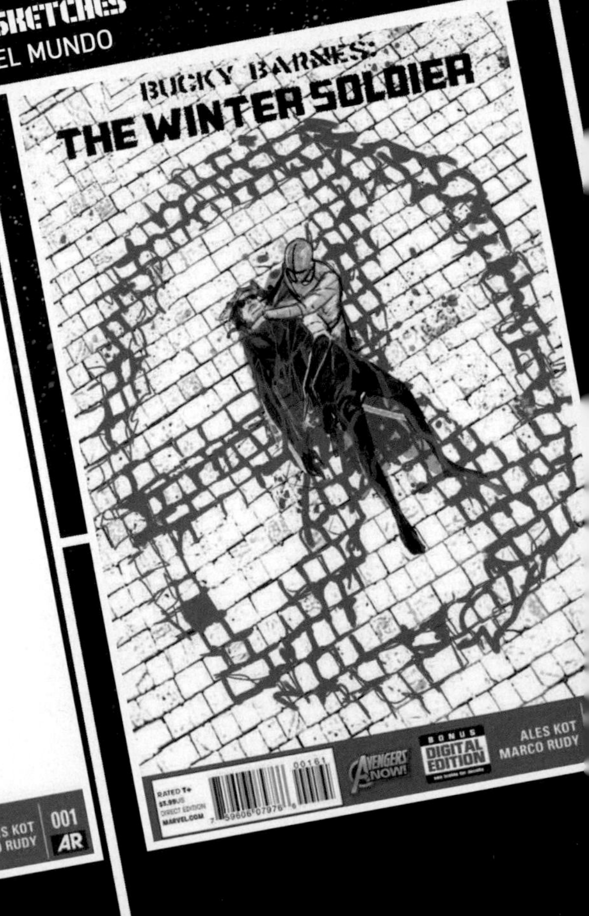
BUCKY BARNES:
THE WINTER SOLDIER
ALES KOT
MARCO RUDY
BONUS
DIGITAL EDITION
AVENGERS NOW!
RATED T+

BUCKY BARNES:
THE WINTER SOLDIER
WACKY FACE PAINT KIT

BUCKY BARNES:
THE WINTER SOLDIER

#7 (ABOVE) & #8 (BELOW) COVER SKETCHES
BY MIKE DEL MUNDO

BUCKY BARNES:
THE WINTER SOLDIER
MARVEL
DIGITAL EDITION
ALES KOT
MARCO RUDY
001
AR

BUCKY BARNES:
THE WINTER SOLDIER
MARVEL
DIGITAL EDITION
ALES KOT
MARCO RUDY
001

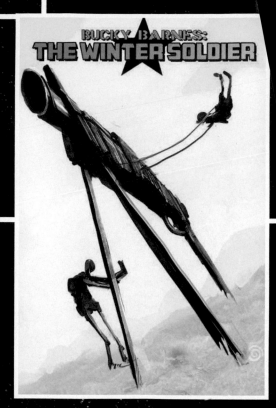

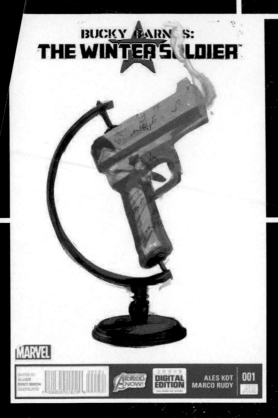

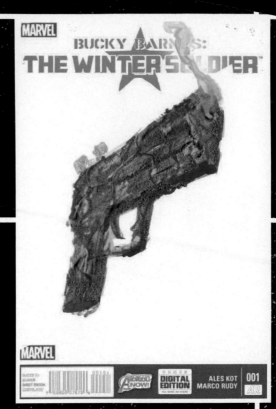

**#8 (ABOVE) & #9 (BELOW) COVER SKETCHES**
BY MIKE DEL MUNDO

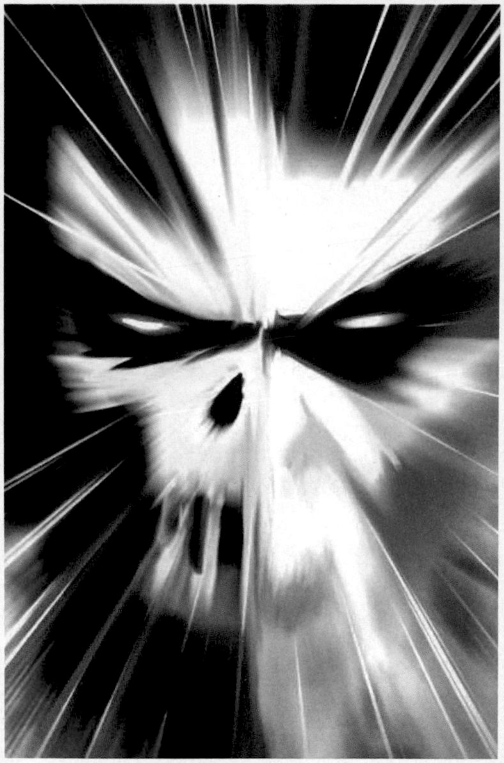

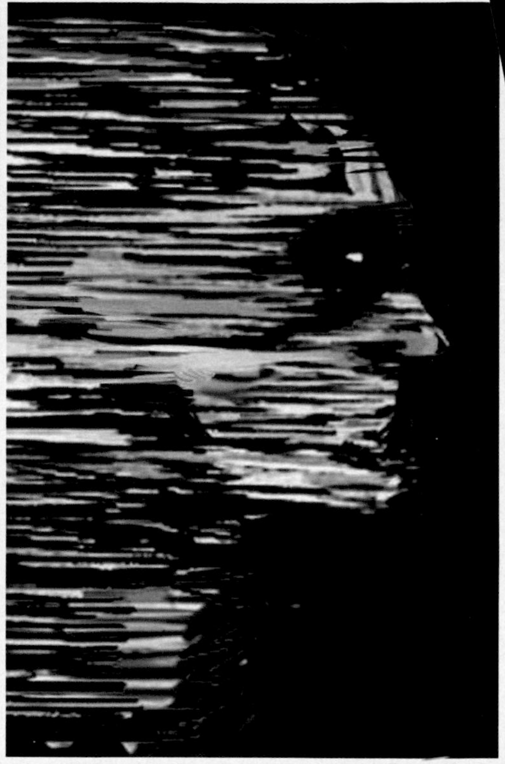

**#10 (ABOVE) & #11 (BELOW) COVER SKETCHES**
BY MIKE DEL MUNDO

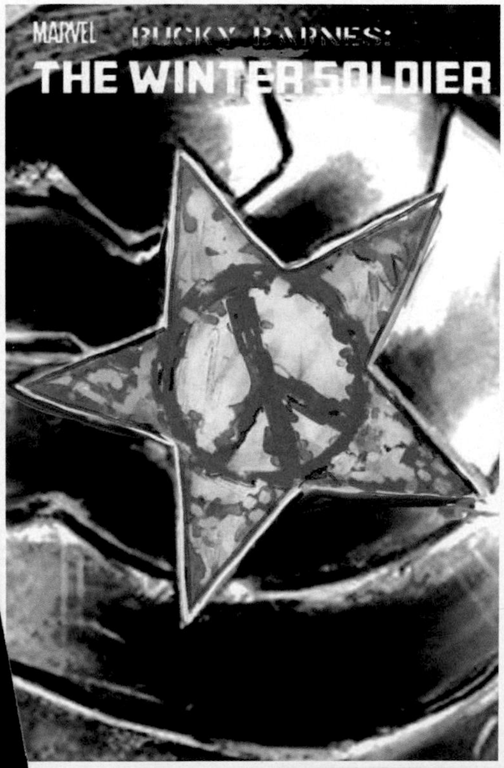
MARVEL
BUCKY BARNES:
THE WINTER SOLDIER

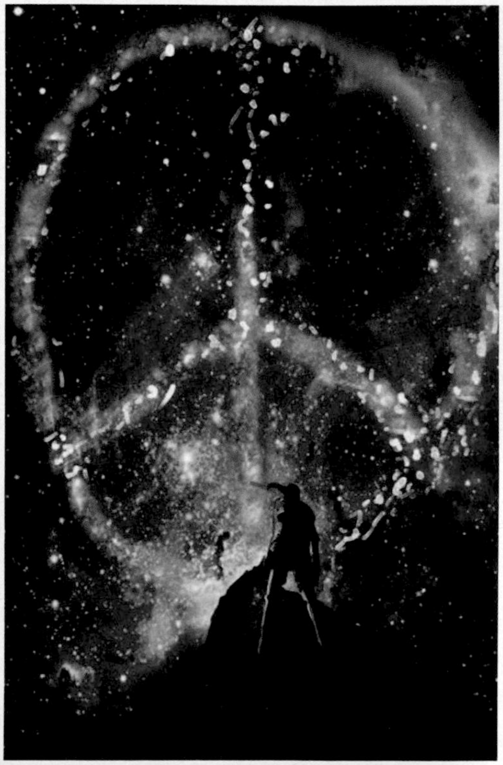

## #6, PAGES 13-14 SCRIPT EXCERPT BY ALES KOT & ART BY LANGDON FOSS

PAGE 13 - LANGDON
Langdon – invent three planets of your own choosing. Any kinds. All I'm asking for is – make them all peaceful, coexisting in harmony. Some of the men, women and non-humans have scars, likely ex-soldiers. It doesn't matter. Everyone is doing fine.

OLD BUCKY (this is just basic text, will be much more layered later): AND IN TIME, THERE WAS PEACE. SOLDIERS BECAME UNNECESSARY.

Old Bucky. He's looking somewhere we can't see – his eyes wet, his chin proud. This is a Soviet propaganda poster kind of a panel, except that it's a snapshot of his life in the moment he realized there was no more war to have. He didn't see it coming. He nearly stopped hoping.

OLD BUCKY: EVEN THE ONES WHO USED TO BE HIDDEN IN THE SHADOWS.

Bucky in his barn, putting together something massive and slightly familiar...a TON of material around, and sketches, papers, and the robot friend we know from #4...Bucky is on the floor, putting things together--

OLD BUCKY: AND AS MY TIME AND ENERGY NEEDED A NEW OUTLET, I BECAME...

The machine, nearly finished, in front of us. Bucky is nowhere in the panel – this is all about the moment, being near-finished with the huge amount of work, from Bucky's POV.

OLD BUCKY: ...CURIOUS.

PAGE 14 - LANGDON
Old Bucky, interacting with the machine, looking in...echoes of the scene in #4 here, please. He's fascinated with it, and operating it, doing the things he has not done for a long time.

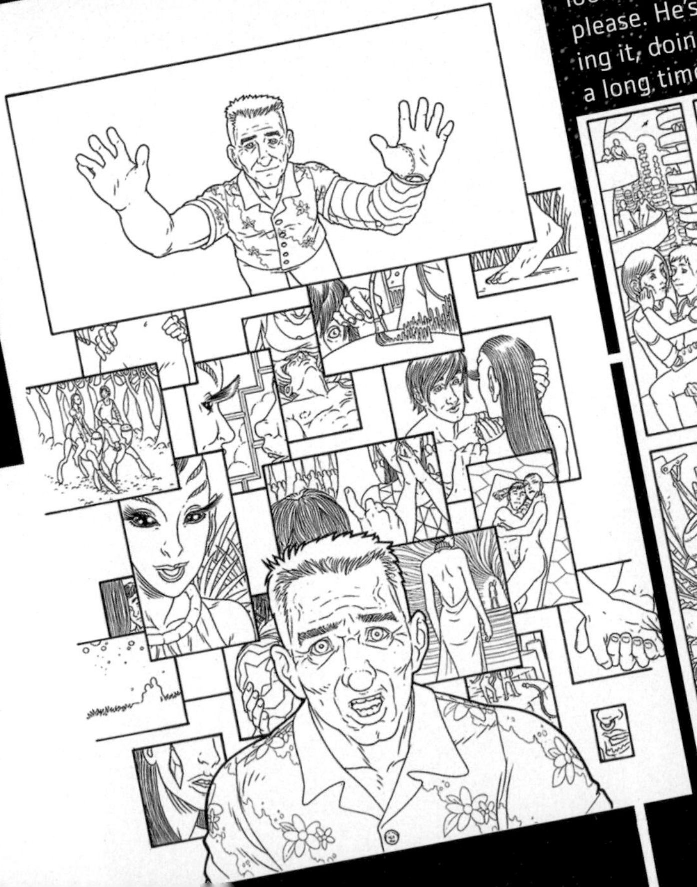

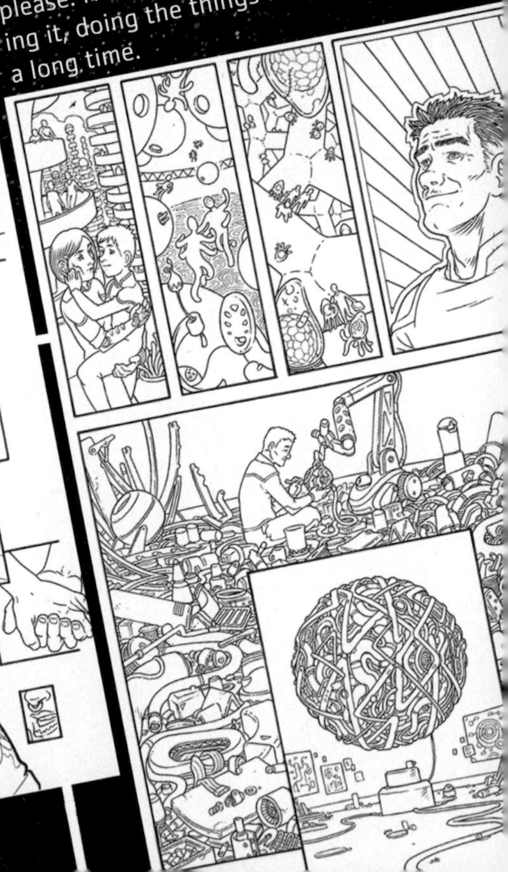

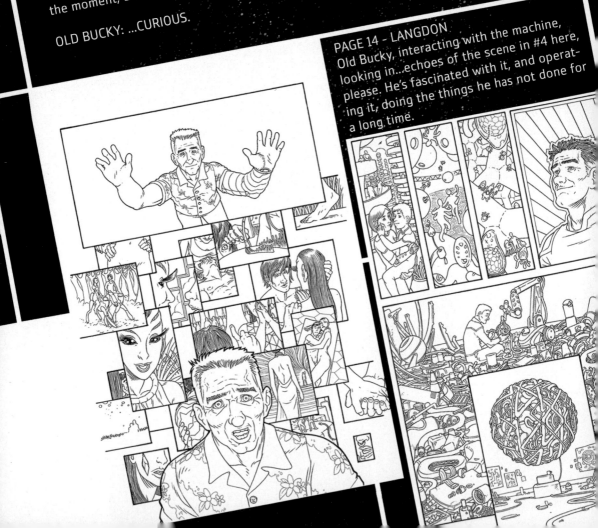